The Future of
Drug
Discovery

Who Decides Which Diseases to Treat?

to Sabine
Riitta
Pinja & Silja

Expert Reviews for The Future of Drug Discovery: Who Decides Which Diseases to Treat?

Tamas Bartfai & Graham V Lees

"A remarkable compendium of hard data and wise prescriptions for the pharmaceutical industry."
—Michael S Brown, *1985 Nobel Laureate in Medicine or Physiology, UT Southwestern Medical Center*

"[This] is a remarkable and timely book ... remarkable, as it is an insightful and careful analysis of the many factors determining success in this challenging area of human endeavor ... [and] timely, as the crisis in drug discovery has already begun ... The authors really prove their credentials with a thorough and expert review of the factors influencing the future of drug discovery delivering a detailed analysis of the biological and technical challenges ... The authors strategize on alternative business models and propose viable choices ... there is light at the end of the tunnel."
—Graeme Bilbe, *Drugs for Neglected Disease initiative, former Senior VP Novartis*, from his *Foreword*

"The future of drug discovery is compromised by interests driven by concerns other than science or health ... This is not an indictment of the pharmaceutical industry, but rather an exposition of various ills that exist in the present iteration of Pharma that need to be remedied so that the future promise of Pharma can be realized. The book is both enlightening and disturbing. It should serve as a call to action to use these facts and suggestions to help Pharma do what we need it to do—to create drugs that are effective in treating human illnesses."
—James H Eberwine, *University of Pennsylvania Perelman School of Medicine*, from his *Foreword*

"This book [offers] thoughtful and at times provocative proposals. [The authors] give a strong wake-up call in favor of continuing efforts and desperately needed investments into research and development to create new innovative medicines. Anyone who is looking for a thorough appraisal of current drug development issues combined with optimistic insight into the challenges, opportunities and specific needs of developing new medicines will benefit from reading this book. For individuals who are currently in or are planning to become involved with pharmaceutical or biotech industries, regulatory bodies or NGOs, academia or any form of biotech-focused financial investment - or just for getting a better understanding of the future of drug development - this book will be an excellent 'starter dose'."
—Eduard E Holdener, *NovImmune, former Head of Clinical Development, Roche-Genentech*, from his *Foreword*

"This book is a must read for students, prescribing physicians, academic and industry researchers, analysts, patient groups, business and science journalists, and importantly, Policy Makers. More than ever before, drug development is a complex scientific, industrial, and societal endeavor that needs the combined attention of Governments, Academics, and Big Pharma; it cannot be left to Wall Street alone."
—Daniel Hoyer, *Dept Pharmacology, U Melbourne, former Distinguished Scientist, Novartis*

"Bartfai and Lees raise critical issues confronting the search for new medicines. Their analysis is cogent, and their proposals thoughtful and thought provoking. For anyone curious about where new medicines come from, and what it will take for the BioPharma industry to bring new treatments to patients with Alzheimer's disease, diabetes, depression, cancer, and more, this is a must read."

—Michael D Ehlers, Senior VP *Pfizer & CSO Neuroscience, former Howard Hughes Investigator, Duke University*

"The global recession has caused unprecedented anxiety in many commercial areas, and the pharmaceutical industry is no exception. Armed with hard facts and their own real life experiences, Bartfai and Lees dissect the clinical needs, the marketplace, and the risk/ benefit ratios of various strategies needed to survive the Valley of Death. In contrast to the worldwide somber mood, they see a glass that is half full and an industry with unprecedented opportunity. Courage is required of the pharmaceutical leadership charged with navigating these waters. The concrete, specific, and clear-eyed analysis of Bartfai and Lees make this an essential reference for entrepreneurs looking for optimism leavened with specific advice on strategies and mindsets that are likely to lead to success."

—Samuel E Gandy, *Mount Sinai Alzheimer's Disease Research Center*

"This insightful (and bracing) analysis provides a detailed 'lay of the land' with respect to the opportunities for and barriers to the development of new medicines by the world's pharmaceutical and biotech industries. Bartfai and Lees outline a set of proposals to revitalize the analysis and development of orphan drugs, to reform US patent guidelines and intellectual property protection, and to shorten the timeline between drug development in biotech and drug implementation by large pharma. Most importantly, they make a compelling case that substantive progress will not be made without restored - indeed, increased and sustained - investment in both basic research and its translational development."

—Greg Lemke, *Molecular Neurobiology Laboratory, The Salk Institute*

"This is an extraordinary, insightful and provocative book that should be read by all those concerned by the progress of biomedicine, from scientists to politicians. It deals with the future of drug discovery and its present-day dramatic contradiction: should we develop new drugs to the benefit of humanity's welfare or should we consider as a priority the financial goals & benefits of pharmaceutical companies? Central to the book, the paradox is very well documented and ably illustrated. The authors demonstrate the unanticipated inverse relationship existing between our greatest medical needs and the number of projects pursued by the pharmaceutical industry. This is particularly true for brain diseases (Alzheimer's disease, schizophrenia, neuropathic pain, etc.) that represent the greatest health burden on the population. A conservative estimate is that, in a typical year in Europe, about 165 million people—38% of the total population of these countries—will have a fully-developed mental illness (H. U. Wittchen *et al. Eur. Neuropsychopharmacol.* **21,** 655-679; 2011). The response of major pharmaceutical companies to this exceptional situation has been, unexpectedly, to cut their programs in brain therapeutics, for the simple reason that they are financially too risky. Yet, and this is an interesting aspect of the book, the authors remain optimistic about the future. Among the arguments they develop in the last part of the book, the basic research on drug design is progressing faster than ever, and new economic models of pharmaceutical industry development may be suggested that would be financially stable. The debate is open in unambiguous terms about the future of drug discovery and development, which is, in my opinion, one of the major ethical responsibilities of today's societies."

—Jean-Pierre Changeux, *Collège de France & l'Institut Pasteur*

The Future of
Drug
Discovery
Who Decides Which Diseases to Treat?

Tamas Bartfai PhD

Professor and Director of
the Harold L Dorris Neurological
Research Center
The Scripps Research Institute
La Jolla, CA, USA

Graham V Lees PhD

Corpus Alienum Oy
Helsinki, Finland

AMSTERDAM • BOSTON • HEIDELBERG • LONDON
NEW YORK • OXFORD • PARIS • SAN DIEGO
SAN FRANCISCO • SINGAPORE • SYDNEY • TOKYO
Academic Press is an imprint of Elsevier

ELSEVIER

Academic Press is an imprint of Elsevier
32 Jamestown Road, London NW1 7BY, UK
225 Wyman Street, Waltham, MA 02451, USA
525 B Street, Suite 1800, San Diego, CA 92101-4495, USA

Notice
No responsibility is assumed by the authors nor the publisher for any injury and/
or damage to persons or property as a matter of products liability, negligence or
otherwise, or from any use or operation of any methods, products, instructions or
ideas contained in the material herein. Because of rapid advances in the medical
sciences, in particular, independent verification of diagnoses and drug dosages
should be made

British Library Cataloguing-in-Publication Data
A catalogue record for this book is available from the British Library

Library of Congress Cataloging-in-Publication Data
A catalog record for this book is available from the Library of Congress

ISBN: 978-0-12-407180-3

For information on all Academic Press publications visit our
website at elsevierdirect.com

Typeset by TNQ Books and Journals Pvt Ltd.
www.tnq.co.in

Printed and bound in United States of America

13 14 15 16 17   10 9 8 7 6 5 4 3 2 1

Working together
to grow libraries in
developing countries

www.elsevier.com • www.bookaid.org

Content

Preface

Why this new book?

Our first book[1] is still very pertinent to the process of modern, target-based drug discovery in Big Pharma and biotech.

Since we wrote the last book, something dramatic has happened that fundamentally changes the path of drug discovery. Previously, a scientific advance into the mechanism of almost any disease led to a dedicated effort throughout the pharma industry to discover molecules that would provide a new, better treatment. Drug discovery followed the path of human endeavor and discovery. Pharma companies were set and willing to tackle almost any disease, providing scientific research had uncovered sufficient detail on the disease process. They were eager to be first to learn of the basic science discoveries made in the government-sponsored academic laboratories.

This is no longer true.

The largest pharma companies have narrowed their sights and have dramatically culled research programs to focus on "reliable" diseases where they are most likely to make a profit. They have discarded many of society's vitally important therapeutic areas. With a clear eye on stock price, shareholder value, and "Wall Street" perceptions, pharma has focused on finances not therapies.

What this means is that the gurus of Wall Street and the financially mindful chiefs of the industry are deciding which diseases to treat without apparent care or concern for society's needs. As an example, we can cite the *Financial Times* report of August 28, 2012, the day this preface was originally drafted. AstraZeneca, the Swedish-British pharma concern, cut its research and development (R&D) workforce by 23% and used $4 billion of its $33 billion sales revenues to buy back stock in order to prop up its

---

1 Bartfai T and Lees GV (2006) *Drug Discovery: from Bedside to Wall Street*. Elsevier/Academic Press: Amsterdam.

stock price, which is very low; the market capitalization was only six times the earnings. This may have been prompted by the projection that by 2016 it would lose 50% of its revenue because of its patents expiring on its largest selling drugs.

Is cutting one's R&D the right strategy for preserving one's long-term viability? AstraZeneca is currently clinging onto a top 11 spot in the world's biggest pharma. The 10 companies above it have also been indulging in R&D cuts and stock buybacks. It is not streamlining based upon any technological development; it is backing away from a whole cadre of diseases that need treatment—some of them urgently. Some diseases, for which we have no effective treatments, will become epidemics. Alzheimer's disease (AD) is a condition looming on many of our horizons. Yet we have no immediate prospect of treating the condition, and pharma has almost universally dropped it from its R&D. There are too few attempts to produce antibiotics, yet the latest estimates are that 50% of new cases of tuberculosis (TB) are drug resistant to present antibiotics. The best antipsychotic drugs are causing metabolic syndrome and diabetes, and few attempts are being made to find safer ones for this prevalent and lifelong disease. Obesity is a growing epidemic, but all recent pharmacological attempts to address the problem safely have failed.

The latest news is that the trials to combat AD by Lilly, which has invested a huge amount in AD drug development, have basically failed to reach both clinical end points. This is regrettably not an isolated incident. Trials by others have brought or are likely to bring similar disappointments. We can almost say this for certain because all of the drugs in development targeting AD are targeting the same molecular mechanism. The protein folding error in AD is common in several diseases, yet we do not honestly know if fixing it is key to AD treatment that will affect, slow, or stop memory loss. The failures, partly stemming from a narrow research focus, reinforce pharma's decisions that AD is too complicated a disease and drug development is long and risky, and even the potentially large payoff is not attractive to remain in this race in the present risk-averse environment that promotes cost-cutting executives, who proudly announce no more new research centers: "We are cutting research and development COST!" Such pronouncements are erroneously applauded by Wall Street and short-term shareholders.

Why would pharma back away from therapeutic areas that should yield multibillion dollar revenues? The reason is relatively simple: the companies cannot see a way to develop drugs for "difficult" diseases in an economically viable way. The trials take too long, the risks are too great, and there are easier ways to make money. They are less motivated to be pioneers. If another company does it, they can copy them with similar drugs. Maybe. But with huge irreversible cuts in R&D worldwide, nothing is certain.

It is, frankly, easy to write a book "revealing" the well-documented excesses of the pharma industry: overzealous sales reps, unsafe drugs, exorbitant prices, advertising to patients, and lobbying of physicians and Congress. Those are separate, important ethical issues. This book is not devoted to them; there are other scandal-oriented authors doing a better job on those plentiful excesses.

Our thesis in this book is that the pharmaceutical industry is still the only source of new drugs. Some, maybe 1–2%, are discovered in academia, but the crucial clinical trials and marketing require the almost century-long experience, as well as the financial muscle, of the industry. There is as yet no other viable candidate in the foreseeable future. Biotechs can be pioneers, but they often do not have the resources to fund a phase 3 clinical trial, which often results in failure. Many successful phase 2 drugs, for which some efficacy and safety have been demonstrated, are just dropped in pharma and not picked up from biotech either, because of marketing decisions, not clinical viability.

The result of these trends is a major gap between the medical need and the focus of pharma companies; this new book is all about this and more. We identify the problems and the reasons behind them. We also offer solutions.

The scientific effort needs to be upgraded. It has, over the past 50 years, cost hundreds of billions of dollars to begin to tackle some cancers. It has been a superb government-led effort, rapidly joined by industry, to understand and begin to tackle HIV/AIDS and in 30 years turn a death sentence to a treatable, severe chronic disease. The abandoned and neglected diseases need major governmental investment if one is to identify new drug targets for pharma to exploit. The government budgets for research have been redirected toward so-called translational research, but the amounts being dedicated cannot fund important trials and government remains a very junior partner to industry in translational research, while it does cutting-edge basic research when it is the only major actor and produces breakthrough results.

Pharma needs to be incentivized. It is impossible to expect pharma to develop drugs that take much more than 10 years to develop, only for its patent to expire shortly thereafter. The tax incentives available for "orphan" or "rare" diseases should be extended to diseases identified as important for society, yet now abandoned. Governments, which have a track record for conducting clinical trials, need to support some phase 3 trials, not just safety and "evidence-based medicine" (EBM) trials.

A number of non-mutually exclusive suggestions are given especially in the final chapter. If an "expert reader" just wants the suggested answers, without full consideration of the questions, then please turn to the second part of Chapter 12 (under Drug development is moving, but not completely, *et seq.*). We hope you will then turn back to the important middle and fully appreciate the essential information in the debate. The majority of Chapter 11 is reasonably essential background in terms of organizing the future of drug discovery (under Filling the strategic vacuum, *et seq.*) An expert reader might be, perhaps, someone who can read Chapter 04 without learning anything.

Society needs to be more aware of what is going on and why they should be concerned. Its elected officials should be cognizant of how to ensure that the economic cost of the looming epidemics does not cripple the economy. The world cannot sustain untreatable infections, worldwide microbial epidemics, and a growing population over 80 with AD who will drain most of our resources, because they need 24/7 care. We need to change course as soon as possible.

We hope this book provokes scientists to lobby for more funds for basic research, for pharma to be reminded that the risks are worth taking, and that government spends more on research in order to reduce and break the trend of increasing healthcare costs. The examples of good new drugs saving lives and reducing suffering, while saving funds as well, are plentiful. We need to use the accumulating scientific data to make new drugs in areas where society needs them most, and not only in areas where pharma presently flocks to make copies of one another's medicines.

Tamas Bartfai PhD

Professor and Director of the Harold L Dorris Neurological Research Center, The Scripps Research Institute, La Jolla, CA, USA

Graham V Lees PhD

Corpus Alienum, Oy, Helsinki, Finland

Foreword by Graeme Bilbe PhD

The *Future of Drug Discovery* is a remarkable and timely book; remarkable, as it is an insightful and careful analysis of the many factors determining success in this challenging area of human endeavor. Bartfai is the insider with a successful track record in both academia and industry, speaking with authority on key issues. The communicator, Lees, demonstrated in the first book (*Drug Discovery: from Bedside to Wall Street*) that a complex theme like drug discovery can be made accessible to an audience less well versed in some of the intricacies of the "art." This book is also timely, as the crisis in drug discovery has already begun.

Societies in the modern world view easy (and sometimes almost free) access to health care as a human right. Accordingly, governments should be invested in making sure that their citizens are healthy, as healthy citizens make vibrant and successful economies. However, the current model of drug discovery, where large, asset-rich pharma companies freely pursue drug discovery and developments in those diseases with a large return on investment, is less and less aligned with the medical needs of an aging demographic and a society facing lifestyle challenges that hugely impact disease.

The drug industry is distinct from other industries. Drug development life cycles are 10-12 years long. The in-position life expectancy of CEOs in Big Pharma is 5-7 years. And no longer are scientific or clinical experts leading these companies. The markets demand quarter on quarter growth in company performance and double-digit returns. As a result, pharma companies are hemorrhaging knowledge workers trying to maintain their profit lines at market expectations. That is a central theme in this book. Key knowledge and expertise for drug discovery and development is disappearing, just when looming epidemics of diabetes and Alzheimer's disease are already measurable and beginning to influence society's ability to bear the cost of care and treatment.

If this book merely described the maladies of the pharma industry and its imminent end, as many treatises in the popular press as well as from analysts and consultants would have us believe, then there really is a dismal future. The authors of this book really prove their credentials with a thorough and expert review of the factors influencing the future of drug discovery by delivering a detailed analysis of the biological and technical challenges. With enough money, time, and insight these factors are all surmountable. Nevertheless, a little more challenging will be aligning the forces to do so and likely building a new model for drug discovery and development.

For several decades, the pharma industry has translated academic research into novel therapeutics for unmet needs. This has been very successfully applied to the diseases attacked so far. Now the challenge for drug discovery and development is to find novel therapies for more complex diseases where validated starting points for drug discovery are harder to identify. Further, well-characterized populations for clinical trials combined with diagnostics and surrogates to enable rapid development or rejection of each therapeutic approach are less readily available. Taken together with a financing model poorly suited to support the development of therapies outside the remit of the pharma industry and a product life cycle of 10-12 years, action must be taken now. It will require the commitment of many sectors and interests, from academic research groups to financial institutions and most likely strategic government funding. Plus the heat needs turning up on the political debate.

In spite of all that, there is light at the end of the tunnel. The authors strategize on alternative business models and propose viable choices. It will require the combined efforts of government, industry, and the markets plus new ways to incentivize and reward innovators. That this is possible is clear. Solutions to two great scourges, the HIV epidemic and some cancers, have been found as a result of recognizing the issues, summoning the political will, providing sustained funding, and aligning all constituencies to a common purpose. Whether this will happen in the near future for other diseases, the authors leave open for us to judge.

Graeme Bilbe PhD
Research and Development Director
Drugs for Neglected Disease initiative

Foreword by James H Eberwine PhD

Facts are facts ... The future of drug discovery is compromised by interests driven by concerns other than science or health. This is one of the basic tenets of Bartfai and Lees' new book *The Future of Drug Discovery*. This is not an indictment of the pharmaceutical industry, but rather an exposition of various ills that exist in the present iteration of pharma that need to be remedied so that the future promise of pharma can be realized.

As a scientist performing fundamental (basic) research, I cannot help but marvel at the process of translating discoveries made in the lab to therapeutics that are used to ease human suffering. The nature of scientific discovery is agnostic to human need; however, when aligned, the results of fundamental science can have dramatic individual and societal impact. There are growing individual and national efforts to reinvent and reinvigorate the field of translational medicine so that results from fundamental studies can be more readily transitioned to the clinic. There are three fundamental decisions to be made in developing therapeutic drugs: What disease area will be targeted? How much of a resource investment should the company provide? When to stop development because of adverse effects or inefficacy of drug action? These three decisions are intricately intertwined, with the first and second among the most important issues discussed in this book.

There was a time not so long ago when drug companies were run by scientists or MDs. This is no longer the case, and now only one of the major drug companies, Novartis, is headed by an MD. The CEOs of the other companies and the trend in CEO recruitment is to hire business professionals. This illustrates one of the themes of the book, which is that medical/research decisions are being made by people without extensive training in the field. While most Big Pharma are publicly traded companies with a fiscal responsibility to their shareholders, the makers of our medicines—the deciders of which diseases will be investigated so that treatments may be forthcoming—must be held to a different standard of success than the simply quantifiable potential profitability of a research program.

In highlighting the impediments to the future of drug discovery, the authors go to great lengths to suggest remedies, thereby providing one of the most thought-provoking chapters of the book, Chapter 12. The suggestions run the gamut of pharma being more open to the rescue of phase 2 drugs that have failed either for their primary indication or because of the testing conditions, to encouraging governments to rewrite patent guidelines (particularly in the United States), thereby allowing pharma to make up for the long development time and high costs associated with the long process from initial patenting to receipt of Food and Drug Administration approval. Several of these ideas are intriguing but will come at a cost to the consumer, and hence warrant serious discussion.

Of course, academic efforts in translational science are also discussed in the book, highlighting academia's overall lack of success in bringing new drugs to the market. This is explained in several ways, including the existence of unfounded biases of academicians concerning the difficulty and scientific worthiness of work done in pharma (making it difficult to work with pharma) and the lack of sufficient government funds for performing the necessary clinical development. While pointing out these inadequacies, the authors are also hopeful that governmental funding agencies and pharma are seeing the need to work together, as evidenced by the Alzheimer's disease clinical trial to be carried out in an extended Colombian family that was initiated by Genentech and jointly funded by the National Institutes of Health, non-governmental organizations, and pharma. Drs. Bartfai and Lees see such collaborations (as discussed in their first book *Drug Discovery: from Bedside to Wall Street*) as necessary and integral to the future development of drugs. Sharing the monetary and failure risks through involvement of multiple groups working closely together seems like a reasonable approach to take on the risks of drug development for complex multigenic diseases, as well as orphan diseases.

One might wonder why Drs. Bartfai and Lees would discuss these pharma issues in this very public manner. In making his arguments, Dr. Bartfai compels us based upon his experience as both a drug company insider and as an academic professor. His unique perspective is amplified by the fact that he is a husband, father, and grandfather. His own scientific work has concentrated on understanding the mechanisms of fever production, which is the leading cause of death throughout the world. I am confident that these humanitarian experiences coupled with his scientific "wherewithal" have driven him to detail the problems that he envisions with the nature of drug development so that this and future generations will have the information necessary to help change the course of drug development.

The Future of Drug Discovery is both enlightening and disturbing. It should serve as a call to action to use these facts and suggestions to help pharma do what we need it to do—create drugs that are effective in treating human illnesses.

Woodrow Wilson once said of America: "We cannot be an ostrich with its head in the sand"; this is Drs. Bartfai and Lees' message to all of us.

James H Eberwine PhD
Elmer Holmes Bobst Professor of Pharmacology
University of Pennsylvania Perelman School of Medicine

Foreword by Eduard Enrico Holdener MD

Tamas Bartfai and I were at Roche when we met in the early 1990s. He was leading CNS Research and I had global responsibility for oncology drug development. Our paths often crossed—in the corridors or at regular internal meetings—and we would discuss the challenges and the opportunities with which we were faced at that time in creating and developing new medicines. Tamas had broad experiences in science, medicine, and R&D at a number of well-reputed universities and as a consultant to top pharmaceutical companies. He had developed his strong opinions by not just trying to solve problems, but also looking preemptively for solutions. Although I never met Graham, based on his scientific, academic, and business credentials, it is not surprising that he and Tamas did not hesitate to dissect the complexities of drug development in the current pharmaceutical environment and provide a framework for a better future.

These highly experienced scientists in the field of drug development have taken on the daunting task of critically reviewing the world of pharmaceutical and biotechnology research and development. This book is the result, offering thoughtful and at times provocative proposals. Looking forward to 2025, Tamas and Graham outline the immediate and long-term changes necessary to better address future patient needs.

They have deconstructed the network and inter-relationships between the pharmaceutical and biotech industries, the regulatory authorities, governments, and nongovernmental organizations (NGOs), as well as the broad range of interests from the investment community. These complex relationships significantly impact all patients, and most particularly those burdened with diseases with no effective treatment options. Through these analyses they were able to identify disease categories with high medical need but alarmingly low investment activities. The reasons for this are discussed in detail.

In spite of all the challenges and the so-called "crisis in pharma," the authors convey an astonishingly high level of enthusiastic support for the "drug development world." Through this publication they want to give a strong wake-up call in favor of continuing efforts and desperately needed investments into research and development to create new innovative medicines, in particular for those diseases where there is continuing or even increasing medical need, such as type 2 diabetes or Alzheimer's disease.

This book is structured to stimulate the reader by using a question and answer style. Even when the reader already has their own burning questions, this book is a great help to find answers or propagate a critical discussion regarding many hot topics. Readers may not always agree with some of the personal views presented by these authors, but at least they will get enough information to make up their own mind. This sort of Q&A approach provides the busy reader with the option to select readings by specific areas of interest. By design, this book is a resource work that does not need to be read from cover to cover. Instead, the reader is offered a practical way to absorb an enormous amount of detail on pharmaceutical drug development in digestible portions.

The authors also discuss what drives decisions to develop or—as happens more and more often—not to develop drugs even when an urgent demand for better treatments, supported by pharmaceutical industry, government, and others, is discontinued. This leads to a detailed discussion of the commercial aspects of drug development, where the authors build a bridge between commercially viable solutions and the needs of special patient populations. They have provided the information necessary to understand where the development of personalized medicine may lead us to, the role of companion diagnostics, and who may particularly benefit from this approach.

This well-written text is supplemented by informative and easy-to-read tables that help the reader to review important historical data and to get a quick overview on many of the themes. The authors critically review the past performance of the pharmaceutical industry, take a clear stand regarding mistakes that have been made, and provide a personal preview of how things could be done better in the future. The upfront introduction for nonspecialists signals a sincere desire to reach out to a broader audience.

Anyone who is looking for a thorough appraisal of current drug development issues combined with optimistic insight into the challenges, opportunities, and specific needs of developing new medicines will benefit from reading this book. For individuals who are currently in or are planning to become involved with pharmaceutical or biotech industries, regulatory bodies or NGOs, and academia or any form of biotech-focused financial investment—or just for getting a better understanding of the future of drug development—this book will be an excellent "starter dose."

Eduard Enrico Holdener MD
Chairman of NovImmune SA and
Emeritus Global Pharma Development Head at Roche

Chapter 00: Introduction

What medicines you will need & why you might not ever have them

"Big Pharma" has not had any financial losses; however, it has been closing research divisions and laying off very qualified and experienced people who were working on the drugs for your future. The investment society has made in educating these individuals, who found once prestigious well-paid jobs in pharma, is now unproductive. After being laid off, some of these scientists are taking their pet projects to existing biotech and to venture capitalists in order to try and set up their own biotech companies. This is by no means easy, as you will find out while reading this book.[1]

Meanwhile, cash-rich Big Pharma has been buying back stock to prop up its stock prices, and Wall Street and company directors appear to approve of this. CEOs that did not participate in this buyback were suddenly "departed" from their jobs.

This means that society will not have many of the medicines it needs, when it needs them.

Aging is the major risk factor for disease

The population is becoming older, and with aging comes an increase in debilitations, such as diabetes, obesity, cancer, pain, cardiovascular disease, osteoporosis, and Alzheimer's disease (AD).[2] In the past, the pharma system was relied on to develop drugs to meet society's needs. Within huge caveats about price and availability, the market has worked in many ways.

---

1 In this book we give many details, which we hope are easy to follow for nonscientists and nonphysicians. For this introduction we might say "diabetes" when we mean "type 2 diabetes mellitus." The word mellitus is often dropped in literature, but it is an extremely important distinction. It means the urine, or "siphoned fluid," is sweet; the much rarer "diabetes insipidus" means that the urine is lacking in taste. Yes, there was a time when physicians tasted the urine of people who urinated too much.
2 And other neurodegenerative disorders.

The Future of Drug Discovery. http://dx.doi.org/10.1016/B978-0-12-407180-3.02002-X

Pharma and biotech are still working on many diseases, but they have given up on too many of them because they are deemed too difficult. Of those listed previously, pharma is investing quite reasonably by pursuing better medicines for cardiovascular disease and osteoporosis; collectively, it is probably spending enough.

It is spending more and working most avidly on cancer and diabetes, with or without obesity. It is also working diligently on some so-called orphan or rare diseases that have relatively few sufferers.

The difficulty with cancer drug development is that many of the drugs make people feel sicker and only extend life by a few months. The new drugs are also very expensive. Despite this, treatment options have improved a great deal in the developed world. Now, obesity drug candidates have been failing because they seem to make patients feel suicidal. Diabetes drugs are proving to be profitable to pharma. One fairly new class of medicines has produced three approved drugs against diabetes in the last 6 years and we have identified 34 other candidates trying to compete with these three. Imagine the amount of money spent developing 34 drugs. If they all worked and were approved, the total investment could be easily $30–60 billion. Unless one of them is an oral pill that can be administered once per week, there will be no "market access."[3] The existing drugs will be too good and too similar. These 34 drugs target one and the same receptor. There are 30 targets known for diabetes, and there are over 300 diabetes projects. If these are to reach approval, then with each drug costing an estimated $870 million in "out of pocket" expenses and $1.8 billion including capitalized costs, this would total more than $270–550 billion. This money is not being spent on innovative new drugs, but mostly on so-called "me-toos."[4] Of course, this money will not all be spent because between 90 and 99% of drug-development projects fail or

3 Market access is one of the newish terms used by pharma consultants to describe the phenomenon that an approved drug will not necessarily become a prescribed, used, profitable drug if it is number 5-15 in its class.
4 Me-toos are drugs that are similar in structure and mechanisms of action to already available drugs, usually from competitors.

are dropped. Many are dropped because a competitor dropped a similar drug, targeting the same target, while others are found to be unsafe or not efficacious.

The remaining two age-related diseases on the list, pain and AD, are hardly being worked on at all. Another newly neglected, in terms of drug development, disease is schizophrenia, which can affect someone from age 20 onward and is arguably more debilitating to the individual than AD. Still, there are many more diseases that should be addressed.

Painful truth & AD

Some companies are working on inflammatory pain, which brought the very efficacious and perceived as very safe Vioxx and Celebrex to market. Vioxx has been subject to many lawsuits since it was found to contribute to cardiovascular incidents that accelerated death in some patients. Merck, which developed the drug, was, in some aspects, allegedly found guilty of being economical with the truth. Pfizer, which developed Celebrex, has now been found by inference[5] to have lied to the FDA[6] about its heart attack data.[7] The irony—if something can be called ironic when patients have died—is that both drugs are probably safe provided they are given to the right patients and they take them at the right dose. The proper selection of patients for clinical trials and treatment is strongly featured in this book.

The type of pain we are referring to is resistant to morphine, which is still the best pain killer known, despite being around for 5,000 years. Drug-development programs for this "neuropathic pain" have been largely abandoned by pharma.

AD is predicted to become an epidemic. Already more people suffer from it than have HIV/AIDS. As more and more people become older, the

---

5   We are not qualified to interpret legal data directly, but the payment of a "fine" could be said to imply compliance or agreement with the accusation or simply represent a concession that the case was not worth fighting. We are not stating any opinion about any drug company being found "guilty," even if reportedly found guilty by any judicial system.
6   The U.S. Food & Drug Administration, which oversees safety and, to a somewhat lesser extent, efficacy of both new and existing drugs.
7   See also Chapter 03.

number of victims is likely to soar, with half of those over 85 having it. This will place a great strain on families and healthcare services, and both their budgets. Families make sacrifices that often mean their contribution to the economy is reduced. Full-time care for individuals requires at least three staff members working 8-hour shifts. It will be a strain on the healthcare system; it is not a sector of the workforce that should be growing so significantly. AD will claim the lives of 10 million baby boomers in the next few decades.

George Vradenburg, co-founder and chairman of USAgainstAlzheimer's (USA2), makes compelling arguments. His estimates are that the United States is only spending $400 million on research on the disease, yet is spending $200 billion on care, which he compared to Jonas Salk deciding to invest in leg braces for polio patients instead of looking for a vaccine. The projected cost of care by 2050 would be $1 trillion. Research spending is insignificant compared with the cost burden. We agree with his estimate that at least $2 billion in annual research on the disease is needed.

Pharma still has some clinical trials running, but the prospect of finding a drug that slows AD progression significantly appears slim. Today, in the face of failing trials, pharma is closing AD drug-development programs because they are too expensive and take too long.

It is common to blame pharma. They are accused of many falsehoods, but it is not all pharma's fault. They have explored the main lead that science has given them, and it does not appear to be working. Some candidate AD drugs have reduced amyloid deposits in the brains of mouse models and improved or even reversed cognitive decline, but while they may decrease the amyloid load in AD patients they have little or no effect on cognitive abilities. Science is not providing enough drug targets; more research investment needs to be encouraged and, actually, demanded if we are to combat AD.

Governments, notably the U.S. government through the National Institutes of Health (NIH), have backed research initiatives in the past. For example, the more than 40-year investment costing many billions of dollars is now bearing fruit in the fight against cancer and many effective drugs have been approved. The massive, compared to AD, annual research budget of $3 billion for HIV/AIDS, has brought extraordinary progress; a fatal disease has turned into a manageable chronic illness in a period of 25 years. The force of nongovernmental organizations and lobbyists has made sure it is not only the rich who are being treated.

AD is especially difficult, which is exactly why society should be looking for a preventative therapy for which familial AD has the best chance of revealing an effective therapy. Recent events including the start of a trial on familial AD, backed with government dollars, in Colombia vindicate our thesis: the model of drug discovery needs correction and adaptation. Drugs important for society need to be vigorously pursued; government needs to accelerate funding of research more purposefully and be involved in financing drug discovery trials, not just in post-marketing trials for safety. Pharma needs to be encouraged, if not actually coerced, into pursuing society's needs, and must select patients much more carefully.

Society, government, and pharma have to work together for common goals, but the new trial developed to delay the onset of AD in a family (a third of whose members are likely to develop AD at the age of 45) is using two drugs against the same target. The basis of the model is good, but if the trial does not work, the model must be preserved for other drug candidates using other mechanisms of action from other companies. Trying to prevent AD is much more hopeful than trying to reverse it. But a preventative drug, even for an ultimately fatal disease, has to be very clean with only minor side effects.

More government action required

The familial AD trial is scheduled to last 10 years. The drug has already been around since 2006. If the patent is not extended it may expire ~3 years after approval. Competition would probably appear in less than 3 years. Patent extension is possible, but why make it a legal argument? Why not simply extend the patent based upon approvals? While many citizens and healthcare commentators and practitioners like it when a patent expires and generics appear, society cannot expect pharma companies to invest heavily over a long period without any chance of recuperating their investments. Short patent life spans mean higher prices.

Another effective erosion against exclusivity during the life of a drug's patent comes from off-label use of another drug approved for another condition. A company can be effectively scooped by a drug not actually approved for the condition in question.

"Fiddling" with patent law, while at the same time making it simpler, is not the only incentive that can be used to entice pharma into not abandoning whole research areas. Anything that is projected to reach epidemic proportions should be granted the same privileges as those given to orphan or rare diseases, for example, tax breaks.

If a foreign force was planning to wipe out 10 million baby boomers, no expense would be spared. AD research and drug development need the kind of lobbying practiced by the defense contractors and the HIV/AIDS activists.

The decisiveness & divisiveness of market access

Pharma is not wholly to blame; the people in *control* of pharma are wholly to blame. The "lesion of the status quo" currently becoming infected is caused directly because pharma is turning its back on its traditional role of providing drugs for society's needs.

Pharma is completely under the control of finance and marketers. Business is dictating its path. The investors and gurus of Wall Street want to return to pharma's traditional double-digit growth, but it is not going to happen. Wall Street needs to curb its ambitions and marvel at the future inventiveness of pharma to carve out a more modest profit from its science-determined future.

Doctors and scientists used to run pharma. A scientific discovery would, with pharma's expertise, turn into a needed and safe drug. Business mentality has turned the industry on its head. MBAs, economists, financiers, and "marketers" are deciding what to spend money on. It does not matter how good a drug candidate might be, it will be scrapped if marketers decide that the drug will not have sufficient market access.

When whole programs are scrapped, which is now the situation we find ourselves in, the intellectual core of the company is lost. Legendary scientists who discovered drugs that earned companies billions over many years are unceremoniously let go.

It is time society decided that decisions should be made by people who care about society and are qualified to make them.

Government can change the future

Government has always been involved in the business of drug discovery. In the United States and probably in the rest of the world, both political parties support the basic research budget and it has often increased when others were cut. Possibly uniquely, in the United States the government often gives more money to health research than is requested by the NIH. Of course, the two sides of the house may be giving money for different reasons, but they recognize the value of the research both for citizens and for companies.

However, if the NIH really wants to become seriously involved in drug development from discovery of mechanisms through drug candidate design to clinical trials, then it really needs to ask for much more. Scientists in academia do not seem to appreciate how much it really costs to develop a drug. The NIH needs to ask for more and the U.S. government needs to give it in order to fund its National Center for Advancing Translational Sciences (NCATS) initiative. Perhaps the NIH should hire a significant portion of the recently laid off R&D scientists who have immediate and current experience in pharma.

In the past decades, government has already paid for extremely costly but important clinical trials to determine the efficacy and safety of drugs and therapies. These long-term studies involving many thousands of patients are simply not affordable for drug companies. It may also be against their interests. It would definitely take government intervention to compare two or more new drugs in parallel in a single large trial.

In Europe, governments, which through their national healthcare programs pay for most of the drugs prescribed, are beginning to insist via their regulatory bodies to approve drugs only if they are superior or more cost-effective. In other words, if a new drug is being considered for approval, then it would have to be superior to charge a superior price. This must be a good development. It should, at the same time, encourage better drug development, or at least lower prices for me-toos, and encourage "first in class" innovations instead of me-toos.

Government involvement in drug development may also serve to make drugs available at more reasonable prices. This has been done before.

Not all is doom & gloom

Along with the good news of a trial by Genentech on familial AD, Novartis has recently embarked on a clinical trial, involving 17,200 patients over 4 years, to show that one of its drugs,[8] already used in other conditions, will exhibit cardiovascular protection. The gamble is brave, but quite rational. The drug is only currently approved for a spectrum of auto-inflammatory diseases including the intriguingly monikered Muckle-Wells syndrome.[9] If Novartis is able to show cardiovascular protection, then the drug will go from near orphan status to mega-market. It is also brave because even if successful, it would need some extension of patent time to make it worthwhile.

Meanwhile, Novartis too is cutting research and laying off highly trained successful drug developers.

What can society do?

We hope this book gives the background and foreground for what the problem is and what the solutions are for developing cost-effective drugs. A major issue being debated here is that if Wall Street and financial considerations are the sole determinants of which medicines pharma chooses to develop, without taking into prime consideration society's needs, then society, including governments, investors, and pharma

---

8   canakinumab (Ilaris).
9   Named after Thomas James Muckle and Michael Vernon Wells, who described it in 1962. It is an autosomal dominant disease that causes sensorineural deafness, recurrent hives, fever, chills, and painful joints.

executives, will not have the medicines they and their relatives need. Not even the richest individuals can "buy" efficient, safe drugs developed for their own needs.

Staying on the current path, governments will be faced with escalating healthcare costs in the face of declining economies.

Chapter 01: Why there will be new drugs despite the ongoing "crisis" of drug development in Big Pharma

Pharmaceutical industry in crisis & consolidation

Pfizer, the largest pharmaceutical concern in the world, acquired the Ann Arbor research site in Michigan by purchasing Warner-Lambert/Parke-Davis in 2000. In 2007, Pfizer closed the site despite having just spent $2 billion to refurbish it earlier in the year. The TV news broadcasts of the time commented that the closure of this research site was motivated because "most medicines were already discovered." Nothing could be further from the truth; this is why we believe that many more medicines will be discovered and used in the treatment of many more diseases in the future.

Pfizer has made one more big acquisition since 2007, buying Wyeth for $49 billion in 2009. However, it has also closed numerous research sites as old and as prestigious as the site in Ann Arbor, which is now re-engineered by the University of Michigan as a science park. Pfizer has been perhaps rightly criticized for acquiring companies for rights to an approved product, not for the companies' own research activities. It was not alone among the large pharmaceutical companies of the world in cutting research activities through to 2011. The major U.S. competitor Merck bought Schering-Plough for $41 billion in 2009, and also closed numerous research sites. Yet neither Pfizer nor Merck, nor any other Big Pharma companies, believe that there is no future in drug development. It is just that the industry is fumbling to find ways to accommodate the expectations of their "spoiled" stockholders, who have been used to double-digit growth and stable or increasing stock prices over the past four decades, yet neither such growth nor improving stock prices have been realized since 2008. Stock prices of major pharmaceutical companies have fallen more than the average of other industrial stocks, despite continuous payments of dividends by the companies. The investors are fully aware of the huge patent erosion on the largest earning drugs from all the major pharmaceutical companies. They also know there are no new products to replace these $3-8 billion a year earning drugs, which for some

The Future of Drug Discovery. http://dx.doi.org/10.1016/B978-0-12-407180-3.00001-5

companies account for large portions, up to 40-50%, of earnings and profits, and which lost patent protection from 2009 to 2012.

The industry also struggles with the effects of the 2008 economic recession. Pharmaceuticals is a very capital-intensive industry, with very long 10-12 year product development cycles, and it is in the middle of a capital-requiring merger and acquisition wave that now comes at a much higher cost than the industry has been used to.

The scarcity of cheap capital for mega acquisitions of $40-50 billion and the scarcity of patience for returns on investment has changed what the industry views as a reasonable risk and as a reasonable time line. This is, however, not so easy to accept for our society as the products of this industry are required to save lives and maintain health. There is a resultant dichotomy between the continued medical needs of society and the former fantastic success of private pharmaceutical companies to bring very useful drugs to the clinic in the past 40 years. The industry's sudden risk aversion will be featured throughout this book as a major theme that needs several innovative solutions. However, the scientific basis necessary for new therapies is being continuously developed despite the less intensive contribution and use by the industry.

There is much talk about the crisis of the pharmaceutical industry that in 2009 spent $92 billion on research and development but had "only" 29 products approved. These products are not all blockbusters selling for a billion dollars or more per year and they may or may not cover the cost of their development over their remaining patent life. So the industry cut 29,000 jobs in 2009, and continued this tactic in 2010, when 26 new drugs were approved, and in 2011 when 34 drugs were approved by the Food and Drug Administration (FDA) although only five are expected by the stock market analysts to reach sales over $350 million per year. In addition, the companies initiated the buying back of their own stock options to support the stock prices. Although these stocks had suffered less than others during the beginning of the recession of 2008-2009, investors thought they were too slow to recover. Yet there can be little doubt that this essential global industry, which, despite complaints of falling profits by investors and managers, remains undeniably profitable in absolute terms. Compared to most industries such as steel, paper, food, and so forth, pharmaceutical returns are at least double, yet the other industries remain active with smaller profits. From governments' points of view, there is an extra importance attached to developments in the pharmaceutical industry as it is one of the pillars of public health and thus of a stable society. There can be no doubt that this industry is not only going to survive but it will also produce new medicines that address diseases that we cannot yet treat, and will provide drugs that treat other diseases better than presently available drugs. In addition, it will provide drugs for diseases yet to emerge or to be diagnosed.

Simply speaking, several of the following important factors for survival as well as continued growth of the industry are stably present:

1. There is a global pharmaceutical market that grows.
2. There is new science, new diagnostics and therapeutics, and new medical and information technology to provide a basis for novel developments.
3. A globalization of healthcare standards is taking place.

Therefore, there will be a growing pharma industry. What it will look like, who will invest in it, who will work in it in which countries, and how the pricing of its products will be negotiated are all interesting questions for which this book provides some suggestions.

Since pharma is not just any industry,[10] it has to accommodate high ethical standards as human lives and human suffering are in the balance of the effects and distribution of its products. Discussions about this industry will always need to encompass ethical aspects on a global scale, along with the economic, scientific, technical, and political aspects.

This book will describe what industrial, academic, clinical, and preclinical researchers all seem to believe: that we will have many powerful new drugs discovered, tested, and marketed and that we are only at the beginning of real pharmacological *prevention* and *treatment* of many diseases.

---

10   See also Chapter 07.

Today we satisfactorily treat only very few diseases. "Satisfactory treatment" means that at the end of the treatment period we restore the treated patient to full health. This means not only that the symptoms of the disease are gone and the consequences of the untreated disease are fully prevented, but also that the successfully treated patient now has the same risk for becoming ill again with the same or with other diseases as if they had never had the disease. We can now achieve this restoration of "full health" only when treating bacterial infections, when the proper antibiotic is found (after identifying the infectious bacteria via increased use of diagnostics) or by the use of broad spectrum antibiotics.

Some experts on the complicated and much internationally debated concept of *health* add to the fully curative medical approaches, such as the early removal of tumors that have not yet metastasized, as success stories of treatments that restore full health. Whether one agrees with this addition of fully successful treatment or not, the total number of fully successful drug treatments is very low compared to the number of diseases where we provide pharmaceuticals as treatment or part of treatment, and even lower compared to the number of diseases where we can diagnose the disease but can offer no treatment or only symptomatic treatment.

Thus, there is a huge remaining medical need to be filled by new drugs, even in diseases where we provide pharmaceuticals as the pharmacological treatment, or part of the treatment, but this treatment is not curative.

The diseases that we can diagnose but can offer only symptomatic treatment include the drug treatments of the 50 "top diseases" (top in terms of number of patients treated and/or top in terms of the income per disease that the pharmaceutical industry derives from selling drugs to treat this disease) such as hypertension, diabetes, schizophrenia, major depression, anxiety disorders, rheumatoid arthritis, HIV, and epilepsy, to mention a few. Only in a few cases do we modify, but not stop, the rate of disease progression. We do not restore health with the current drugs in these diseases.

There is a disproportionate use of U.S. data in this book, and there are several reasons for this. Firstly, there is easy availability and transparency of data, even in comparison to Europe, where often the conscious (governmental) price control of drugs plays direct and indirect roles. Secondly, the U.S. market is now the largest pharmaceutical market and rarely are drugs developed that will not be introduced there. Thirdly, the U.S. research expenditures by governmental and private enterprise lead drug development, even if the share of European, Japanese, Chinese, and Indian research and development is increasing. Fourthly, the U.S. pricing is the earnings leader for most pharma companies and the decisions to engage in a drug-development project are strongly influenced by the U.S. medical and sales views. Fifthly, the United States is home to most large pharmaceutical companies, generic companies, and biotech companies; thus, trends from the United States affect events in the long product cycle of 10–12 years. Even if other governments made huge decisions and investments in a 15-year window, the United States would still remain important. Sixthly, in judging trends one needs to consider that although living standards and healthcare is better in Norway, Sweden, Finland, the Netherlands, Germany, Switzerland, and so forth, than in the United States, these countries are small and homogenous in comparison to the United States. Finally, when Chinese, Indian, Russian, and Brazilian leaders describe their aims, it is to reach U.S. and not Norwegian standards, and while the latter would be better, it is even farther away.

For patients diagnosed with any of the other ~500 diseases not in Table 1.1 listed by the FDA or the 700 rare or so-called "orphan" diseases, the pharmaceutical industry does even less. Why? Simply because there is no good scientific basis for treatments, or, what is more often the case, the industry has made the calculation that working on a drug treatment for a "smaller" indication/disease is not economically feasible, that is, not profitable or at least it does not easily fit within the historical double-digit growth and profit targets. The industry set these financial targets decades ago after World War II when healthcare in general and drug lists were expanding from almost nowhere, and the stockholders have come to expect such growth and profits.

We will discuss under the "future of the industry" this "catch-22." The entire industry has locked itself into a promise of growth that it cannot

Indication	Prevalence (millions)
Hypercholesterolemia	112
Hypertension	84
Type 2 diabetes	25.8
Major depressive disorder (MDD)	22.3
Neuropathic pain	**18**
Alzheimer's disease (AD)	**5.3 (projected 2035: 42 million)**
Chronic obstructive pulmonary disease (COPD)	**17**
Stroke	**5.8**
Rheumatoid arthritis (RA)	3.1
Schizophrenia	**2.2**
Multiple sclerosis (MS)	0.4
Cancer overall	11.7
Breast cancer	2.7
Ovarian cancer	1.2
Prostate cancer	2.5
Colorectal cancer	1.8
Melanoma	0.7
Bacterial infections	**240 (worldwide 4 billion)**
Malaria	0.002 (worldwide 2.6 billion)

Table 1.1: The top diseases: prevalence of diseases in the United States
These data are for a population of 303 million. A significant number of the population is sick, is diagnosed, and, if treatment is available and effective and if they are insured, they will be treated. The diseases in bold type are ones where the industry effort is grossly inadequate and where the profit motive trumps medical need (see also Table 4.1). Obesity is not listed because there is no agreement on whether it is a bona fide disease or a risk factor for many diseases such as cardiovascular disease, diabetes, and so forth. Malaria is a reminder that the United States is a strange mirror at times. There are 2,600 malaria cases in the United States per year, while the world struggles with this disease. However, the U.S. prevalence number is reflected in the six research projects sponsored in the United States by companies, while the U.S. government and U.S. nongovernmental organizations (NGOs) participate and, in some cases, lead the international efforts to prevent and treat malaria; this is not a pharma industry initiative.

Company	2009 revenue	2009 employees	2009 RPE	2012 market cap
Roche	$47.35B	67,695	$699,460	$149.63B
Bristol-Myers Squibb (BMS)	$18.80B	28,000	$671,770	$59.77B
Eli Lilly	$21.83B	40,360	$541,030	$49.07B
Johnson & Johnson (J&J)	$61.89B	115,500	$535,900	$190.54B
AstraZeneca	$32.80B	63,000	$520,700	$59.35B
GlaxoSmithKline (GSK)	$45.83B	99,913	$458,700	$113.49B
Novartis	$44.26B	99,834	$443,410	$140.92B
Pfizer	$50.00B	116,500	$429,260	$179.27B
Abbott Labs	$30.76B	73,000	$421,360	$104.00B
Sanofi Aventis	$41.99B	104,867	$400,410	$106.58B
Merck	$27.42B	100,000	$274,280	$134.68B
Bayer	$22.30B	108,400	$205,720	$51.39B

Table 1.2: The top 12 drug companies by revenue, per employee earnings, & market capitalization
Revenues and employee earnings data are from 2009; market capitalizations are as of August 2012 at the NYSE. The total pharma and biotech company capitalization is close to $3 trillion, making up a very important portion of the total economy, and is even more important because of the life-saving nature of their products. The earning per employee and the project portfolios encompass both proprietary and generic drugs in different portions and are discussed in subsequent chapters.

sustain for many reasons outside of its own competence, and then by means of mergers and acquisitions, life cycle management of old drugs, and so forth, tries to find miraculous growth and profits. This "holy grail" of the pharma industry, high stock prices and double-digit growth, is not easily achievable. Eventually, at least 2-3 of the top 10 companies will have to admit this, as did the Merck CEO Kenneth Frazier in February 2011. He announced that at best single-digit growth is to be expected and that stock buyback for billions will be used to try to lift stagnant or sinking stock prices, as had also Pfizer and GlaxoSmithKline (see Table 1.2). When the industry sets realistic financial goals then perhaps we will have an industry that is essential to our society, and is still more profitable than, for example, the steel industry, but does not adhere to unrealistic self-ascribed financial goals to which it is held accountable by the analysts and stockholders.

Why is there a strong belief that new future medicines will come?
In the gloom of steady layoffs, one needs to outline why one should believe in a strong future for the industry. The basis for this optimism has several sources, as summarized in Table 1.3.

Why there will be many new drugs in the future
1. The scientific basis for the design of novel treatments of diseases is steadily increasing; government spending on basic research continued to increase even during the financial crisis in 2008 and onward.
2. The number of scientists with experience in drug development is increasing in the developed and developing world alike.
3. Past significant success. a. The last 40 years have shown that we can develop useful and possible-to-pay-for drugs that dramatically change mortality in all kinds of large and small disease entities when we focus our priorities scientifically, financially, and politically. b. The diseases where the standard of care could be changed include some very common diseases such as cardiovascular disease, diabetes, rheumatoid arthritis; some much feared diseases such as cancer, hepatitis C, HIV; and some genetic diseases that were deadly such as Gaucher's disease, hereditary angioedema, and so forth. c. This medical success, which was accompanied by massive economical success for the investors of the fully private pharmaceutical industry, forms a strong foundation to believe that this industry, despite discussions of crisis, will continue to develop new drugs.
4. New, constantly mutating pathogenic microbes, especially bacteria and viruses, continuously impose a renewed demand for novel drugs for which they are not yet resistant. a. This race to outmaneuver infectious agents is never ending and dictates the development of new antibacterial and antiviral drugs. b. Both the heads of the FDA and the European Medicines Agency (EMA)[1] warned in the fall of 2010 that we are dangerously behind nature and its mutating microbes in developing new antibiotics, with possible dire consequences globally.

Why there will be many new drugs in the future

5.	New diseases can be diagnosed with new technologies and after being diagnosed will require drug treatment.
	a. Known diseases are diagnosed better and, more importantly, earlier, permitting more effective and, at times, different treatments.
6.	Recognition of the value of preventive medicines (e.g., statins for cardiovascular disease) is increasing and such medicines are being sought for type 2 diabetes, obesity, AD, and so forth.
	a. For example, it is now estimated that in the United States alone there are ~820,000 fewer cardiovascular disease deaths a year because of
	i. preventive use of statins, and
	ii. disciplined control of hypertension, even when this control is far from complete.
7.	Significant improvements in synthetic organic chemistry[2] permit with great efficacy the total synthesis of natural products that were earlier deemed impossible to turn into drugs because of the difficulties and cost of synthesis; for example, the 2010-approved drug for metastatic breast cancer, eribulin mesylate (Halaven), is a synthetic analog of a natural product with more than a dozen chiral centers and had been deemed impossible as a commercial product 10 years ago.
8.	Society has a need and wish to act as healer.
	a. There is no political party and no election process where healthcare and its delivery are not being discussed prominently, right after food-energy and national securities.
	b. Society in developed countries, in its post-industrial, post-Internet phases, is turning to biology:
	i. There is interest in health and life span extension as never before.
9.	Recognition by governments and NGOs that health is a global issue leads to prepaid vaccine development and drug-development programs with guaranteed purchases from pharma to treat diseases of the developing world in an ever-increasing manner.
10.	Smaller pharma and biotech companies pick up smaller diseases, where Big Pharma competition is less strong and where they may also benefit from orphan drug status with favorable tax conditions.
	a. They show that treatments for these diseases are possible to find and that it is often much more profitable than Big Pharma marketing departments calculated.
	b. The start of modern treatments for multiple sclerosis (MS) started from Biogen with interferon beta[3] in 1996; now MS is one of the most active fields of drug development, with Big Pharma[4] amply represented as well as the now big biotechs Biogen Idec and Teva Pharmaceutical Industries.

(continued on next page)

Why there will be many new drugs in the future

11. Big Pharma is acquiring risk-reduction techniques, permitting it to remain successfully in drug development:
    a. It now realizes that testing a drug in a small indication in a well-defined patient population may teach a great deal about the properties of this drug, its behavior in man, and its side effects, and that this knowledge then significantly increases the likelihood of success of a larger trial in a larger indication, where failure might easily cost $500 million to $1 billion. Thus, we see examples of bigger and bigger pharma going into orphan or small diseases with a drug that is also intended for a big indication.
        i. For example, Novartis had an anti-IL1b antibody approved in the treatment of the orphan disease familial Mediterranean fever and learned how it works, and at which dose, before entering it into a type 2 diabetes trial and myocardial infarction prevention trial ~100–1,000 times the size of the Mediterranean fever trial.
        ii. Other companies insist on "precision medicine" for the first trials of their drug candidates, selecting a patient group based on genotyping, or phenotyping in such a manner that it can decide whether there is a meaningful biological signal produced by the drug before deciding on the several hundred million dollar multiyear phase 3 trials.
        iii. A much greater emphasis is being put on finding, developing, and using *biomarkers* that, while not the clinical end point, can *predict* the effects of the drug.
        iv. Companion diagnostics are becoming more common to help enrich the study group with patients most likely to benefit.

12. The total medicines market is rapidly increasing, with new patients diagnosed and treated.
    a. In China, India, and South America, previously uncared for patients are increasingly receiving the most modern drug therapies as their countries reach higher living standards and produce diagnostics and drugs.
    b. Even in the United States there is a large expansion, with the Health Care and Education Reconciliation Act of 2010 (aka the Affordable Health Care Bill) adding another 31 million patients to the most high-priced market.

Why there will be many new drugs in the future

13. Thus, with an annual increase in the global medicines market of ~4-5% and with little exposure to economic cycles of recession, pharma remains a very profitable high-tech industry that is not raw material dependent and is politically not very vulnerable.

   a. Thus, while it is capital intensive, we believe that there will be capital for drug development, albeit while under continued pressures from investors to increase earnings. Pharma can be assisted by government:

      i. by reducing liability, as has happened with vaccines,

      ii. by prolonging patent life spans, or

      iii. by giving tax breaks such as with drugs for the treatment of orphan diseases.

Table 1.3: Why we will have many new drugs in the future
See text for detailed explanations about some of the points in Table 1.3.

---

1 Also known as the European Agency for the Evaluation of Medicinal Products (EMEA).

2 Sometimes it is not necessary to bring out a new drug to make improvements. In 1954, the future Nobel laureate Robert Burns Woodward of Harvard synthesized strychnine. Strychnine, for its size, was thought to be the most complex known molecule. It is found in the beans of *Strychnos ignatii*. Woodward's synthesis took 29 chemical steps and yielded 0.009%. In 1994, Viresh H. Rawal and Seiji Iwasa synthesized it in some 12 steps with a 22% yield, a 2,500-fold increase.

3 Recombinant interferon α-2a and 2b were originally approved in 1986 to treat an even smaller indication—hairy cell leukemia—in oncology, which was then almost exclusively a small company therapeutic area.

4 The first oral MS drug was approved in November 2010; it was from Novartis. Biogen Idec, Merck, and Pfizer will follow closely behind.

Scientific progress in biology is strong and scientific knowledge is steadily increasing. This means that understanding the physiology of humans at a whole body, organ, tissue, cell, and molecular level is becoming more detailed. Increased understanding of molecular detail is the prerequisite for modern drug development and thus, unlike advances in cellular imaging, as spectacular as the images might be, only the molecular detail provides real addressable drug targets. In the 1990s, researchers made the assumption that discovering, by itself, a change in the genome or in the transcriptional profile associated with a disease was a cue for an actionable drug-development project. However, only 10 years after the human genome project finished in 2001 and ~15 years after the interrogation of cellular transcriptional profiles with microarrays and other methods like sequencing have we started to appreciate that identifying genetic and transcriptional changes associated with disease is important. Still, it is no guarantee that it alone can form the basis of a successful drug-development project; rather, it is an inducer and a prompter of such a project. While in the 1990s biotechs were founded on identifying a disease-causing mutation, today one needs to show how the effects of this mutation will be dealt with using a drug molecule in a safe and efficacious manner before a company is financed.

Nevertheless, as we will discuss in the section "Biomarkers" in Chapter 08 and in Chapter 09, "Personalized medicine," the diagnostic value of discovering genetic changes and of following transcriptional changes with disease and treatment is enormous for both drug development and drug treatment follow up. The progress in biology coincides with, and is assisted by, the progress of information technology that is required to handle the ever-increasing data we can collect from a single patient visit. The new emergence of systems biology, a modern version of physiology, emphasizes the patterns of reactions and pathways that are used by nature in different cell types. Identifying such pathways and their chemical, biological, and structural commonalities in multiple cell types and tissues suggests that drugs developed for one disease may be used successfully in others because underlying cellular pathways are similar or identical. This is most common in the therapeutic areas of oncology and inflammation.

How can small companies, providing the financing climate is good, fill the spots deemed too small economically by large pharma? A good example is the success of enzyme replacement for small genetic diseases that was pioneered by the Genzyme Corporation. Genzyme is active in orphan drugs for indications with fewer than 200,000 patients in the United States.[11] The company is very valuable today, based on the high

---

11   In Europe, the equivalent is a "rare disease," as determined by the European Medicines Agency (EMA), where prevalence is no more than 5 in 10,000 people in the European Union (EU), which is currently approximately 250,000 people.

prices for these successful "biologicals," or recombinant enzymes, to replace the enzyme deficiencies, at least in the periphery. Indeed, after a yearlong take-over struggle, Genzyme was bought by Sanofi Aventis for $20 billion in 2011, even as generic competition by credible actors such as Merck and Teva was brewing. This example shows that the extremes of diseases in terms of patient numbers, such as cardiovascular disease, with hundreds of millions, and some rare diseases, with, say, 10,000 patients, are often well served. For example, as a result of large scientific and drug-development investments, cardiovascular drugs were developed that serve ~100 million of the 300 million Americans. At the opposite end of the spectrum of diseases, for rare diseases that are almost always genetic, scientific investments in recombinant technology and the generosity of the Orphan Drug legislation bear fruit.

When Amgen made its first sales projections for erythropoietin (EPO) used to treat patients with low red blood cell counts after radiation therapy for cancer, it was projected to generate $300 million per year. However, EPO sells for $5 billion a year. It should, however, be added that the extensive marketing of EPO (and its high price) have been called into question by the UK authorities, who believe that EPO is overused, particularly in dialysis patients with increased mortality and, of course, unnecessary cost. Hence, the new UK guidelines will lead to reduced use of EPO, but the bulk of its sales will remain from its main use to boost hemoglobin.

There are many examples of drugs that were misjudged by Big Pharma with respect to earning potential in one indication, and this has enabled biotechs successfully to enter the market.

Many pharma companies seem defeated by how good generic drugs are and are becoming. Chemical innovation may present opportunities for pharma companies to stay ahead. The generic drugs, good as they are, are also a testament to the success of the pharma industry. There are no generics without the original patented drugs. It is remarkable that big pharmaceuticals make generic competitors of the original drugs of their Big Pharma competitor—an ultimate form of compliment; GSK's first generic drug (Alli) was a reduced dose copy of orlistat, Roche's breakthrough weight-loss drug, Xenical.

Safe drugs in new indications: one does not always need new drugs for new therapies

There are many examples of safe drugs that find new indications, reach many patients, and generate larger than expected sales. When, for example, a small epilepsy drug is projected to sell for $200 million, it may sell 3-4 times more because it is used "off label" in mood stabilization, pain treatment, and so forth, providing it is shown to be safe; the most prominent example is gabapentin. The first successful tyrosine kinase inhibitor in oncology, Gleevec, was projected to sell for a maximum of $300–500 million per year and be useful only in a special form of leukemia. However, because of the commonalities of cellular pathways in various cancer cells and because it is a less specific drug than we thought it was, Gleevec is now used in a whole range of cancers and sells for over $2 billion per year.

The examples of higher than expected earnings on drugs become incorporated into the thinking and action of Big Pharma, which either acquires the smaller companies (which happens often) and retains some of their best people temporarily (with golden handcuffs) or partly adopts the same thinking, which has happened at least in a few cases in recent years.

Ideally, we should prevent rather than treat diseases and there is a strong scientific drive toward this goal. But, rising healthcare costs counteract any talk that we should treat "nonsymptomatic," and thus healthy-appearing, people, as expeditiously as we treat everyone diagnosed with the already overt disease.

This is a poor man's dilemma: never having enough funds to prevent any disasters as the funds at hand have to be used to meet more expensively the acute problems.

Of course, one must remember that vaccination programs are the best example of preventive medicine at its most effective, cheapest, and best. Childhood vaccinations have become so accepted and expected that governments have taken over the liability costs in most countries for most vaccines that are part of vaccination programs. However, the most important preventive medicines list would be very incomplete without pointing out the several hundred million doses of annual influenza vaccines used to prevent complications in a nonsymptomatic population of aged persons and in people suffering from other diseases such as respiratory and cardiovascular disease.

This book will deal with medicines and not vaccines, which are a very special set of medical products deserving separate books, and there are indeed many books about the science and policy and politics of vaccine development and of vaccination.

Preventive drugs: large, long, expensive, convincing trials

Because our society is not that poor and there is a strong, growing scientific basis for preventive medicine, we implement piece-by-piece preventive medicine and early diagnosis programs, such as mammography and prostate and colon cancer screenings. The cost of these programs is being continuously questioned. They remain because early detection is the best guarantee for successful treatment. However, more intelligent screening methods that focus on those most at risk are continuously sought after to reduce cost. The dilemma is well illustrated in the case of gastric cancer that has an approximately five times higher prevalence in Japan than in the United States, making it economically justifiable to screen in Japan. This results in gastric cancers being discovered at an early stage, which can then be treated surgically and with drugs, while the ~20,000 cases in the United States per year do not justify screening and gastric cancers are diagnosed at a more advanced stage (III to IV), and, as a result, mortality from this type of cancer is 50%.

When we can be convinced that preventive medicine in large diseases exists and is effective, we have and are spending $10-15 billion a year on it. The famous "4S" study sponsored by Merck in Scandinavia showed that Merck's cholesterol-lowering drug simvastatin could reduce the incidence of myocardial infarction and could reduce mortality. This study was the first in "evidence-based medicine" (EBM).[12] It followed 4,400 patients and took 6 years to complete. It established the statin market not only for Merck but also for Bristol Myers Squibb and Pfizer-Warner Lambert, which also sell statins. Pfizer's Lipitor sold over $6 billion per year and the expiration of the patent protection in 2011 of its largest selling, blockbuster drug had an enormous impact on the largest pharma company.[13]

The emergence of solid data on disease prevention from EBM trials of this size, duration, and quality can be used to establish rational recommendations. It places preventive drug treatment, drug pricing, and how useful and economically worthwhile it is for society and the individual on more solid ground.

The large clinical trials sponsored by governments in Europe and the United States often transcend the questions on the efficacy and safety of a single drug from a company, and affect our concepts of disease and its drug treatment. A good example of how convincing for doctors, patients, and politicians a large comparative study on prevention can be is the study from the National Center on Diabetes Prevention at the Centers for Disease Control and Prevention in Atlanta. The review article[14] compared 56 studies from 20 countries on prevention of type 2 diabetes, which results to a large extent from the obesity epidemics that are spreading

---

12   See also Chapters 03, 07, and 11.
13   See also Chapters 04 and 06.
14   Li R, Zhang P, Barker LE, Chowdhury FM, & Zhang X (2010) Cost-effectiveness of interventions to prevent and control diabetes mellitus: a systematic review. *Diabetes Care*. Aug; 33(8):1872-1894. The authors "found strong evidence to classify the following interventions as: (I) Cost saving 1) ACE inhibitor (ACEI) therapy for intensive hypertension control ...; 2) ACEI or angiotensin-receptor blocker (ARB) therapy to prevent end-stage renal disease (ESRD) ...; 3) early irbesartan therapy ... to prevent ESRD ...; 4) comprehensive foot care to prevent ulcers ...; 5) and 6) multi-component interventions for diabetic risk factor control and early detection of complications ...; (II) Very cost-effective 1) intensive lifestyle interventions to prevent type 2 diabetes among persons with impaired glucose tolerance ...; 2) universal opportunistic screening for undiagnosed type 2 diabetes in African Americans between 45 and 54 years old; 3) intensive glycemic control as implemented in the UK Prospective Diabetes Study ...; 4) statin therapy for secondary prevention of cardiovascular disease ...; 5) counseling and treatment for smoking cessation ... 6) and 7) annual screening for diabetic retinopathy ...; and 8) immediate vitrectomy to treat diabetic retinopathy ..." (abridged).

all over the world, presenting, quite possibly, the largest threat (second only to Alzheimer's disease; AD) to people, the healthcare system, and society.[15]

Age as a risk factor & keeping costs in check

Society in developed countries has an increasingly aging population with many chronic diseases for which today the *most important risk factor is age*. This is true for cancer, AD, and other neurodegenerative diseases; the pressure on healthcare is growing. At the same time we are told that the expenditures for healthcare as a portion of the total economy have to stop increasing lest we will not be able to educate our young, put out the fires, and defend the borders of our countries. Can this be done: treating more patients, treating them better, and not increasing healthcare cost?

The answer is that it most likely can be done. Advanced drug treatments that start early as preventive treatments or treatments of earlier diagnosed disease can be more efficient and will improve healthcare cost wherein drugs account only for ~15–18% of the cost. Well-chosen, efficacious early treatments can reduce the cost and risk of medical interventions of hospitalization and of lost productivity. Good drugs pay for themselves in many ways.

Drugs are not made in anyone's cellar or house laboratory anymore and their design, synthesis, production, testing, and approval are among the most complex and most regulated, long-term human activities carried out in a large and complex industry. It involves pharma, healthcare, hospitals, insurance, government, and patient–doctor interactions.

This book will address the opportunities and risks facing the drug-producing part: the pharma industry of this greater societal equation. We describe the opportunities as presented by increased scientific and technological prowess in diagnosing diseases and understanding disease processes, and making drugs that can prevent, cure or slow down, or

---

15 It should be noted that currently it is estimated that 80% of obese people will not develop type 2 diabetes.

interfere with the disease, and the risks arising from the drugs themselves. No drugs offer benefits without risks. The pressures put on this industry are from expected profits, governmental and international regulations, and surely ethics. It is thought to be, and should be, an ethical industry whose products affect the very well-being and suffering of humans. The reach is increasingly widespread as pharmaceutical products approach food in their global use. Yet this industry is treated many times by investors, managers, and politicians as if it manufactured some gadget without which we could live well, and in a few years when this product and this "need" are forgotten, we will live equally well. This is not the case: we continuously need drugs for our ills and for those of us who surely will fall ill.

Newly orphaned diseases: more government needed

As a direct result of pharma companies' growing risk aversion, many of the industry's giants have decided to drop entire research programs. Whole diseases have been dropped from their research profiles. It is as though these diseases are now "orphaned" despite a much higher prevalence than the original definition (see Table 1.1). Pharma companies would be able to afford to continue many more programs but reduce their scope in order to maintain their stock prices in the short term.[16]

Admittedly, some of the necessary trials are long and potentially very expensive, but governments can afford to conduct the trials. It is not as if they have never been involved in large, long, and important trials that changed the practice of medicine and thus general health and expenditure on health. Throughout this book governments will be requested to extend their involvement. The long-term trials of hormone replacement therapy from the Women's Health Initiative and a number of trials conducted in the UK through its National Institute for Health & Clinical Excellence (NICE) are a testament to the importance of noncommercial trials.

16   Bartfai T & Lees GV (2011) Pharma TARP: a troubled asset relief program for novel, abandoned projects in the pharmaceutical industry. *TheScientificWorldJournal*. Feb 14;11:454-457.

We are not talking about rare diseases, and we are certainly not talking about cancers or diabetes where Big Pharma is seriously involved with several hundred ongoing trials, which all have difficulty recruiting patients because of the competing trials. We are talking about large indications like pain, AD, schizophrenia, and antibiotics to treat bacteria strains that have become resistant to today's antibiotics. Studies in these areas can be at worst self-financing and at best profit generating.[17]

---

17 Ibid.

Chapter 02: The need for medicines grows

Small molecules & biologicals

The description of any stock offering in a large or small pharmaceutical company states that the medicines market is growing. Demography and science meet economy and politics in this generic statement as seen in Table 2.1, which summarizes the factors behind the growth of pharmaceutical sales.

There are numerous publications dealing with point 1 in Table 2.1 concerning emerging markets, and to drive home the point it is worth remarking that in India there is now a larger middle class than in Germany.

Factors that underlie the growth of pharmaceutical sales
1. Increasing global population, and increasing middle class in the large new markets of India, China, South America, and Russia, as well as the United States healthcare reform, which should add over 31 million previously uninsured patients into a market of high prices.
2. Increasing age of population in developed markets, partly reflecting the improved medicines of the past 40 years—"pharma creates pharma market"—since for many major diseases age is the most important risk factor.
3. New diseases can be treated, often with expensive biologicals at $20-100k per year.
4. Diagnostics market grows even faster (5-8%) than pharmaceutical markets (3-4%) and new diagnostics define new patients, often earlier in the disease progression, meaning that different drugs can be used, often at higher efficacy.
5. NGOs and governments act more widely as drug purchasers for poor countries in Africa and Asia.
6. Obesity and AD spread has taken epidemic proportions and underlies large medicine markets

Table 2.1: The factors that underlie the growth of pharmaceutical sales
Observations from the first decade of this century; the picture is unlikely to change soon.

The Future of Drug Discovery. http://dx.doi.org/10.1016/B978-0-12-407180-3.00002-7

Thus, the purchasing power for drugs in India is greater despite the larger German GDP. Differences in cultural and family ties explain why the Indian market for expensive biologicals to treat certain cancers is bigger now than the German market, while in 1999 the Indian market was negligible. Identical arguments could be made about the growth of the Chinese pharmaceutical markets and the per capita income, while still lower than in Europe, does not reflect the fact that families pull together financial resources differently in Asia to buy expensive treatments than in Europe, where more people expect the government-sponsored healthcare systems to carry the cost.

The aging population

Point 2 of Table 2.1 concerning the aging population in developed countries has been thoroughly discussed in macroeconomic terms. But it is for fear of reprisals for failing the measure of political correctness, and for our horrific history of eugenics of the twentieth century, that it is seldom pointed out that, in the developed countries, in the last 6 months of our lives we spend more on medical care than in our entire lives up to that point. Often the results, as measured in life quality at the very end of our lives, are abysmal. Changes in our philosophy of how we deal with death might inevitably help to ease this unevenness of how lifetime healthcare spending is allocated and lifetime medicine cost is distributed.

Nevertheless, the population's increasing age in most countries increases the disease burden dramatically because not only Alzheimer's disease (AD) and other neurodegenerative diseases but also cancer, hypertension, and so forth increase with age. Age is the most potent underlying factor known.

Thus, it would be wrong to think that the growing average age does not have a very broad effect on medical and drug needs. Consider that over 70 years of age everyone has symptoms of osteoarthritis and over 85 years of age every second person suffers with AD. Life expectancy is increasing, but not throughout the world. Some shocking examples can be found in Africa, where the life expectancy is now below 50 years and is still falling because only 14% of the HIV/AIDS sufferers are being treated fully or adequately. Mortality in patients with HIV/AIDS and subsequent tuberculosis is extremely high among young adults, while at the same time, in the same countries, child mortality from bacterial infections and malaria remains high. In Russia, after a long period of falling life expectancy following failing societal support of the ill during a period of large changes, life expectancy is now, in 2012, stabilizing.

Rare or "orphan" diseases

A rare or orphan disease has a prevalence of fewer than 200,000 affected individuals in the United States (see the National Institutes of Health-U.S. Food and Drug Administration; NIH-FDA, National Organization of Rare Disease database of 1,200 diseases). It includes cystic fibrosis, which affects 1 in 31,000, Gaucher's disease, which affects 1 in 50,000, and others such as Fabry's disease, Hurler's syndrome, Hunter's syndrome, Dupuytren's contracture, Huntington's disease, Swyer syndrome, Miller–Dieker syndrome, hereditary tyrosinemia, Mediterranean fever, and so forth. From the patients' point of view, the lack of interest of Big Pharma in these rare diseases was good news. This allowed the smaller biotech companies to work on these diseases, especially because the competition from Big Pharma between 1980 and 2010 was very low. The scientific basis for understanding the genetic cause of rare diseases is often good, and the biotechs were able to demonstrate that biologicals, which provide replacement for faulty or absent proteins, can be effective. These biologicals often have good safety profiles and could be developed with less capital, fewer people, and faster in 5-7 years than small molecules that take on average 10-12 years.

Because of the work of biotechs, which became in many cases deservedly rich, Gaucher's disease is now treated with enzyme replacement therapy from Genzyme-Sanofi and other companies will follow with so-called biosimilars (i.e., drugs similar to those already approved from competitive companies). Soon the disease might also be treated with small molecules, which took 25 years longer to develop than the recombinant enzyme that is administered by infusion. Today ~40% of patients with cystic fibrosis will reach adulthood compared to a small percentage 25 years ago. There are new breakthroughs expected to improve this survival rate. For example, in January 2012 a small molecule treatment developed by Arena-Vertex, which will benefit only 4% of cystic fibrosis patients, or ~1,200 in the United States, was approved in record time by the FDA. The price tag for this nonbiological pill is reported to be close to $300,000 per year.[18]

The pharma industry has, through these and many other examples, learned that a company that addresses an orphan or rare disease can be highly profitable even when the total number of patients is so low, for example, 10,000, which is much lower than the definition limit of 200,000 for an orphan disease in the United States. In these cases we, society and insurers, are willing and able to pay for very expensive medication for orphan diseases. One real drawback for these low-prevalence diseases is, however, the lack of a screening program,[19] although severe genetic diseases are diagnosed in close to 100% of cases where medical supervision is available. Chapter 10 discusses the issue of how much we can or should pay for drugs and how these sums relate to the total cost of healthcare and to the concept of "quality-adjusted man-year" in different countries with different health insurance systems.

Notwithstanding the cystic fibrosis drug mentioned earlier, it is noteworthy that the most expensive drugs today are all protein drugs: biologicals. They are produced in bacteria or in mammalian cells at a higher cost than small, chemically synthesized molecules can be made. However, the cost of goods, although higher for biologicals than for small molecules, does not explain the tremendous price differences between the majority of expensive small molecules (~$3,000-6,000 per year) and

---

18   Although the manufacturer has committed to make it available for free in the United States for patients who have no health insurance and annual household income of under $150,000. See also Chapter 09.
19   As discussed in Chapter 01 for gastric cancers.

the biologicals (~$200,000–400,000 per year) used to treat orphan diseases (see Table 2.2).

It is worth noting that the first protein drugs were not expensive and were produced by purification of natural sources, such as donated blood. Insulin was purified from pig and whale pancreas and plasma products, and coagulation factors, plasma expanders, and several hormones were obtained from a cheap starting material—human blood from volunteers. Regrettably, in the mid-1980s, human blood purchased very cheaply from poor countries in, for example, the Caribbean, was sometimes infected with HIV. Problems of virally infected serum products and blood have

Drug	Indication	Annual cost	Company
Soliris (eculizumab)	paroxysmal nocturnal hemoglobinuria (PNH)	$409,500	Alexion Pharmaceuticals
Elaprase (idursulfase)	Hunter's syndrome	$375,000	Shire Pharmaceuticals
Naglazyme (galsulfase)	Maroteaux-Lamy syndrome	$365,000	BioMarin Pharmaceutical
Cinryze (C1 esterase inhibitor)	hereditary angioedema (HAE)	$350,000	ViroPharma
Myozyme (alglucosidase alpha)	Pompe's disease	$300,000	Genzyme
Arcalyst (rilonacept)	cryopyrin-associated periodic syndromes (CAPS)	$250,000	Regeneron
Fabrazyme (agalsidase beta)	Fabry's disease	$200,000	Genzyme
Cerezyme (imiglucerase)	Gaucher's disease	$200,000	Genzyme
Aldurazyme (laronidase)	Hurler's syndrome	$200,000	Genzyme, BioMarin Pharmaceutical

Table 2.2: The most expensive biologicals used to treat orphan diseases
Data are from 2010.

occurred in almost every country. Part of this was because of lax testing routines, but part of it was because the rapidly mutating virus was escaping detection by antibodies. PCR-based screens today provide for much better, although never complete, safety of human blood-derived products; the residual problem is we just do not know all the viruses we should screen for.

Drug development: adding biologicals

The development of novel medicines in the past 25 years has run on two parallel and complementary developmental tracks.

1. Synthetic small molecules have been produced by medicinal chemists as they have developed drugs during the past 130 years using methods of synthetic organic chemistry to assemble molecules in 6-12 or more steps of chemical synthesis. More recently, small molecule drug discovery has developed in rapid tempo by incorporating computational chemistry, robotization, structural chemistry, and so forth.[20] Such methods continue to make small molecules, of molecular weight 600 Da or smaller, that will be taken most often as oral tablets.

2. Protein drugs, that will be injectable—either intravenously (tPA, Remicade, Avonex, etc.) or subcutaneously (insulin, Humira, etc.)—are produced as recombinant proteins and no longer purified from organs and tissues, as was the case between 1920 and 1985. Vaccines contain one or more viral or bacterial proteins or dead microbes and sometimes even whole live, but weakened, attenuated microbes. Acellular vaccines contain microbial proteins as the antigen to prompt an immune response and prepare the immune system for future infections.

Until 2000, the common assumption of drug company marketers was that as most patients are afraid of injections given by medical personnel,

---

20   See, for example, Bartfai T and Lees GV (2006) *Drug Discovery: from Bedside to Wall Street*. Elsevier/Academic Press: Amsterdam.

they would be even more afraid of having to inject themselves. Drugs that require injections will always be harder to market than drugs that can be taken as oral tablets or capsules. Thus, in therapeutic areas such as metabolic disease, cardiovascular disease, inflammation, neurology, psychiatry, and dermatology the marketers vetoed the development of biologicals. Now, we have very successful biologicals for the treatment of multiple sclerosis (MS), rheumatoid arthritis (RA), psoriasis, and several different types of cancers as a result of small biotech companies taking the initiative to develop efficacious protein drugs. These are often so potent that the small drug volumes needed can be injected subcutaneously; an administration made widely accepted by insulin pens. This suited biotechs as they lacked the large infrastructure to develop small molecules, while recombinant protein technology was more familiar to small biotech and academia than to Big Pharma until the mid-1990s.

The string of biologicals started long ago with insulin and coagulation factors as purified proteins, after heterologous expression was introduced by Paul Berg from 1972 to 1981, continued in October 1982 with biosynthetic insulin formulation (Humulin from Lilly) and in 1985 with recombinant growth hormone (Omnitrope from Sandoz). This has replaced Kabi's well-selling purified growth hormone for the treatment of dwarfism, which was prepared from pituitaries of deceased persons and thus never really free from the risk of viral contamination. The recombinant tissue plasminogen activator (tPA), introduced in 1987 by Genentech, has become an important drug to treat myocardial infarction. The recombinant interferons (Biogen's Avonex (interferon beta-1a) and Schering-Plough's Intron A (interferon alpha-2b, developed by Biogen) have become breakthrough drugs in neurology for the treatment of MS (see section "Treatment of MS"), where the biologicals have made inroads. Then came the big indications: RA, [Centocor's Remicade, the anti-tumor necrosis factor (TNF)-α infliximab], Immunex's Enbrel (TNF inhibitor etanercept), BASF's Humira (TNF inhibitor adalimumab), and type 2 diabetes (Byetta, glucose-dependent insulin secretion enhancer exenatide[21] from Amylin Pharmaceuticals and Eli Lilly). This was despite the fact that Remicade and Enbrel were administered intravenously and Humira and Byetta were administered subcutaneously by injection, and despite the very large price difference from the existing oral drugs. Importantly, the original findings often came from government-supported research labs, and these innovations were carried forward by biotech companies. Big Pharma became involved in many of these innovations through either cooperation or acquisition, since clinical development and marketing needs the dollar muscle of Big Pharma to maximize the distribution. Biologicals are often discovered in government-funded laboratories and exploited by the private sector.

The very high efficacy and low safety concerns associated with these biologicals, together with some of the later ones like Humira and Byetta requiring only subcutaneous injection and not intravenous infusion, made the point that patients in all therapeutic areas (not only in oncology or in acute myocardial infarction) accept injectable drugs, and that insurers and patients accept the much higher prices when superior efficacy is shown. The trend of the biologicals market expanding alarmed the large pharma companies, yet for 15 years after the recombinant protein technology was introduced they still refused to develop recombinant protein drugs and relied on their superior medicinal chemistry. Ironically, the preclinical research of the Big Pharma companies has used recombinant proteins to test the small molecules in development; thus, the technology was familiar but they refused to learn about the administration, large-scale preparation, and marketing of biologicals. In addition, there was an exaggerated fear of the potential liabilities arising from immune responses to the recombinant protein drugs. Since the early 1990s, ~20% of approved drugs each year are biologicals. Biologicals became such big-selling drugs and invaded all therapeutic areas that Big Pharma had to

---

21 Exenatide was developed from the original hormone exendin-4, which was discovered in the saliva of the Gila monster, a venomous lizard native to the southwestern United States and northern Mexico. It is allegedly sometimes referred to as "lizard spit." The drug is now produced by direct solid phase synthesis of the peptide.

incorporate them. What better way to do this than by buying the biotech companies that had pioneered researching, testing, and marketing them? Thus, Roche bought Genentech; AstraZeneca bought Cambridge Antibody Technology and MedImmune; Merck bought Schering-Plough; and Pfizer bought Pharmacia, which had combined earlier with Kabi, and later bought Wyeth, a major player in recombinant proteins for treatment of hematological disorders and in the production of vaccines.

This means that the discussions and the competition between biologicals and small molecules to treat the same disease have effectively been internalized into the big companies. It is a clear trend that pharmaceutical companies still want to find small molecules that have the same or higher efficacy as the biologicals but are orally available. When we have truly equal efficacy of oral and injectable drugs for the same indication, it is likely that the first line of therapy will be the oral drug. Big Pharma, even when it has acquired an effective and high-priced biological to treat a disease, continues to look for an oral drug and, sometimes, the knowledge acquired developing and marketing the biological for the indication is key to the success of discovering the small molecule oral drug: the real skill and love of big, chemistry-based, pharmaceutical companies. Examples of this are the JAK2 inhibitor from Pfizer for RA where anti-TNF therapies are successful; the oral drug Gilenya from Novartis for the treatment of MS where interferons are successful; or BG-12 (dimethyl fumarate), the small molecule from Biogen Idec that is also used for the treatment of MS.

Treatment of MS

We chose the history of treatments for MS, for which small molecules were introduced in the 1960s, biologicals introduced from 1996 to 2007, and new small molecules again in 2010, because it helps to consider these changes in focus and methods of the industry through the case of a well-diagnosed, but very hard to treat, severe disease. There are scientific, industrial, marketing, and insurance payment issues surrounding this disease and the development of its treatment. It is helpful to follow how oral drugs gave way to higher efficacy biologicals and how oral small molecules can come back when they finally match the efficacy of the biologicals and show similar safety.

MS is a small, devastating, neurodegenerative disease with ~350,000 patients in the United States. This intermediate prevalence of ~1:1000 is also found in Europe's ~860 million population; there are ~2.4 million sufferers worldwide. The neurologists who treat MS have reliably diagnosed this disease since the early 1950s, even before the 1980s when their diagnostic tools expanded to include imaging techniques that permitted lesions in the brain to be viewed and new lesions produced by this severe neurodegenerative disease to be quantified. However, the drugs available were associated with such bad side effects that intent to treat was low and was largely limited to diagnosis and management of secondary symptoms.

As a result of the great success of basic research and the biotech and pharmaceutical industry, over the past 25 years the number of treatment-responsive patients increased 6- to 8-fold. Parallel to these therapeutic achievements, the expenditure on patients with MS has risen 20-fold because many of the breakthrough new treatments are expensive biologicals. However, the last entry of new drugs is a highly efficacious oral drug that is now being priced close to the biologicals it beats, and not to other small molecules.

The success of biologicals in the treatment of MS has made this disease one of the most popular indications to target among first the biotech companies and medium-sized pharma companies alike. When beta interferon was introduced by Biogen-Schering-Plough in 1996, it made a huge medical difference in the treatment of several forms of the disease (relapsing remitting, progressive, and relapsing progressive). It represented the result of 13 years of work between these two companies: a small biotech with top scientists and a medium-sized pharmaceutical. Today, development of biologicals is about twice as fast as it was 15 years ago, but the clinical trials, of course, remain as long as clinical trials in a given condition have to be—a favorite toxicologist colleague used to point out that "nine pregnant ladies cannot deliver a baby in one month"—thus, the toxicology studies and clinical trials take a long time, setting the minimum development time even for biologicals at 7 years or more.

The discovery of new medicines for MS treatment (see Figure 2.1) has many important lessons that we will touch upon in this book in relation to how the treatments, how the companies, and how the regulators have changed in the past three decades. MS was treated until the 1990s with immunosuppressive high-dose cortisol therapy. The past 15 years have seen the entry of disease-modifying biologicals of two classes, beta interferon and glatiramer acetate (Copaxone from Teva Pharmaceuticals), and then a third class, natalizumab (Tysabri from Biogen Idec and Elan) a therapeutic antibody. In 2010 the oral disease-modifying drug fingolimod (Gilenya from Novartis) was approved to reduce relapses and delay disability progression in patients with relapsing forms of MS. Already an additional new oral drug, BG-12 from Biogen Idec, a company already in a dominant position in the MS market with its biologicals, is awaiting approval.

The list of MS drugs (Table 2.3) currently in clinical use is instructive about how the benefit to risk ratio has to improve, that is, how the drugs that are approved have to meet higher and higher standards in

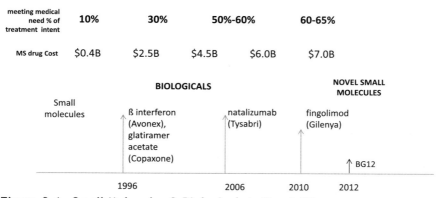

Figure 2.1: Small Molecules & Biologicals to Treat MS
The introduction of biologicals and the latest oral treatments have brought increased fulfillment of the medical need and a huge increase in drug cost. Medical need is met to a six times higher degree than 30 years ago.

Multiple sclerosis drugs currently in clinical use: small molecules, peptides, proteins, & new small molecules	
Novantrone (mitoxantrone)	small molecule cytostatic agent, immunosuppressive; injection
Copaxone (glatiramer acetate)	mixture of polypeptides; injection daily
Avonex (interferon beta-1a)	small protein; infusion weekly
Betaseron (interferon beta-1b)	small protein; infusion weekly
Extavia (interferon beta-1b)	small protein; infusion weekly
Rebif (interferon beta-1a)	small protein; infusion weekly
Tysabri (natalizumab)	therapeutic antibody affecting immune response; infusion
Gilenya (fingolimod)	immunosuppressor by restricting lymphocyte exit from lymph: oral

Table 2.3: MS drugs currently in clinical use
The pharmaceutical path to the creation of a $7 billion market from one of $100 million in 15 years, as of March 2012. Fingolimod was derived from a natural immunosuppressive product in an entomopathogenic fungus that is an alleged eternal youth nostrum in traditional Chinese medicine.

terms of efficacy. For the latest approved drug, Gilenya, there are data to show that it reduced relapses in 70% of patients over a 4-year period. When the first MS drugs were approved, 90- and 180-day trials were run against placebo, with a response rate of just 30%. The reduction of relapses by 30% in these 6-month trials was sufficient for approval. Safety has also improved dramatically from the high cardiotoxicity of Novantrone, a cancer drug, to the safety of the beta interferons. Some of the higher efficacy drugs such as Tysabri and Gilenya, however, have come with safety issues. A rare incidence of progressive multifocal leukoencephalopathy has been reported in Tysabri cases, which scared patients and physicians. Possible acute heart rate increase with Gilenya requires patients to be observed when the drug is first administered. Despite these risks, one cannot help but conclude that, while there is no cure for MS, the symptom treatments have improved dramatically simply because small companies such as Biogen and Teva brought forward efficacious treatments compared to the standard of treatment in the early 1980s. In addition, the agreement between the FDA and the companies using the best clinical research led to quantifiable surrogate end points to follow the effect of drugs on disease progression using brain imaging of gadolinium-positive stained lesions. The real clinical end points are the number of relapses and the time intervals between them, and so forth, but when the FDA approved an imaging-based parameter as a surrogate measure, the drug developers in bigger companies, who had frowned upon MS as a small-market and hard-to-follow disease, became keener with a new quantitative clinical end point. Counting relapses and determining their amplitude, or trying to measure disease progression with scales that take into account several parameters, is inherently a much more difficult prospect.

Several other small molecules, Merck's cladribine (Litak/Movectro), and Biogen Idec's BG-12, are in clinical trials.[22] This huge success for MS patients and clinicians is also a huge economic success for biotech and pharma. The sales in 2009 of MS drugs were $7 billion and for 2012 are expected to reach at least $8 billion.

One has to add that there remains much to do in MS treatment; ~30% of patients are nonresponders to all MS drugs available today. In addition, some patients develop tolerance to some of the drugs, and the oral drugs have possible severe side effects. Thus, drugs with better safety profiles are clearly needed. None of these treatments are curative, but they do stop the symptoms of the disease and slow disease progression, sometimes very efficiently, but not fully.

Yet, the development of drugs to treat MS is one of the success stories worth examining and re-examining because it shows that new science, new diagnostic techniques, better clinical trials, and the economic success related to delivering a drug where medical need is high all show that we will continue to develop new drugs even for less prevalent diseases.

---

22 However, initial excitement for oral cladribine for MS has been muted and in June 2011 Merck withdrew it since the FDA wanted more data on risk-benefit and safety.

Treatment of RA

Areas where science has propelled the introduction of biologicals have seen large improvements of medical care and simultaneously huge rises in the price of treatment. One such important case is the breakthrough in understanding the role of the pro-inflammatory cytokines TNF-α[23] and interleukin-1 (IL-1) in RA. RA is a major disease with an incidence of 1 in 108 in the United States, amounting to ~2.6 million patients with ~3 times more women suffering from it than men. The introduction of anti-TNF therapies, then the IL-1 receptor antagonist, and now rituximab (Rituxin, an anti-CD20 antibody discovered by IDEC and initially approved in 1997 for B-cell non-Hodgkin lymphomas) have radically changed treatment for moderate and severe cases of RA. These treatments significantly slow the destruction of joints that can lead to invalidity if untreated. The RA drugs Remicade (approved in 1999), Enbrel (1998), and Humira (2002) all sell for ~$2-5 billion per year and the annual bills per person are well over $20,000, yet we all believe that this is worth the price. While it is estimated that newer introductions of biosimilars will soon reduce these prices by an estimated 15-50%, they will remain very profitable drugs. It is in many ways illuminating how the development of RA drugs has proceeded and where it is headed today: Chapters 03 and 04 also touch upon these issues.

Before the introduction of biologicals for RA in 1998, the rate of RA incidence and the number of patients diagnosed was the same as it is now. RA is easy to diagnose as the symptoms of pain associated with movement and joint deformation are so obvious. The treatment options were nonsteroidal anti-inflammatory drugs (NSAIDs) like ibuprofen and disease-modifying small molecules. This class of oral therapies included the cancer chemotherapy drug and anti-metabolite methotrexate, developed in the 1950s, or immunosuppressing drugs such as cyclosporine, and sulfasalazine—all cheap, small molecule medicines. These are low molecular weight substances with minimal to moderate effects on severe

---

23   Bruce Beutler was awarded the 2011 Nobel Prize in Physiology & Medicine for his work on innate immunity and cytokines.

disease and its progression. In the case of NSAIDs, there are good effects toward the concomitant pain. Later entries in this class, such as the COX-2 inhibitors Vioxx and Celebrex, had serious cardiovascular side effects, including mortality, and Vioxx has since been withdrawn (see Chapter 03). Steroids, like cortisone, are also used to combat RA.

The first anti-TNF antibody, infliximab (Centocor's Remicade)—a mouse-human chimeric antibody—was approved for the treatment of RA in 1998 (and in the same year for the treatment of moderate and serious Crohn's disease). By 2002, a fully human antibody adalimumab (Abbott's Humira) with a higher affinity for TNF also came onto the market. While it was expected to cause less antibody-induced immune response, this had not been a real problem with the mouse-human chimeric antibody, infliximab. But, thanks to its higher affinity, adalimumab radically improved the mode of administration; infliximab and etanercept (Pfizer's Enbrel), a TNF receptor blocker, are intravenous infusions at the doctor's office, while adalimumab is administered as a subcutaneous self-injection by patients. Etanercept is, however, not an antibody, but a fusion protein that also blocks TNF signaling, and it is comparable in its efficacy and in its mechanism of action to infliximab. Those companies that missed the anti-TNF "boat" to launch an RA drug onto the market could make a blocker of IL-1 signaling by a recombinant IL-1 receptor antagonist, for example, anakinra (Amgen's Kineret) approved in 2001, or the anti-IL-6 antibodies, such as tocilizumab/atlizumab (Hoffmann-La Roche & Chugai's Actemra) approved in 2010. From 1997, the anti-B-cell, anti-CD20 antibody rituximab (IDEC's Rituxan) has also been shown to be effective in RA and approved for its treatment (see Figure 2.2).

Pfizer may have changed the RA treatment landscape again in March 2011 as it successfully finished the phase 3 trials in RA of tofacitinib, a small molecule Janus kinase 3 (JAK3 inhibitor, an oral pill, that has shown similar efficacy as the biologicals approved for treatment of severe RA; long-term safety remains to be followed).[24]

---

24 See, for example, the story of Vioxx in Chapter 03.

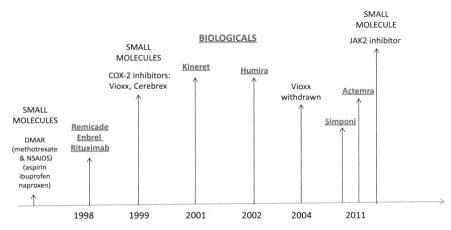

Figure 2.2: RA: History & Cost of Treatments during 1998-2011

The ups and downs of RA medication from oral small molecules to intravenous and subcutaneous biologicals (bold) then to better small molecules. Cost is indicated by the length of the arrows. The sales increased from $2-13 billion since the introduction of biologicals. Remicade (Centocor/Janssen Biotech, approved in 1998 for Crohn's disease), Enbrel (Immunex/Pfizer, 1998), and rituximab (IDEC/Biogen, 1998) are all given intravenously. Later came the subcutaneous applications such as Humira (Cambridge Antibody Technology/ BASF/Abbott, 2002). They all interfere with TNF signaling; Humira is an antibody to TNF. Kineret (Amgen, 2001) is an intravenous IL-1 receptor antagonist. Simponi (Centocor/J&J, 2009), like Humira, is a high-affinity TNF antibody, and also subcutaneously administered. Actemra (Genentech/Roche, 2010) is an intravenous IL-6 inhibitor. All of these medications can be considered disease-modifying anti-rheumatic drugs (DMARDs), although many have been approved beyond RA for other inflammatory diseases such as psoriasis and Crohn's disease. The small molecules before biologicals are generally nonsteroidal anti-inflammatory drugs (NSAIDs), except for methotrexate, which is an anti-metabolite. Cost is indicated by the length of arrows.

The biologicals to treat RA are all used as add-ons to methotrexate, the generic cheap, immunosuppressive, anti-inflammatory small molecule. However, it has limited efficacy and serious side effects such as teratogenicity and penicillin interaction. Because of its very low price and measurable efficacy and because patients worldwide are taking methotrexate, it is almost impossible to run a new RA drug clinical trial

The need for medicines grows   47

without it. In richer countries, almost everyone with moderate to severe RA is on methotrexate, as well as on a biological such as Remicade or Humira.

As with MS, where gadolinium imaging helped companies to judge the efficacy of the drugs, the improved diagnosis and the agreement on what constitutes treatment success in RA were essential components in the decision of several companies to join the race to develop new RA drugs. Thus, the agreement of the clinicians and regulators to use the American College of Rheumatology (ACR)-30 scale[25] for characterization of the disease state and the quantification of the radiologic study of joint degradation played an important role in this impressive development of several new drug classes for RA that earlier was treated with old, cheap, and highly ineffective drugs. These drugs were at times dangerous too; ~50% of the bleeding ulcers were "credited" to overuse of older NSAIDs by RA patients.

The scientific recognition that the same inflammatory cytokines (TNF and to lesser extent IL-1) play key roles in the inflammatory and often severe skin disease, psoriasis, and in the chronic inflammatory disease of the gastrointestinal system, Crohn's disease, have led to clinical trials with anti-TNF and anti-IL-1 drugs in these diseases. Upon showing efficacy of these biologicals, where earlier NSAIDs and steroids ruled, the anti-TNF biologicals were approved for treatment of both psoriasis and Crohn's disease. These are great successes for pharma companies that would have not necessarily aimed at psoriasis as an indication that has many topical treatments, which are moderately effective, and use steroid-based drugs. But now there are significant anti-TNF sales for the treatment of severe psoriasis patients. These developments have changed the clinical outcome

---

25 "...[the] (ACR)-30 scoring system ... evaluates the following domains: patient function, patient/parent assessment of well-being, physician assessment of overall disease activity, number of joints with active arthritis, number of joints with limited range of motion, and erythrocyte sedimentation rate (ESR). Improvement in any three of these domains by 30 percent and worsening in not more than one by 30 percent is considered to be improvement." From The Effectiveness of Disease-Modifying Antirheumatic Drugs (DMARDS) in Children With Juvenile Idiopathic Arthritis (JIA) http://www.effectivehealthcare.ahrq.gov/index.cfm/search-for-guides-reviews-and-reports/?productid=404&pageaction=displayproduct

for patients with psoriasis covering >30% of the body surface; they also changed the administration of these treatments. Most dermatologists were not used to administering drugs intravenously; rather, they were accustomed to prescribing topically applicable creams and foams, and, even less often, orally available steroids. They were also not used to prescribing drugs that cost $20,000 or more a year. These developments have changed how dermatologists treat their patients. The changes, which were embraced by younger physicians faster, changed the income of some of the dermatologists dramatically, but also their risk acceptance; namely, that all of the anti-TNFs carry a warning that they increase the risk of severe infections significantly and require knowledge of, or control of, whether the psoriasis patient ever had tuberculosis. These issues and intravenous administrations were new to dermatologists, as was the ability to do something life-changing for patients who suffer from psoriasis. Biologicals, like small molecule drugs, when found efficacious and safe (or reasonably safe) are tested in many indications and find new uses.

The race to make the best, cheapest, and safest drug for RA patients is not over. Today, we do not cure the disease although we now significantly change disease progression. The safety of the drugs is a problem even for the biologicals. Anti-TNFs do not come with this robust efficacy without affecting the body in several powerful ways, and they are known to permit reactivation of earlier tuberculosis that otherwise lies innocently dormant, encapsulated as tubercles in patients' lungs. Thus, people with a positive tuberculin test are not eligible for anti-TNF therapy. This is a problem of different proportions in different countries with, for example, the Russian and Eastern European populations more commonly being TB-positive than those in the United States.

Recombinant proteins as treatments
Recombinant proteins expand the market and, being expensive, they expand the pharma companies' earnings even more.

Recombinant proteins, known as highly potent medicines that are safe from off-target side effects, take a shorter time to develop than small molecules. As drugs with high earning potential, they send an important message for pharma companies to consider, and, it seems, they got the message. All Big Pharma now develop and sell recombinant proteins as drugs. The ability to develop new recombinant proteins in new indications has resulted in a significant development in major pharma companies. Pfizer, AstraZeneca, Roche, Novartis, and Merck, the very companies that were, until 2005, betting on their superior medicinal chemistry knowledge, now have, through multiple acquisitions, full-fledged recombinant protein arms. One should add that several large pharmaceuticals, such as GlaxoSmithKline (GSK), Merck, Sanofi-Pasteur-Merieux, and Pfizer-Wyeth, were already in possession of biological production know-how through their vaccine production, but the vaccine production and development has always been an isolated part of these conglomerates since vaccines are tested, distributed, and priced differently from other biologicals.

Future recombinant proteins as treatments

Through the introduction of biologicals into such a large indication as RA, the market and the value of the market have been dramatically expanded. Initially it was thought that recombinant proteins would be used in diseases where very small amounts of a peptide or protein are needed, and mostly in endocrinology where a hormone such as insulin is used in very small quantities in the treatment of diabetes mellitus. But now recombinant protein technology and protein engineering technology are producing drugs that are used in every therapeutic area and in vaccine production (see Table 2.4). The large increase in the indications that we can address—not only enzyme, hormone, and coagulation factor deficiencies, but also in indications such as inflammation, various cancers, and macular degeneration—represents a significant increase in the market value. The number of available agents in this "recombinant DNA-recombinant protein revolution" will increase, affect, and enrich life sciences and the pharma industry, as well as improve outcomes for the patients.

In the coming decade, the fruits of individual patient genome sequencing, improved imaging, and knowledge management techniques will improve

Recombinant proteins produced for therapeutic & vaccine purposes	
Hormone replacement	Growth hormone (GH), insulin
Growth factors	Growth hormone (GH), insulin-like growth factor 1 (IGF-1); erythropoietin (EPO); granulocyte-macrophage colony-stimulating factor (GM-CSF)
Active enzymes	Tissue plasminogen activator (tPA or PLAT) to dissolve clots in myocardial infarction and embolic or thrombotic stroke; alpha-galactosidase A or agalsidase alpha (Replagal from Shire) and beta-glucocerebrosidase or agalsidase beta (Fabrazyme from Genzyme) replacing faulty enzymes in the lysosomal storage inherited diseases, Fabry's disease and Gaucher's disease, respectively
Coagulation factors	Factor VIII, factor IX, factor X, thrombin
Therapeutic antibodies	Used in inflammation, oncology
Cytokines	Beta-interferon, alpha-interferon, IL-2, IL-1ra, IL-11, etc.
Vaccines	Several vaccines are composed not of (live or denatured) cells of the microbes but of selected microbial proteins that can cause similar immune reaction as the whole microbe, but where the side effect profile is often improved and where production costs are much higher

Table 2.4: Larger groups of recombinant proteins produced for therapeutic & vaccine purposes

diagnosis, treatment selection, and follow up, and will open new disease areas for drug development.

The question is not whether we will run out of diseases to treat or whether microbes will stop mutating and thus reduce the need to develop new drugs; rather, the question is what does the industry, that is, its investors and managers, believe about the future, where it takes 10–12 years from discovery of the scientific basis through business decisions to product? It also costs $1 billion per project with a >90% risk of losing the entire investment in this project, and liabilities can cost more, especially when drugs are withdrawn. The future of drug development as a private

The future requirements of drug development as a private industry
Improve drug discovery process, in particular clinical trial processes, to reduce further the risk of expensive failures from today's very high rate.
Shorten the time from the start of a project to approval of drugs.
Charge a price that will provide the profits to keep this high-tech, long product development time, high-risk industry going.
Protect the patent life of compounds so that earnings continue.
Protect proprietary drugs from generic competition.

Table 2.5: The future requirements of drug development as a private industry

industry depends on how much of the industry believes that it can achieve several financial goals (see Table 2.5).

The industry is fighting on many fronts to improve profit while it attempts to limit competition. It is fighting against shortened patent times and against generics and biosimilars. It, of course, continues strenuously to do what it has always done to improve the efficiency of its discovery and trial processes. Some of this has led to large-scale outsourcing of aspects of preclinical and clinical research from the United States and Western Europe.

Pharma, governments, & nongovernmental organizations

The pharma industry is a significant industry in the economic lives of most developed countries and its dealings with governments are very complex. This is partly because the products of the industry are necessarily approved and controlled by government and international agencies, and partly because in most places the major and/or ultimate purchasers of most of the products of the industry are governments. In countries like the United States, Switzerland, France, the UK, and Japan, the industry has considerable political lobbying muscle that comes to the forefront when important decisions are made. This book will elucidate some publicly known examples.

In some critical areas for our society the governments, international organizations, and nongovernmental organizations (NGOs) have stepped in to secure a market for existing and new drugs. Development, production, and distribution of vaccines, key broad spectrum antibiotics, and drugs for malaria and sleeping sickness have all benefited from such actions. This is important for global health and for political stability in our inter-related world. Pharma industry has now accepted and contributed to these actions even if it did not initially welcome them. There was conflict between the U.S. government and pharma industry in 1996–1997 over making HIV drugs for Africa that is now resolved because the initiatives have created a market where there was no market or just a small market in Africa. However, the industry recognizes that these governmental and NGO purchases set a limit on the "upside earning potential" in markets such as the middle classes of the world. It also is finding that the increasingly socialized medicine markets of Western Europe are driving a hard bargain with drug prices and more and more often conduct comparative, evidence-based studies (see Chapter 03) to examine whether the new, more expensive drugs deliver more than older, cheaper drugs in terms of safety and efficacy. They, in effect, force the companies to prove that the new drugs represent a significant advance.

The large viral diseases such as influenza and hepatitis C attract sufficient attention from pharmaceutical companies based on their profit projections. In the case of flu medicines, one must not forget the bonanza of more than $10 billion over the past years that Roche and GSK experienced when the drugs they developed to treat flu—the neuraminidase inhibitors Tamiflu and Relenza, respectively—became highly coveted high-price items that were stockpiled by governments for the bird flu epidemic. Nevertheless, despite this commercial success, Roche has stopped both antibiotic and antiviral development. The number of companies researching new antibiotics that are so essential for public health is becoming smaller, and this is a real concern.

When Big Pharma, now often in groups of important companies, leaves or never even enters a disease area (see Table 2.6), there is a space of opportunity for smaller companies, as we discussed above in relation to therapies for MS. The newer problem arising in 2011 and beyond, however,

Therapeutic area	Core of 20 in 2000	Core of 10 in 2011
CNS	20 (100%)	4 (40%)
Cancer	20 (100%)	10 (100%)
Anti-infectives	18 (90%)	3 (30%)
Cardiovascular	18 (90%)	9 (90%)
Respiratory/allergy	15 (75%)	4 (40%)
Metabolic disease	14 (70%)	8 (80%)

Table 2.6: "Core" therapeutic areas of research for top companies
Between 2000 and 2011 the number of large companies fell by 50% (20 to 10) through mergers and acquisition. The percentage of companies involved in antibiotics discovery fell from 90 to 30% of the active companies, in CNS from 100 to 40%, and in pain from 80 to 20%. The drop in anti-infective research from 18 companies to 3 could be considered a disaster. With each merger and acquisition, R&D departments are always lost, so in all of these cases there is a more precipitous drop than the data show (cf. Table 4.2).

is that the small companies will run out of venture capital support when it becomes clear that their drug candidate is not going to be taken over or licensed by a Big Pharma, even after successful phase 1 and 2 trials. It is this issue that will be critical to solve in the years to come if we want to maintain drug discovery in the private form of the past with firm regulatory influence from government.

The way to ensure that clinical trials will be carried out in a competent manner in diseases when there is a present medical need and a small company has a compound that passed phase 2—and thus has some promise to treat a disease for which presently no or inadequate treatment exists—is via government "interference." The need for new drugs is growing and society cannot afford that drug-development projects are put on indefinite hold because Big Pharma investors and management have changed the definition of what risk is adequate.

Chapter 03: Medicines are becoming better: some of the breakthrough medicines of the past decades

Significant progress since WW II

In the 1950s, when the university-educated grandmother of one of the authors[26] (T. Bartfai) returned from the physician she would say that she felt lucky because the physician not only could diagnose her problems but also thought that there may be some drug therapy that may ease the pain, although not without lots of side effects. She was happy and satisfied with the state of medicine as provided for her in a poor central European country right after WW II.

Today, we expect that all our medical (and sometimes not "medical," but "presented to doctors") problems can be diagnosed, rectified, or, at the very least, significantly addressed and ameliorated, with drugs that would be efficacious, fast acting, and without side effects. How we have become, since WW II, so demanding is a story of politicians' and scientists' promises. In percentage of GDP, indeed, money spent on healthcare is four times more when compared to the 1950s, and with more drugs come more demands. We had a "war on cancer," we had a "fight against polio," and we had a "campaign against HIV/AIDS." Several of these expensive, sustained efforts have been very successful. We have significantly improved survival, indeed progression-free survival, in leukemias, certain lymphomas, breast cancer, and prostate cancer. Apart from isolated outbreaks, largely because people refuse to vaccinate their children, we have eradicated polio from the world, except in Pakistan where certain religious extremists prevent

---

26 G.V. Lees' grandparents did not survive WW II.

vaccination,[27] and in 25 years we have turned HIV/AIDS from a deadly disease into a treatable chronic disease, with which people can live 15 years or longer if they are given access to drug therapy.

The new medicines introduced between 1965 and 2010 not only addressed previously untreatable diseases but also became safer and easier to administer.

This unbroken series of 30–40 years of success based on breakthroughs in life science research, discovery, information technology, and imaging made the pharmaceutical industry and its stockholders rich and powerful. It is also the major reason for the much talked about "crisis of the industry," which is characterized by fewer genuine new drugs being approved (see Tables 3.5–3.7) and for the spectacular and expensive failure of drug candidates in phase 3 trials (see Table 5.4, which highlights the most expensive phase 3 failures of 2010 by indication and company).

Simply, we raised the bar for new medicines to be approved and used. We raised the starting point to a very high level when making new drugs. For example, for new antihypertensives the bar is extremely high. There are so many (approximately 250) available blood pressure-lowering drugs, many working with different mechanisms of action, and all of them by now are available as generic, cheap oral medicines. Indeed, efficacious and safe antihypertensive drugs in all five different major antihypertensive drug classes are sold, such that if we measured and diagnosed high blood pressure in the whole world, we could cheaply and safely supply every person on the globe with drugs without breaking the bank, and thus reduce heart attacks, stroke, kidney disease, and diabetes significantly. This is being recognized by governments and nongovernmental organizations

---

27   Efforts to vaccinate children in some regions of Pakistan in 2012 resulted in the deaths of a foreign doctor in July in Karachi, a community health worker shot in October in Quetta, and five Pakistani females shot on December 17, four in separate coordinated incidents in Karachi, and one in Peshawar. Another car carrying workers was fired upon. Pakistani police help enforce vaccinations but are unable to offer security to the 80,000 plus field workers. Several clerics have claimed that the vaccination program, while compulsory by law, is a Western or CIA plot to make people infertile, and seemingly ignore the reduced incidence of the disease, which has fallen since 1994 from 20,000 to under 30 in 2005 and about 60 in 2012.

(NGOs). Infectious diseases like HIV and tuberculosis, and typically tropical diseases such as malaria should be diagnosed and their treatment assisted in poor countries; we should also provide help in the treatment of hypertension, diabetes, schizophrenia, and epilepsy. All of this could be done relatively cheaply and safely with efficacious, cheap generic drugs, with which we have decades of experience.

The great beginning & the feared end of extremely profitable drug discovery

For the rich markets it means that any new drug must address some aspect of efficacy or safety that none of the older drugs alone or in combination can. It would have to be relatively cheap, and it would have to compete with the safety record of the older drugs. Ubiquitous beta blockers, to reduce blood pressure and heart rate, have been used by 400 million patients for over 40 years in every thinkable and unthinkable drug combination. How can the pharmaceutical industry compete with that? One way would be if we could cure hypertension, and not simply accept it as an age-related pathophysiology; our generic cheap and efficacious drugs only treat the symptoms of the disease.

The same is true in other large diseases like major depression (MD).[28] The monoamine oxidase (MAO) inhibitors of the 1960s (efficacious but dangerous in combination with red wine and cheese), and the tricyclic antidepressants from the 1960s and 1970s (efficacious but causing dryness of mouth and other side effects, and today mostly used in pain management), were successfully replaced in the 1990s by the selective serotonin reuptake inhibitors (SSRIs) including zimelidine (Zelmid[29]), fluvoxamine (Luvox), fluoxetine (Prozac), and a series of "me-toos" such as paroxetine (Paxil), citalopram (Celexa/Ciprami), vilazodone (Viibryd), escitalopram (Lexapro, etc.), and the largest selling sertraline (Zoloft/Lustral), as well as the

---

28 Or, major depressive disorder (MDD).
29 Zimelidine (marketed as Zelmid, Zimelidine, or Normud) was discovered by Nobel laureate Arvid Carlsson and developed by Astra. It was withdrawn after 2 years, but paved the way for the class of me-toos of equal efficacy but better safety.

serotonin-norepinephrine reuptake inhibitors (SNRIs) such as venlafaxine (Effexor) and duloxetine (Cymbalta, etc.). Most of these are now generics and prove a difficult hurdle to overcome for new antidepressants because they are cheap, efficacious, and generally safe. They also beat anxiolytics like the benzodiazepines in treating chronic anxiety indications. However, for acute anxiety SSRIs are not providing a robust treatment before a 14-21 day treatment period.

One must admit that the standard of care in many large indications is high, as far as symptom treatment goes. Generic drugs increasingly occupy these large indications leading to the debate about the "end of drug discovery," whereas the debaters really mean the "end of extremely profitable drug discovery," that is, double-digit growth for decades.

Drug discovery recovery, phase 1

Insulin, discovered in 1923, was the first "biological" used as a drug. The introduction from the 1980s and 1990s of new biologicals such as erythropoietin (EPO) in oncology, tissue plasminogen activator (tPA) and urokinase for myocardial infarction, growth hormone (GH) for dwarfism, interferon beta in multiple sclerosis (MS), and the large number of therapeutic antibodies to treat different forms of cancers and rheumatoid arthritis (RA) has addressed different diseases that are in the middle range in terms of the number of patients affected with very selective and safe drugs. Our willingness to pay $20,000-100,000 per patient-year to treat these diseases made the biologicals an economically safe bet for small and, latterly, big companies.

Biologicals were, and are still, popular drugs to develop through their high selectivity, which limits "off-target" side effects and makes them safer than many small molecule drugs. Their development on average has been 4 years shorter and much cheaper than that of small molecule oral drugs. Playing safe, i.e. trying to reduce clinical trial failures, at least through lack of safety, for Big Pharma means engaging in making biologicals.

Today, the situation is such for the insurers and for the pharmaceutical companies that there are drugs available for most large indications and middle range indications that can be expected to bring in sales of $600 million per year or more, because of the large number of patients taking them or because of the very high price we pay for them, keeping in mind that the number of patients is low.

These drugs, particularly the ones approved in the past 10 years, besides showing reasonable efficacy and more than a 30% response rate, overall exhibit safety that far exceeds anything patients had been treated with earlier. The drugs of today are significantly better than those of the previous decades.

Drug discovery arrested?

Indeed many drugs approved in the 1960–1970s, and before, would not be approved today. This includes our favorite anti-inflammatory, antipyretic pain killer, aspirin, which was synthesized by Felix Hoffmann at Bayer and first sold in 1899, and is not yet approved by any regulatory agency. Still, it is widely recommended by physicians and pediatricians and used in low doses even as a preventive medicine in cardiovascular indications.

Aspirin, which is very cheap and quite efficacious for several common ills, sold over the counter is credited with over 300,000 stomach bleedings a year. Yet, as the list of indications in which aspirin is employed shows, it was found safe enough and cheap enough to be tested in several large indications and remained popular in those indications as its risk-benefit ratio is deemed acceptable. Today, no pharma executive would propose registering and selling it and no one would buy it at non-generic prices, for no other reason than because ibuprofen, another cheap anti-inflammatory antipyretic pain killer, is also available as an over-the-counter drug, although its safety profile is not much better.

The chase for ever safer drugs can fool us sometimes, as in the case of COX-2 inhibitors. There is a good intellectual, scientific reason why selectively inhibiting COX-2 (the enzyme held responsible for inflammation and pain) would be better than inhibiting both COX-1 and COX-2. Existing NSAIDs[30] such as aspirin—available long before the COX enzymes were described—inhibit both classes of enzyme, and inhibiting COX-1 is suspected of causing aspirin's adverse gastrointestinal effect. The first selective COX-2 inhibitor celecoxib (Celebrex from Searle-Monsanto/Pharmacia-Pfizer) was approved on December 31, 1998; Merck followed shortly after on May 27, 1999, with rofecoxib (Vioxx). Without going into great detail (see our earlier book *Drug Discovery: from Bedside to Wall Street*,[31] pp. 165–168, the articles in Wikipedia for reference, and many litigious-lawyer websites), Merck voluntarily withdrew Vioxx on September 30, 2004, based upon emerging data from its self-financed post-marketing phase 4 trial. Both Merck and the Food and Drug Administration (FDA) were accused of responsibility by relatives of patients who allegedly died from cardiovascular events related to the use of Vioxx. It would be extremely misguided for a drug company knowingly to launch a drug that will be withdrawn and litigated against; the penalties are too severe. Any revenues are quickly overtaken by investment, legal costs—running at $600 million or so annually—and settlements.

While it is evident that Merck defended its position and many lawsuits were dismissed, Merck came to an agreement in 2007 whereby they set aside $4.85 billion to settle some 27,000 lawsuits. The scandal over the heart attacks could be linked to this COX-2 inhibitor, but it is extremely difficult to know whether the physicians prescribed the drug appropriately, or whether the patients took the drug for too long at too high a dose. Did they take it together with another drug metabolized by the same cytochrome P450 enzyme, which ~75% of drugs utilize, despite it evolving for completely different reasons? That would have the effect of increasing the effective dose. Lawyers, who seem to relish the idea of drugs being withdrawn, were encouraged by the initial jury award of $250 million, despite it being 10 times more than Texas law allowed. It is evident that some data were withheld and others fabricated externally to

---

30   Nonsteroidal anti-inflammatory drugs.
31   Bartfai T & Lees GV (2006) *Drug Discovery: from Bedside to Wall Street*. Elsevier/Academic Press: Amsterdam.

Merck. But what is the underlying reason? Societal/patient need, coupled with the pressure from shareholders and the desire to discover efficacious drugs, can be overwhelming. While potential conflicts of interest are inevitable, since experts are necessarily involved on all sides, it does not mean the drug companies encourage any fabrication or misinterpretation of data. Vioxx has actually been approved for reintroduction but Merck has elected so far not to re-launch it. On November 22, 2011, Merck was also fined $1 billion for false marketing of Vioxx, because it marketed Vioxx for off-label use to treat RA despite it not being approved for the indication.

Somewhat ironically, it seems that data behind the launch of celecoxib were fabricated by the same scientist(s), yet Celebrex has not had to be withdrawn. Again ironically, the lesser specificity and efficacy of Celebrex over Vioxx reduces its risk. However, Pfizer, which has via acquisitions become the owner of Celebrex, has in 2012 been accused of lying to the FDA about Celebrex. While inhibiting COX-1 underlies adverse gastrointestinal effects, it also serves as a cardiovascular protective.

However, the Vioxx story and subsequent scandals involving two other large companies, GlaxoSmithKline (GSK) and Eli Lilly, concerning other drugs for different large indications such as diabetes, depression, and schizophrenia, have shaken the confidence of patients, doctors, and investors in the largest and oldest pharmaceutical companies on the most important issue: Would they endanger patients by letting them take drugs known by the company to be dangerous? In 2012 GSK was handed a fine of $3 billion, the biggest in history, for "encouraging" off-label use including administration to children, for which these particular drugs were not approved.

The popular opinion is, unfortunately, that industry-wide the pharmaceutical companies are not behaving ethically and they deny or suppress data that endanger large-selling drugs' continued sales; they try to undermine the credibility of investigators who uncover such data; they fight the regulatory agencies to the bitter end about withdrawing drugs; and they fight viciously in court the victims of drug-induced death and illness. While the companies' reputations suffer, the reputation of doctors has also taken a serious beating. It has shown how much they are tied to certain companies to promote their drugs. Perhaps based upon the reputation of the safety of drugs, they inevitably prescribed drugs to inappropriate patients without adequately explaining the risks.

One may ask why any authors should write about this in a chapter entitled "Medicines are becoming better." The answer is simple: the revelations of cases such as Vioxx, rosiglitazone (Avandia from GSK, used in treatment of diabetes but with cardiovascular risks), olanzapine (Zyprexa from Eli Lilly approved to treat schizophrenia and bipolar disorder), and so forth have contributed to our having ever safer and safer drugs.[32] It will be discussed that the companies are more careful, the regulators are more thorough, and, unfortunately in our view, in some countries like the United States, where one can solicit cases, the lawyers are more aggressive. But the overall outcome is better drugs. Had we wanted a best-seller book, we could have joined the ranks of authors lambasting the industry. But we would like this industry to continue to make drugs, just better ones.

The Vioxx story, running from the start of research in 1991 through approval in 1999 to withdrawal in 2004, shows that the drive for more selective and thus safer drugs sometimes fails because the biology of humans is far more complex than we understand. The failure is not shameful, but the cover-up is.

The drug ibuprofen, the enormously popular generic, inhibits two closely related enzymes, COX-1 and COX-2. While we are happy with the efficacy of this cheap drug, physicians and the industry badly wanted to limit the gastrointestinal side effects and create a blockbuster drug to treat more safely RA and pain of inflammatory origin.

---

32   The thalidomide (Contergan/Thalomid) scandal of 1961–1962 similarly strengthened the hand of regulatory agencies regarding safety requirements and improved the science of early drug testing. The FDA had, incidentally, refused approval of thalidomide, predominantly due to the lack of resources to process the application; not because of superior insight. Nevertheless, the FDA prevented this tragedy happening in the United States; having regulatory agencies is useful.

The background to the Vioxx story is extremely illustrative. It was shown by basic researchers that the efficacy stems from inhibiting COX-2 and that the COX-1 inhibition is responsible for many of the side effects and contributes almost nothing to the therapeutic effects. Capitalizing on these scientific data, first Searle (later acquired via Monsanto by Pharmacia and then by Pfizer) and then Merck developed the selective COX-2 inhibitors Celebrex and Vioxx, respectively. These were pushed by successful marketing and sales departments into becoming multibillion dollar drugs within 18 months of their launch, because any patient could feel that they were efficacious pain killers, and the restrictions on how many ibuprofen tablets are safe to take did not apply. Patients may have thought they did not have to limit the dose because they detected no adverse effects of exceeding the recommended dose. The anti-inflammatory (swelling and swelling-induced pain reduction) and pain-killing efficacy was felt in 30 minutes by the patient and required no complicated instruments to detect the effect nor advanced statistics to prove an effect. This led to a huge and, even by industry standards, extensive promotion by two of the largest companies in the United States. Soon millions of prescriptions were filled for each of these "COX isoform" selective COX-2 inhibitors. Anyone who was willing to look at the statistics could see that, besides the large number of treated and satisfied patients, there was a small group of Vioxx patients with increased frequency of myocardial infarction and also death occurring on Vioxx at a higher rate than expected. Some physicians, including some of Merck's consultants on COX-2 development, warned the company that selective inhibition of COX-2, although seemingly an improvement over ibuprofen, may increase the cardiovascular risk, because the products of COX-1 and COX-2 enzymes need to be balanced for cardiovascular safety and need to be present alongside the anti-inflammatory effect. The letters from these consultants had been systematically ignored and allegedly left in the drawer of a research executive. Research physicians in 2001, 2 years after the approval and introduction of Vioxx, compared 1,064 treated patients and found 34 deaths compared to the control group where there were only 12. Finally, this study was published by the *Journal of the American Medical Association,* which is highly respected but has Merck as one of its best paying advertisers. Then the whole case blew open leading to the FDA investigation, voluntary withdrawal of Vioxx by Merck, and then Pfizer's withdrawal of Bextra (after paying $1 billion in fines for promoting the drug), the follow-up to Celebrex. Label warnings on Celebrex were strengthened and its sales were seriously limited. From ~138,000 patients, over 2,000 deaths could be connected to their taking Vioxx.

This is the way our medicines become better. Firstly, companies now clearly realize that even the largest ones among them can be brought to their knees by litigation around one or two unsafe drugs that were pushed by their marketers and executives into very large populations of patients and could hurt many. Drugs with poor efficacy do not become safety risks, either because they flunk the clinical trial by not showing efficacy or they miraculously are approved because a misleadingly small trial showed some random efficacy. Physicians realize soon enough that there are better, more effective drugs to treat the same disease and they stop prescribing the less efficacious or non-efficacious new drug. Thus, while it hurts the top line of the annual report to discover lack of efficacy and sales of any drug, it has more benign and more predictable consequences for the company. The lack of sales does not break a large pharma company if it has many other well-selling products. But unsafe drugs like fenfluramine-phentermine (fen-phen) caused the fall of American Home Products, then the number three U.S. drug and vaccine maker, and more recently Vioxx shook Merck and Zyprexa shook Lilly.

As a consequence, companies take less risk in pushing drugs. There is dramatically greater safety consciousness in the companies' clinical trials and even of its marketers.

Secondly, these cases of withdrawn drugs, and the litigations around them, teach the physicians the value of meta-analysis of many, smaller, published studies on the same drug that, despite many limitations of putting together data obtained in different studies, permit them to look at the statistically relevant, truly large number of patients who have all taken the same drug even if the studies were called differently. The meta-analysis can reveal a barely discernible trend in many small studies. The results may become a statistically significant, reliable piece of information about the efficacy and safety of a widely used drug. Steven Nissen at the Cleveland Clinic and his colleagues worldwide have made a major impact on drug safety with systematic meta-analyses of large drugs used to treat type 2 diabetes, a steadily increasing disease. Long-term use of the diabetes drug rosiglitazone (GSK's Avandia)[33] was shown significantly to increase the risk of cardiovascular incidents and of myocardial infarctions leading to its withdrawal in Europe in 2010, while the FDA permitted restricted uses in the United States, but its sales have dropped.

Thirdly, the FDA, the European Medicines Agency (EMA), and other regulators have also elevated their attention level about safety studies that fail to reveal those drugs that may become unsafe over long-term use.

The Vioxx, rosiglitazone, and other cases have led the EMA and FDA to ask for better pre-approval and also better and longer post-market analysis of side effects and of mortality, despite the protestations from the companies that it delays entry into the market—and the start of earnings—for important new drugs in the field of obesity diabetes.

Diabetes drugs were earlier approved after relatively short trials of 3-6 months because their effects on serum glucose and insulin levels could be shown in a few days or weeks, and sustained for a few months, during which the (cardiovascular) safety risks were not obvious. However, since patients often will take these drugs for the rest of their lives, it is important to know if after 5-10 years of taking this drug their risk of cardiovascular disease has significantly increased, or if they indeed encountered disease more frequently than others with similar diabetes and are similarly overweight. Subsequent to Nissen's meta-analysis of

---

33 Nissen SE & Wolski K (2007) Effect of rosiglitazone on the risk of myocardial infarction and death from cardiovascular causes. *N Engl J Med.* June 14; 356:2457–2471.

rosiglitazone data, and against protest from GSK, which conducted many post-marketing studies to fight the results of these meta-analyses, the EMA decided that the benefits no longer outweighed the risks of the use of rosiglitazone.

We are seeing more and more often these types of communications:

In September 2010 the EMA, the European Union (EU) body responsible for monitoring the safety of medicines, recommended the suspension of the marketing authorisation for rosiglitazone (Avandia, Avandamet and Avaglim) from GlaxoSmithKline. The EMA has concluded that the benefits of rosiglitazone no longer outweigh its risks and the marketing authorisation should be suspended across the EU.

The EMA has advised that patients who are currently taking rosiglitazone-containing medicines should make an appointment with their doctor at a convenient time to discuss suitable alternative treatments. Patients are advised not to stop their treatment without speaking to their doctor. NICE does not recommend the use of drugs without marketing authorisation. Therefore, as a result of the EMA's decision, NICE has temporarily withdrawn its recommendations on the use of rosiglitazone in this guideline.

Some large companies like GSK and Johnson & Johnson (J&J) respond by reducing the portion of their income that is dependent on sales of proprietary drugs and focus on devices and generic drugs with lower risks. An executive bitterly complained that one cannot be sure which drugs in clinical trials will make it, and now it is clear that one can no longer count on the income of a multibillion dollar drug that has been on the market for many years. This is the reality of the pharmaceutical industry that prizes its product to take into account both the trial data and the withdrawal risks.

Meta-analysis matters: new twist on old information
The medical scientists who carry out meta-analyses have had to learn that data are notoriously difficult to extract from companies. The publication difficulties they encountered taught them that many of our best medical

journals, which depend on advertising revenue from pharma, that is, almost all journals for physicians, are hard to convince to publish critical information about large-earning drugs of large advertisers. But it is not impossible. When it happens, if the study is well done and includes many trials and a large number of patients with clear outcomes, it has dramatic effects on drug sales and, ultimately, on the safety of drugs.

A completely new twist concerning what was really happening in clinical trials has appeared in 2012. Scientists used the Freedom of Information Act to request and receive from the FDA the data used in the approval of drugs in 1997 and 1998. They re-analyzed it and came to completely different conclusions. We will see many of these studies undermining the drugs that were apparently wrongly approved.

While drugs on the market are far safer and also often (although not always) more efficacious than drugs approved 20-30 years ago, there is much that remains to be done.

New uses for safe drugs
In cases of diseases described in points 3-5 of Table 3.1, which cover reasons why some diseases are not yet treatable, one has to see and hope that the spillover from successful areas of drug development will come to provide patients with drugs in those diseases where directed research activity is low or has stopped. Many times drugs developed for other indications provide unexpected relief for patients with diseases that were not directly targeted. For example, in wet macular degeneration, which causes loss of vision mostly in the elderly, the leading drug for treatment is a drug developed for oncology to block development of new vessels, which tumors need to grow. New vessel formation is required for both solid tumor growth and wet macular degeneration. The same vascular endothelial growth factor (VEGF) blockers, such as the therapeutic antibody bevacizumab (Avastin from Genentech-Roche) and the much more expensive antibody fragment ranibizumab (Lucentis, also from Genentech, but marketed outside the United States by Novartis) now save the sight of several hundred thousand patients. Ophthalmological

	Reasons new drug development must and will continue
1	The drugs that show efficacy and safety are, with few exceptions, treating symptoms of the disease and *not curing the disease or significantly modifying the course of the disease.*
2	For many diseases, we have a *large portion of nonresponding patients*, up to 30–40% of those diagnosed with the disease; thus, clearly there is room for new drugs probably with new mechanisms of action that may show therapeutic effect in the present nonresponders.
2a	One special case of nonresponding is the development of resistance of the pathogen, i.e., the microbes that were successfully targeted with the available drugs have become resistant to these treatments and their combinations, and new antibiotics and antivirals are continuously needed.
3	There are many diseases that are *not addressed by any drug therapy today* because they have fallen in the estimation of the marketers, they are too large, too widespread to qualify for orphan drug status, and yet they are too small to assure a "reasonable" financial return given the expected pricing.
4	The *cost of trials*: The duration, enrollment size, and uncertainty of conducting good clinical trials are such that the financial risk is deemed too high by the companies. In these cases improved drugs with higher expected response rate and higher degree of efficacy can dramatically reduce the required size of the trials.
5	There is *not a good enough scientific basis* yet to propose and develop a robustly efficacious and safe drug treatment for diseases where we have not yet identified the molecular mechanisms that can be targeted with drug therapy

Table 3.1: Reasons new drug development must & will continue

patients had to accept injections into the eye instead of drops, which, while psychologically easier to take, had much lower or no efficacy. Here, there is easy comparison provided by injecting one of the two affected eyes with bevacizumab (or ranibizumab). When there is clear efficacy and the patient can literally *see* the difference between nontreated, treated, and placebo, one can convince the patient to pay for the drug and to tolerate injection into the eye and remain on the drug, that is, come back for a new series of injections. It is almost impossible to beat efficacy, as one of our mentors said.

Subsequent to large well-designed clinical trials, Lucentis was approved for treatment of the wet type of age-related macular degeneration (AMD) in 2006 and for diabetic macular edema (DME) in 2012. The much cheaper Avastin is used off-label by ophthalmologists. The use is scientifically driven. Genentech-Roche also conducted clinical trials with Avastin in non-small cell lung carcinoma that showed efficacy and thus gained approval in 2004. Its initial 2008 approval for metastatic breast cancer was revoked in 2011 because, while it slowed progression, it did not extend life nor improve the quality of life.

Off-label use in other indications

Many drugs, particularly cheap generic drugs, are used off-label. For example, as was mentioned earlier, there is a broad use of tricyclic antidepressants in neuropathic pain treatment. In almost all cases the physicians looking for treatment in an underserved patient population turn to *safe* and cheap drugs that can be combined with the drugs their patient presently takes.

Crucially, the drug should be safe, which means the same for expensive and cheap and for old and new drugs, that is, we know which doses to use, how and when to administer it, which drug combinations are permissible, and who might be at risk using this drug. The patients should be pretested, selected, and subgroups at risk excluded from treatment as necessary.

Over and over again safe drugs are tested in many underserved indications where the industry has failed to achieve good therapeutic efficacy because the industry has not tried or so far has not succeeded. Thus, the off-label use most often involves very safe drugs that are generic and have been administered over a long time to a large number of patients. This is not to say that the FDA should not continue to bring to court the companies that, as a matter of policy, willfully promote off-label use of their drugs. It is necessary to conduct well-designed trials to support the claims for the safety and efficacy of their drug in a not yet approved indication. Such trials are necessary as they contribute to the understanding of both efficacy and safety of the drug in a special patient population targeted in the new indication.

An example where a big company paid $2.3 billion in penalties for promoting sales for a large off-label use is that of pregabalin (Lyrica). In 2009, according to the U.S. government: "Pfizer was found guilty of misbranding drugs with the aim to defraud or mislead." This drug and its predecessor gabapentin were originally approved in small trials of 60-522 patients for gabapentin and 26-100 patients for pregabalin for adjunctive treatment of epilepsy. Actually showing that gabapentin or pregabalin is effective against pain would involve much larger pain trials where the outcome would be far from certain, as in pain a much more heterogeneous patient population is treated.

However, pain clinics have rapidly recognized their usefulness in some large pain indications like neuropathic pain, where there are almost no drugs to offer patients. There were good publications on the efficacy of pregabalin in neuropathic pain treatment and expert meetings, most supported by Pfizer. Thus, pain doctors extended its use long before Pfizer had taken the risks of a large pain trial. Many pain trials have failed, leading to companies such as GSK, Roche, and Novartis openly declaring that they have stopped developing drugs for the treatment of pain. This is not because there is no market or medical need, but because they see no reasonable way forward to predict from preclinical animal data which drug candidates will fail in the large trials costing several hundreds of millions of dollars.

Pregabalin was finally tested in clinical trials in neuropathic pain in diabetic neuropathy in 2004, and in the smaller indication, fibromyalgia, in 2007. It was approved to treat these neuropathic pain states as the first such drug, but its sales in these indications and the sales of the other Pfizer drug gabapentin were measured in billions of dollars before the approval. These were known to be safe and efficacious drugs and the company went for the easier approval route with shorter, cheaper, and better controlled trials in partial epilepsy. This is a common clinical trial strategy because the company is assured that it has an efficacious drug that is safe in a larger number of patients, prior to a costly trial in a huge indication. Pfizer avoided carrying out clinical trials formally to prove that the drug was safe in pain patients and efficacious in certain types of pain. Meanwhile its marketers were already busy selling the drugs for pain treatment. However, this somewhat disingenuous promotion to physicians of off-label use was not occurring with a drug with limited safety; instead, the drug was considered very safe. During the final discussions it became clear that Pfizer had been afraid that a formal pain trial might fail. Indeed, 90% of pain trials have failed in the past 10 years, because of the following:

- The drug does not have a robust effect
  - o The efficacy of most pain drugs is measured on a visual analog scale where 0 is no pain and 10 is excruciating pain, and the best drugs bring people from 7 to 4 on this scale, thus clearly not very efficacious and requiring large groups of patients to demonstrate statistically measurable effects
  - o Often because it is underdosed in an attempt to limit side effects
- The enrollment into pain trials includes a very heterogeneous group
  - o Some had this pain for a short time and some for many years[34]
  - o Most of them are already taking many other drugs, etc.

If the clinical trial in neuropathic pain failed and the results then reported at many meetings, which had earlier served to promote off-label use, then the ongoing off-label use bringing in billions of dollars would dry up. Pfizer, however, understood that, for example, in diabetic neuropathy patients, while the drug is efficacious as shown from off-label use, the safety of this drug in this patient group, with vascular, retinal, and kidney problems, was not established. It could have been a very dangerous agent

---

34 When pain is chronic, it leads to neuronal reprogramming and it becomes harder to treat, at least with the same drugs that are efficient when the condition is acute.

for these patients; thus, both efficacy and safety in larger off-label use would need to be established.

This does not negate the often observed situation that patients may benefit from drugs that were not designed to treat their disease.

The most horrific and illuminating example is that of thalidomide (Contergan/Thalomid), produced by Grünenthal, a medium-sized German company. It was used as a sedative to treat morning sickness in pregnant women. This use caused one of the greatest medical tragedies, with ~10,000-20,000 children born with malformed limbs, leading to teratogenicity and mutagenicity screens being introduced to drug development. Today this very drug, which was discovered in the late 1950s in Europe, is used to help leprosy patients with their skin lesions. Since 1999 it has been approved to treat leprosy after careful trials conducted by Celgene, a U.S. biotech. None of the larger companies would go near leprosy or to a drug that has failed with such horrible consequences. Yet Celgene has produced benefits for leprosy patients. Thalidomide is prescribed with serious "black box" warnings and preventive tools to avoid pregnancy and thus teratogenic damage to the fetus. When used in this way it is an efficacious and cheap way to treat symptoms of a terrible disease.

Most examples of "repositioning a drug" are not spanning the horrors of side effects and the horrors of disease quite as widely, but there are examples of expanding the indications for thalidomide, particularly in immunology, to several diseases through new trials.

Rituximab (Rituxan) is used in the treatment of lymphoma and in severe RA.[35] Transplantation drugs like cyclosporine and immunosuppressors like the mTOR (mammalian target of rapamycin) inhibitors found their way to the treatment of renal and other carcinomas[36] and are in trials for treatment of the neurodegenerative Huntington's disease. In these cases the drug is approved for an indication and the drug's target protein

---

35 See Chapter 02, section "Treatment of RA."

36 For example, everolimus (Novartis' Zortress/Certican) was approved in 2011 for pancreatic cancer—one of the worst and hardest to treat cancers—and is marketed in oncology as Afinitor.

becomes implicated in the other disease mechanism. In another indication the drug may be used as an experimental tool, firstly, to prove the disease mechanism; then, after clinical trials, the drug can become approved and be used in further indications: the basic scientific evidence is followed by clinical evidence.

Life cycle extension by repositioning

This kind of "life cycle extension" or "repositioning" for drugs is part of the workings of drug companies that want to maximize sales and profits of a drug that they spent hundreds of millions of dollars to develop and that has a limited patent protection, in each of its indications. Finding new indications, not only the pediatric indication that is most commonly pursued but also truly different indications, is a very profitable way to use the assets of a drug company: it is using the approved drugs it already knows how to manufacture and use in the clinic.

The problems with new indications are often related to pricing the same drug in different indications and finding different formulations when possible and needed. But all of us agree that this process is positive for patients and companies alike. The biggest benefit comes when the newly treatable disease previously had no other treatments. Often, opening drug treatment in a disease where none was known before will lead to a rapid increase in diagnosed cases and expansion of the market and also to development efforts of other drugs by other companies. This is because the successful trials establish the paradigm, the end points of treatment necessary for approval, and the ways to measure this.

As described in Table 3.2, there are multiple factors contributing to better, safer, and more efficacious drugs in a limited number of indications, while other indications are completely, or almost completely, ignored despite large medical need, and in some cases despite likely large returns for a successful launch of a new drug. A problem for our society exists where for-profit companies alone decide which diseases should be treated with drugs. This will be further discussed in Chapters 04, 05, 07, 11, and 12.

	Key reasons for new & improved drugs
1	Pharma is a financially attractive industry; the pharma companies are highly specialized after a 100-year development and will continue to look for new drugs to make; contrary to talk about it not being profitable, it is highly profitable (albeit less so than 5 years ago); and there is a financial initiative to make new drugs.
2	Inter- and intra-company competition exists to invent new drugs to treat diseases that are not being treated or to treat diseases through new mechanisms of action and provide therapy for untreated diseases and nonresponding patients or treatment-resistant cases.
3	Inter- and intra-company competition exists to replace approved drugs in financially attractive indications.
4	Greater emphasis on drug safety at the FDA (especially long-term drug safety); discussions on benefit–risk ratio are now major criteria in the approval discussions.
5	Greater emphasis on drug safety within the companies (fear of litigation).
6	Large public trials: EBM[1] goes beyond in size and duration what private companies can and will sponsor; these trials can elucidate risks and benefits and equivalence of drugs in more convincing ways than privately sponsored trials because of the public sponsorship and because they are usually larger and longer trials.
7	Meta-analysis emerges as an important tool of judging safety over longer time periods and many trials.

Table 3.2: The key reasons for new & improved drugs

1 See later in this chapter, section "Evidence-based medicine requires large & long public-funded trials," and also Chapters 01, 07, and 11.

Inter- & intra-company competition to replace approved drugs in financially attractive indications

When a company has decided to be active in a therapeutic area it then has to decide for which diseases it wants to develop drugs and whether there are already existing drugs, in which case the coming drug clearly has to compete in terms of efficacy, safety, and, today, very seldom in terms of price.

	Ways to improve drugs
1	To provide symptom treatment, as do most of today's drugs
2	To improve also the response a. Of the degree and magnitude of the therapy b. Of the onset of the therapy
3	To reduce side effects
4	To eliminate the need for pretesting
5	To make it possible to apply the drug in combination therapies
6	To make it easier to dose the drug to reduce the number of doses taken daily from, say, three to one
7	To move from injectable to oral drug or patch
8	To find a mechanism of action and a drug that *cures the disease*—or—*modifies disease progression*—rather than just *treating symptoms*

Table 3.3: Ways to improve drugs
Any and all combinations of these improvements may assist the new drug not only to be approved but also to win a larger market share. It leads to better drugs for diseases where we already have drugs. Numbers 1-7 represent progress to become "best in class"; number 8 would represent a new class of drugs—this class would be preferably disease modifying in a condition where we have only treatment for symptoms.

The strengths and weaknesses of the already existing drugs are there for all to see by reading the approval letters of the FDA and EMA that clearly explain for which indication and for which dosing regimen the drug is approved and whether it is a stand-alone treatment or an adjunctive treatment used with other approved drugs. They also explain all the clinical and preclinical results upon which the approval was based. Particularly important is when the drug receives a warning label for safety issues in certain patients, or in combination of other drugs, and so forth, or when the label prescribes testing of genotype or of other parameters before the start of treatment.

These are the issues to which those who aim to surpass an approved competitor drug must pay attention, especially while planning to exploit the same mechanism of action (see Table 3.3).

Pricing policies

It is a peculiarity of the pharmaceutical market (and also of the medical device market) that price does not often enter into the discussion as patented drugs seldom compete on price, although this undoubtedly will come. There is serious consideration given to competing with generic drugs and biosimilars that cost significantly less. This consideration leads to competition within companies to develop drugs that will "cannibalize" the sales of their own leading drug. Hopefully, a new drug will successfully compete with the original drug once it has become a generic, but most importantly will keep other companies' drugs at bay for this indication, that is, the company's franchise is protected.

Novartis provides a significant example (as quoted from *FiercePharma* December 8, 2009[37]):

In the first head-to-head comparison of Novartis' Tasigna[38] and its older medicine Glivec,[39] Tasigna results showed statistically significant improvement over Glivec in every measure of efficacy, including major molecular response, complete cytogenetic response, and prevention of disease progression. Tasigna is currently approved for second-line use for the treatment of chronic myeloid leukemia [CML].

The overwhelming positive data are a dose of good news for Novartis, which will see sales of Glivec erode when it goes off-patent in a few years. Glivec is Novartis' second-best selling drug, with $3.7 billion in sales in 2008. Novartis intends to file worldwide applications for Tasigna for newly-diagnosed patients with Philadelphia chromosome-positive CML in chronic phase.

---

37   Novartis'Tasigna beats Glivec in leukemia study – *FiercePharma*, http://www.fiercepharma.com/story/novartis-tasigna-beats-glivec-leukemia-study/2009-12-08#ixzz0ziK24bxZ
38   Nilotinib.
39   Imatinib, also known as Gleevec in the United States.

Considering the already low rates of progression to advanced disease and the excellent long-term survival of patients on Glivec, the efficacy and safety profile of Tasigna at 12 months is fantastic news and brings promise for further improving the outcomes of patients with Ph+ CML," David Epstein, President and CEO of Novartis Oncology and Novartis Molecular Diagnostics, says in a statement.

To this optimistic statement from the company executive, one must add that Gleevec, an Abl-type tyrosine kinase inhibitor used in oncology, was a groundbreaking drug, and by Novartis developing its own follow-up compound, the company is capitalizing on its know-how in the area to compete with other companies, which with their follow-up or me-too compounds wanted to erode Gleevec's market share.

New competition to successful drugs in an established disease area almost always comes from drugs based on new scientific knowledge that focus on a new mechanism of action. Such drugs may cure the disease, slow disease progression, or reduce symptoms in presently treatment-resistant patients. Chemical innovation that brings new compounds that use the same mechanism as the already established drugs also can be very important for patients if the new compound has a better side effect profile or is easier to administer, or both.

Those companies, both small and big, that compete with drugs at the clinical trial stage (i.e., before approval of the drug) will find all the information they initially need from the Pharmaceutical Research and Manufacturers of America (PhRMA) and in the very useful clinicaltrials.gov database. These data sources have replaced much, but not all, competitive intelligence that is still an important part of following the competition. Companies may adjust predictions about the properties the drug needs to have to be superior to the other company's drug. They also reveal the expected end date of the trial, what the recruitment rate is, and, most importantly, the problems competitors' compounds have encountered. The potential competitor needs to consider whether or not its own drug suffers from the same drawbacks. Not all Big Pharma companies opposed (and vilified) the clinical trials database, although not all supported its launch. It lists the indication; the inclusion and exclusion criteria of patients; the drugs used concomitantly; and the design, duration, and size of trial. One notices repeatedly that a drug candidate does not always advance from phase 2 to phase 3, even though phase 2 was finished years ago.

Thus clinicaltrial.gov is enormously useful when looking to start a clinical trial. One can judge from the size of the trial how large a signal and how large a responder rate is expected, and one can understand from exclusion criteria certain already known drug interactions. Also, the timely passage from phase 1 to phase 2 to phase 3 suggests that the drug is performing as expected, because even big companies, and definitely small companies, publish results of successful phase 2 data. Unfortunately for patients, clinicians, regulators, and competing companies, we are left in the dark when a company stops a trial. Why did your competitor stop a drug-development project? This becomes a hotly debated point in each company. Did they abandon the drug target? Is there a mechanism-based risk they discovered? Is the drug target good, but their molecule faulty? Do they now have a better (backup) molecule that will come? These are no longer million dollar questions; these are billion dollar questions. The regulators may find answers but they are prohibited from publicizing these in case they distort competition and penalize the company who was first, by saving both money and effort for those who are following. This is all well if it were, say, manufacturing plastic plants for cemeteries, but in drug development, new patients enrolled in a trial will now take risks with the other companies' drugs. In case of major drug target-related dangers the regulators may warn all other companies, but the sacrifice of the patients who took the chance to be "volunteers" on the first drug is not being well used for all mankind. But this should be easy to fix.

The people who so eminently run clinicaltrials.gov would be in the best position to enable competitors to receive safety-related information of failed trials. The FDA in one-on-one meetings does sometimes suggest safety tests that reveal that the FDA has learned from the failure of a competitor's trial, but this is not an automatic nor necessarily consistent procedure.

Greater emphasis on long-term drug safety & benefit-risk ratio

Even the most libertarian politicians do not propose that we abolish the FDA or the EMA. The need for these regulatory agencies remains, and time after time it becomes obvious that the industry cannot and should not regulate itself. Another argument in Europe and also in the United States, where the number of patients covered by Medicare increases, is that society in the end will take care of those hurt by medicines. The companies remain private and distribute their earnings to stockholders, representing numerically a very small portion of our society. Even if in some cases litigation makes them pay for the suffering and for the cost of corrective treatments when possible, ultimately, in most cases, society acts as the final insurer. Society, through regulatory agencies, should be able to protect its citizens from harm and itself from unnecessary costs. This is best done by regulatory agencies that have their own internal significant scientific competence and that also work with outside experts. These academic and clinical experts must be independent from both the industry and politicians.[40] This has been possible in most cases, with some notable but very few scandalous exceptions, for example, HIV-infected blood supplies, and Servier's obesity drug, benfluorex (Mediator).

The credibility of the FDA and the EMA arises from their lack of connection to the profit motive of the companies and of the high scientific and clinical competence that the agencies and their *ad hoc* committees have. It would be even better if the companies, through fees, would not finance the FDA, but that the FDA would be supported through taxes. Since 2010, the FDA has been strengthened by the long overdue collaboration on the scientific basis of drugs with the National Institutes of Health (NIH), presently the largest government-supported basic and clinical research institute in the world.

---

40 The best academic researchers are sought by both by the industry and the government as experts, and fortunately there is a broad cadre of excellence and there is significant autonomy among these people such that it is possible to recruit independent expert panels.

In whichever country the regulatory agencies lose credibility, the development and approval of novel drugs becomes difficult and somewhat redundant because the richest markets of the European Union, United States, Japan, and Canada will insist on new clinical trials at sites they trust and can control. Much time and money is lost when trials done elsewhere are repeated. With every failure of an earlier approved drug, the credibility of the approving country falls deeper. This is a hard issue for countries that have decided to build large and, hopefully, exporting pharmaceutical industries like Russia, India, and China; the regulatory agencies in these countries need to have the same credibility or better than the FDA and EMA enjoy today.

The FDA and EMA are continuously accused of being responsible for the "crisis" of the industry—fewer and fewer approved drugs—while the cost of R&D is increasing, reaching $92 billion in 2009. In December 2010, the outgoing EMA chief accused the industry in his turn for throwing away ~$62 billion (as reported in *FierceBiotech*[41]):

> The outgoing chief of the European Medicines Agency took a moment to do the math on the $85 billion the industry spends on drug R&D each year. And he concluded that the vast majority of the money is simply wasted.

> *How many [new drugs] are approved each year—six, seven, eight, nine maybe? If the value of these few new drugs is worth 10, maybe 20 billion U.S. dollars, then where is the remainder of the $85 billion going?" asked Thomas Lönngren ... "Maybe we could use this $60 billion in a better way?" ... Lönngren says drug regulators around the world are likely to cooperate more closely in coming years. "The evolutionary momentum of this is unstoppable.*

He is not too happy with the R&D priorities at Big Pharma companies, either.

---

41   EMA chief blasts $60B in wasted R&D spending each year, *FierceBiotech* http://www.fiercebiotech.com/story/ema-chief-blasts-60b-wasted-rd-spending-each-year/2010-12-16#ixzz1bs7vukHS

In an interview with Dow Jones in London, Lönngren concluded that reducing the amount of R&D money devoted to CNS therapies is a mistake, especially considering the consequences of a rapidly aging population. And he had some sharp words for big drug companies for pulling out of antibiotics in light of the spread of treatment-resistant bacteria.

Moving the goalposts

The industry asks: How are we to develop a drug in a 10–12-year process when the FDA and the EMA are changing the goalposts about what benefit-risk ratio a newly approved drug has to achieve at the time of its approval, not at the time of the start of the project?

The issue is that the FDA is indeed changing its position on safety (or long-term safety to be more precise). It increases the demands when new scientific data from large studies or from meta-analysis of many small studies show that safety aspects of long-term use were not addressed when approving drugs from huge companies held in high repute with a 100-year tradition. Even such resourceful companies cannot fully foresee the safety problems that may arise from sustained use of their drugs. Companies that want to remain in the market as credible sources of new drugs have to work with the regulators on long-term use. When new scientific evidence that affects drug safety becomes available anywhere in the world, regulators have to take it into account. Approval should always be conditional on long-term safety trials and analyses confirming continued approval. Perhaps if the pharmaceutical companies explicitly agree to this they would be more cautious in marketing, physicians would be more cautious about prescribing the drug over the long-term, and the companies' lawyers would not be required to defend the indefensible as plaintiff's lawyers are obliged to be less aggressive. Perhaps, a more cooperative relationship would emerge to society's benefit. It matters not if the drug under review was started as a development project earlier than these scientific data became available. No executive whose heart started a pathologic process 10 years ago leading to the executive's heart infarct today (i.e., 10 years after the start of the process) would like to be treated at the medical standard of the time when the pathological process started. Rather, they all want to be treated at the latest standard, and rightly so. We all should use the globally available, latest scientific data to make decisions that affect health. We should use the most modern medicine for the treatments with the best benefit-risk ratio of the day.

It is true that the FDA now insists on long-term study of the cardio-vascular safety of diabetes drugs, a class of large volume, large-selling drugs that must be very safe for the several hundred million patients who take them worldwide, and whose numbers now explode because of the obesity epidemic (see Chapter 05). While it is true that before the rosiglitazone meta-analysis it was not clear that such long-term safety concerns may affect diabetes drugs, now that we know this, it is impossible not to take this into account at approval and while prescribing drugs.

Weight loss drugs kept waiting[42]

The industry is upset about the risk-benefit arguments that keep efficacious weight loss drugs from approval. Rimonabant from Sanofi-Aventis (Acomplia or Zimulti) and the competitors from Merck, Novartis, and Pfizer are all delayed by the FDA.[43] They work as inverse agonists of the cannabinoid-1 (CB-1) receptor. Endocannabinoid receptors[44] are involved in pain and pleasure sensations and mediate some of the effects of cannabis/marijuana. These drugs, by blocking these pleasure-related effects, increase neurological and psychiatric conditions including suicidal ideation, the symptoms of which are much harder, but not impossible, to measure than the weight loss the drugs are designed to cause. The expert panels[45] have clearly stated that suicide risk, particularly in younger women, is too high a price to pay for weight loss, while agreeing that obesity is a

---

42   See also Chapter 11.
43   EMA initially approved Acomplia but withdrew authorization. See http://www.ema.europa.eu/docs/en_GB/document_library/EPAR_-_Summary_for_the_public/human/000666/WC500021282.pdf
44   Cannabinoid receptors and their endogenous lipid ligands.
45   It is piquantly interesting that the deliberations of the expert panel can be followed live on a webcast, and thus all scientists working on competing drugs are tuned in and hopefully learn something from this collective effort to judge the safety and benefit of candidate molecules.

serious risk factor for type 2 diabetes. While type 2 diabetes is a severe disease, only 20% of obese people will develop it. Indeed, the FDA has always measured risk–benefit when drug approval was discussed, but it was not usually expressed in these clear terms as stated by today's regulators.

Thus, the FDA and EMA are doing what they should: their best to protect the safety of patients.[46] If safety standards change and a drug is no longer passing the safety hurdle, the company should see this as a business risk. If the disease is severe and no other drugs are available, the drug still may be approved but with a warning label. If there are competitors that pass the safety hurdle, then it is the classical business risk that a competitor is better and your product sales will suffer.

Meanwhile, it is feared that obesity will affect almost 50% of Americans, including 1 in 3 children. The projected cost in just medical bills is projected to climb to $500 billion in the next 20 years. Currently it is already 10% of the health bill. The non-medical costs are also considerable.

Evidence-based medicine requires large & long public-funded trials[47]

Large public trials have become larger and longer than those sponsored by private companies. These trials can elucidate risks to benefits and the equivalence of drugs in more convincing ways both because of the public sponsorship and because they are larger and longer.

Large and long-term trials are not new and wealthy self-confident companies used them in the past to create huge markets. For example, the usefulness of statins was established in The Scandinavian Simvastatin Survival Study (now called the "4S study") in the 1990s. Over 5.4 years the study examined Merck's cholesterol-lowering drug simvastatin (Zocor) on mortality and morbidity in coronary heart disease. With 4,444 patients with moderate hypercholesterolemia it was a model study in evidence-based medicine (EBM). It also established important statistics for

---

46   Under earlier, yet still recent, Republican administrations, there was a lot of pressure on the FDA to approve drugs; this was a major strain on the FDA and one of the least favorable aspects of lobbying Congress. Ill-informed politicians (i.e., a large number of them) erroneously equate FDA approval as good for business.
47   See also Chapters 01, 07, and 11.

discussion on the value of preventive medicine. It found that the number of patients to treat with simvastatin to avoid one myocardial infarct was 34.[48] This long study—5 years longer than the time needed to establish that serum cholesterol levels indeed lowered enough for approval in severe hypercholesterolemia—has been the basis of the largest bonanza for Big Pharma in selling cholesterol-lowering drugs. At their peak year, Zocor and Pfizer's Lipitor were selling for $10 billion per year to treat not a disease, but a risk factor for a serious disease, as rich societies should do when they can afford it, and in the early 1990s some societies felt rich.

While the individual companies carry out clinical trials to establish the usefulness and sometimes the superiority of their product in a disease, the publicly financed trials may compare products from different companies, and are most often far longer in duration and larger in enrollment than privately sponsored trials. This makes their results count even more in debates over drug safety. The best recent example, which has shaken the industry, physicians, and postmenopausal women, was the early discontinuation of a trial designed and implemented by the Women's Health Initiative (WHI).[49] The WHI planned two studies on the benefits of hormone replacement therapy (HRT). The first, an Estrogen Plus Progestin,[50] involved an astonishing 16,608 healthy menopausal women aged 50–79 years. The second, an Estrogen-Alone Study,[51] involved 11,000 healthy menopausal women who had had a hysterectomy. The results were so compelling that both trials were stopped prematurely, and the results made immediately available. Long-term use of estrogen plus progestin, a synthetic progestogen, was found to increase the risk of invasive breast cancer, coronary heart disease, stroke, and pulmonary embolism.

---

48   Randomized trial of cholesterol lowering in 4,444 patients with coronary heart disease: the Scandinavian Simvastatin Survival Study (4S) (1994) *Lancet*; 344:1383–1389. (PMID 7968073)

49   http://www.nhlbi.nih.gov/whi/index.html

50   The Estrogen-Plus-Progestin Study, http://www.nhlbi.nih.gov/whi/estro_pro.htm; Questions and Answers About Estrogen-Plus-Progestin Hormone Therapy, http://www.nhlbi.nih.gov/health/women/q_a.htm

51   NHLBI Advisory for Physicians on the WHI Trial of Conjugated Equine Estrogens Versus Placebos, http://www.nhlbi.nih.gov/whi/e-a_advisory.htm

Long-term use of a conjugated equine estrogen developed by Wyeth-Pfizer (Premarin, named because of its source in PREgnant MARes' urINe) had no effect on breast cancer incidence, but did show a slight risk of thrombosis and stroke, which was unacceptable in a trial carried out on healthy subjects. These hormone-substituting drugs are still available and may still be prescribed for shorter term acute symptoms. Indeed there were noteworthy benefits of estrogen plus progestin, including fewer cases of hip fractures and colon cancer. The advice was:

Menopausal women who might have been candidates for estrogen plus progestin should now focus on well-proven treatments to reduce the risk of cardiovascular disease, including measures to prevent and control high blood pressure, high blood cholesterol, and obesity. This effort could not be more important: heart disease remains the number one killer of American women.

The study results were published in the daily and weekly press and started a re-evaluation of HRT, with the whole world reducing its use by ~65–75%. It has mostly hurt one company, Wyeth, which dominated HRT, but it was not the only company producing such drugs. The results probably contributed greatly to Wyeth becoming vulnerable to takeover and the very acquisitive Pfizer obliged.

The WHI, in addition to enabling safety studies, enables drug discovery because its rich sample bank is available to researchers and it now contains samples from ~27,000 postmenopausal women. The WHI itself is also following the volunteers. This would be difficult for a private company, but not for the U.S. government-sponsored institutes: the NIH and the National Heart, Lung, and Blood Institute (NHLBI) that launched the WHI in 1991.[52]

Similarly, other publicly sponsored studies can outlast not only the attention span of pharma companies but sometimes the life span of the

---

52 From the NHLBI Web site: "The National Institutes of Health (NIH) established the Women's Health Initiative (WHI) in 1991 to address the most common causes of death, disability and impaired quality of life in postmenopausal women. The WHI addressed cardiovascular disease, cancer, and osteoporosis."

pharma companies themselves. Cardiovascular health safety can thank the prospective study that started in 1948 for many important insights. Now every child should know that smoking is damaging to their (cardiovascular) health, but it had to be scientifically proven in a large cohort over many years. This was accomplished in 1960 in NHLBI's Framingham Heart Study (FHS),[53] which continues to study cardiovascular disease and its management, and thus can be among the first to discover long-term risks, not only of smoking and lifestyle but also of chronically used drugs that bring acute benefits but may have negative effects over a long period. The FHS, in collaboration with Boston University, has broadened its scope now to include some neurological diseases such as Alzheimer's disease.[54]

Worldwide drug safety benefits from national drug approval procedures and reimbursement differences between the different countries. These differences bring into play different regulatory agencies and what may be overlooked by one will hopefully be found by another. When this happens, the safety concern in one country becomes international within days. If a credible agency stops a drug, almost no other agency dares to continue to permit its use, at least not until additional studies are carried out.

In the UK, where the National Health Service (NHS) pays for and dispenses most medicines, a key question for the government is how to achieve the highest quality care with a minimum of cost, and thus recommendations, or, more properly, "guidelines," on care pathways are given to physicians. These recommendations determine which drugs are to be used as first-line and second-line therapies, which combinations of drugs are effective, and which combinations are cost-effective. This is done based on the NHS's own large, well-designed studies, which many times compare older, generic cheaper drugs and newer, strongly advertised more expensive drugs. Safety is a major consideration in trying to decide whether there are real medical benefits in the use of a particular newer drug. Thus, the National

---

53 http://www.framinghamheartstudy.org/about/index.html,   http://www.framingham
heartstudy.org/participants/original.html,   and   http://www.framinghamheartstudy.org/
about/milestones.html
54 http://www.framinghamheartstudy.org/participants/pr/10_0511.html

Institute for Health and Clinical Excellence (NICE) is working on EBM recommendations, and its studies are often exemplary. While they may not be welcomed by the companies when NICE does not find sufficient reason to use the newer drug, these studies benefit patient safety worldwide.

> *NICE has to ensure that the NHS provides treatments that bring benefits which are value for money. As fulvestrant has not been proven to be cost-effective, we cannot justify diverting NHS funds from other areas of healthcare in order to fund its use.*
>
> Sir Andrew Dillon, Chief Executive of NICE

Gains of & from EBM

EBM is gaining ground everywhere. For example, the National Institute of Mental Health (NIMH) sponsored the Clinical Antipsychotic Trials in Intervention Effectiveness (CATIE) study. The study found that *older antipsychotics were just as effective as newer ones*. The newer ones are invariably very expensive and, considering that the number of prescriptions reflects the high prevalence (7.2 per 1,000) of this chronic mental illness, it is an expensive choice. Overall, in 2002 in the United States the cost of schizophrenia was estimated to be $62.7 billion, with $22.7 billion spent on direct healthcare costs ($7.0 billion outpatient, $5.0 billion drugs, $2.8 billion inpatient, and $8.0 billion long-term care).

This has not only cost implications but serious safety implications as well, since the best selling ($4 billion per year) olanzapine (Zyprexa from Lilly) is not only more expensive than older typical antipsychotics but it also has potentially serious side effects. The older antipsychotics cause a higher incidence of extrapyramidal side effects, such as Parkinson's disease-like symptoms. In contrast, olanzapine was shown first in 2001 and then repeatedly by clinical scientists to cause weight gain, type 2 diabetes, ketosis, and death through ketosis. Worse was that Lilly seems to have played down and suppressed knowledge of and information about these metabolic side effects. In 2005, the FDA finally issued a *black label warning* for olanzapine because of the metabolic side effects. These effects are particularly aggravating as the treated patients are often young women and men, as the disease debuts after 18–22 years of age. Today the safety of antipsychotics has become a serious issue, as discussed in Chapter 05.

Lilly has since settled several large class action law suits for failing to warn about the risks of severe weight gain, diabetes, hyperglycemia, and pancreatitis. It has also been fined for promoting the same drug for treatment of dementia for which it has not been approved. Lilly thus became one of the major pharma companies that has had its safety consciousness significantly raised.

Not all companies have learned their lesson. In May 2012, Abbott Laboratories pleaded guilty to the charge that it promoted its antiseizure drug Depakote (valproic acid) for unapproved uses as treatment for dementia and schizophrenia. The allegation was that Abbott trained sales representatives to promote non-FDA approved use between 1998 and 2006, often directly to nursing homes. As well as a $700 million forfeiture and $800 million spent in civil settlements via the principal case, it agreed to pay $100 million to consumers via the Virginia Consumer Protection Act—a total of $1.6 billion at the time of writing.

Numbers of annually approved drugs

The entities that develop drugs today are arguably in turmoil. Large pharma companies and large biotechs are shaken but alive, and still profitable, albeit less so than 10 years ago; and continue to produce new drugs. However, the scope of their activities and interest is—as we will relentlessly document—unfortunately shrinking, with many of society's important therapeutic areas being abandoned by Big Pharma, as decisions by Pfizer and GSK exemplify.

Firstly, this analysis must start with the recognition that the new drug approvals of 2009–2011 are largely the result of project decisions made between 1995 and 2002, under a completely different set of economic, political, and emotional conditions set by the countries that invest in drug development. They thus reflect the thinking of company managements during that period. Over 90% of these managements have been replaced by now, as the industry turnover of executives is about 6–7 years; this is a major problem in an industry with product development cycles of 10-12 years.

Secondly, it is important to understand that the therapeutic areas, wherein projects were pursued in 1995-2002, when the projects leading up to this approval list were first initiated, such as cardiovascular medicine, neurology, and psychiatry, to a large extent fell out of favor with executives by 2010, simply because the large number of failed clinical trials in the past 5-6 years led to the conviction that it is too risky and too difficult to achieve a New Drug Application (NDA) in these indications. Thus, the therapeutic areas of the NDA list sharply differ from the list of areas that, for example, AstraZeneca, GSK, and Pfizer chose to pursue in 2011 (see Table 3.4 and also Tables 2.6, 4.2, and 4.3.)

Today the weight of oncology and inflammation in project portfolios is being questioned as a result of huge recent medical and financial successes in these areas, for example, Gleevec, Avastin, and Herceptin, in oncology and the anti-TNF therapies such as Enbrel, Remicade, and Humira in RA.[55] Meanwhile, the recognition that in niche areas such as ophthalmology and dermatology substantial profits can still be made keeps these indications

Areas in which drugs were approved	
Neurology-psychiatry	5
Oncology	5
Cardiovascular disease	4
Inflammation	4
Dermatology	1
Infection	2
Ophthalmology	2
Pain	2
Malaria, lice	2

Table 3.4: The therapeutic areas in which drugs were approved in 2009

---

55   See Chapters 02 and 06.

on the list now as 10 years ago. This is not just because in these areas almost no disease goes undiagnosed and unreported, but also because the efficacy of these drugs is so obvious.

The distribution of the approved drugs in 2009 and 2011 (see Tables 3.5-3.7) between biologicals and small molecule drugs shows that the industry in 1995-2002 had already heavily shifted toward biologicals as a drug class that may have a better safety profile. Thus, despite biologicals' non-oral delivery problems, they have a greater chance of becoming approved drugs; consequently, 7 of the 27 NDAs of 2009 are biologicals (5 are natural products), 10 of the 21 NDAs of 2010 are biologicals (4 natural products), and 11 of the 35 NDAs of 2011 are biologicals (2 natural products). Twenty-six of the approvals over this 3-year period were orphan drugs. While this is in and of itself good news, it probably means that the number of patients served by all these approvals has declined.

The number of new drugs approved has shrunk, especially as compared to the golden days of the 1980s when about 60 new drugs were annually approved, and when one considers that some of the molecules are not novel or newly discovered. Recent years have seen 25-30 approvals, despite the increasing expenditures, making the cost per approved drug much higher. The companies rationalize current reductions in R&D expenditures as a savings arising from the merger of R&D units of the merged companies and difficulties in borrowing money, although interest rates are at historical lows. In actuality, companies have cut R&D expenditures in the past 3 years, by up to 20% in some large companies.

It is important to reflect on these lists of approvals in the so-called "pharma crisis years." In 2010 the industry made 29,000 FTEs[56] redundant and R&D budgets were slashed by billions of dollars.

The crisis might be better referred to as a "disappointment" for those convinced that less than double-digit growth and profits are not worth living for.

---

56 Full time equivalents, commonly referred to as staff, i.e., actual people.

	INN (trade name)	Marketed by	Indication(s)	Notes
1	milnacipran HCl (Savella)	Forest Laboratories/ Cypress Bioscience	fibromyalgia; (MDD in some countries outside the United States)	small molecule; SNRI
2	febuxostat (Uloric)	Takeda	gout; hyperuricemia	small molecule; xanthine oxidase inhibitor
3	everolimus (Afinitor)	Novartis	advanced renal cell carcinoma	priority review natural product; mTOR inhibitor
4	artermether and lumefantrine (Coartem)	Novartis (first developed in China)	malaria (used in 80 countries)	priority review natural product; artemisinin-based combination therapy (ACT); orphan drug
5	benzyl alcohol (Ulesfia)	Sciele Pharma	head lice	old small molecule in new preparation (lotion)
6	golimumab (Simponi)	J&J/Centocor	rheumatoid arthritis (RA), psoriatic arthritis, ankylosing spondylitis	biological; human antibody from library; immunosuppressive TNF inhibitor
7	abobotulinumtoxinA (Dysport)[1]	Ipsen/Medicis	cervical dystonia	biological; natural product toxin; blocks neuromuscular transmission by decreasing ACh release; orphan drug
8	iloperidone (Fanapt)	Vanda Pharma	schizophrenia	small molecule; multiple receptor antagonistic atypical antipsychotic
9	tolvaptan (Samsca)	Otsuka Pharma	hyponatremia	small molecule; selective competitive vasopressin receptor 2 antagonist

(continued on next page)

	INN (trade name)	Marketed by	Indication(s)	Notes
10	besifloxacin HCl (Besivance)	Bausch & Lomb	bacterial conjunctivitis	small molecule; 4th-generation fluoroquinolone antibiotic
11	canakinumab (Ilaris)	Novartis	cryopyrin-associated periodic syndromes, a spectrum of auto-inflammatory syndromes	priority review biological; human antibody (from library) targeting interleukin-1 beta; orphan drug
12	dronedarone (Multaq)	Sanofi-Aventis	atrial fibrillation	priority review small molecule; multichannel blocker
13	prasugrel HCl (Effient)	Eli Lilly/Daiichi Sankyo	"'blood thinner" for patients undergoing angioplasty	priority review small molecule; thienopyridine class ADP receptor inhibitor
14	saxagliptin (Onglyza)	AstraZeneca, Bristol-Myers Squibb	type 2 diabetes	small molecule; dipeptidyl peptidase-4 inhibitor
15	pitavastatin (Livalo)	Kowa Research	high cholesterol	small molecule; new statin; HMG-CoA reductase inhibitor
16	asenapine (Saphris)	Merck/Organon	episodes related to bipolar disorder; acute schizophrenia	small molecule; multiple receptor antagonistic atypical antipsychotic
17	interferon beta-1b (Extavia)	Novartis	symptoms of multiple sclerosis	biological; blood-brain barrier improving anti-inflammatory

18	vigabatrin[2] (Sabril)	Lundbeck	infantile spasms (West syndrome); complex partial seizure add-on therapy in adults	small molecule; gamma-vinyl-GABA inhibitor of GABA transaminase; orphan drug
19	bepotastine ophthalmic (Bepreve/Talion)	ISTA Pharmaceuticals/ Tanabe Seiyaku-Senju	ocular itching due to allergic conjunctivitis	small molecule; antihistamine
20	telavancin (Vibativ)	Theravance/ Astellas	MRSA-related skin infections	natural product; synthetic derivative of vancomycin, bactericidal lipoglycopeptide
21	pralatrexate (Folotyn)	Allos Therapeutics	relapsed peripheral T-cell lymphoma	priority review small molecule; folate analog metabolic inhibitor; orphan drug
22	ustekinumab (Stelara)	J&J/Centocor/ Janssen-Cilag	moderate to severe plaque psoriasis	biological; human antibody; anti-interleukin 12 and 23
23	pazopanib (Votrient)	GSK	renal cell carcinoma, soft tissue sarcoma	small molecule; multi-tyrosine kinase receptor inhibitor; antitumor growth and anti-angiogenesis
24	ofatumumab/HuMax-CD20 (Arzerra)	GSK	chronic lymphocytic leukemia	priority review biological; chimeric monoclonal antibody (CD20); early-stage B-lymphocyte activation inhibitor; orphan drug
25	romidepsin (Istodax)	Gloucester Pharmaceuticals	cutaneous T-cell lymphoma	natural product; HDAC inhibitor; anti-apoptotic depsipeptide; orphan drug

(continued on next page)

	INN (trade name)	Marketed by	Indication(s)	Notes
26	ecallantide (Kalbitor)	Dyax Corp	sudden attacks of hereditary angioedema	priority review biological; 60-AA polypeptide; mimics antibodies to kallikrein; orphan drug
27	capsaicin (Qutenza)	NeurogesX	management of neuropathic pain	natural product; 8% capsaicin patch; orphan drug

Table 3.5: FDA approvals in 2009

In this and the following two tables, drugs are listed with International Nonproprietary Name (INN; or in some cases the U.S. adopted name; USAN) and (usually U.S.) trade name in parenthesis. Some of these may be approved for other indications and some will be marketed by other companies. The listed company is not always the one that discovered the medicines. Twenty-seven drugs were approved by the FDA in 2009 compared with 25 in 2008. Eight approvals had priority review. There were seven biologicals (four antibodies, of which three are fully human antibodies); five were natural products. Nine are orphan drugs. No more than four of these drugs are expected to earn more than $1 billion per year. Some major companies did not have any new drugs approved, e.g. Pfizer.

1 See also Xeomin in Table 3.6 for 2010.
2 Vigabatrin was synthesized in 1974 and developed by Merrell Dow. It was originally "launched" in 1989 by Marion Merrell Dow at the 18th International Epilepsy Congress in New Delhi and was initially only available in the UK. It has had a checkered history because of adverse effects, especially on vision, but its approval as an orphan drug for potentially catastrophic infantile spasm is because the benefit outweighs the risk. For more see Shields WD & Pellock JM (2011) Vigabatrin 35 years later—from mechanism of action to benefit-risk considerations. *Acta Neurol Scand.* 124 (Suppl. 192): 1-4. ©2011 John Wiley & Sons A/S.

	INN (trade name)	Marketed by	Indication(s)	Notes
1	tocilizumab (Actemra)	Roche/Chugai	RA	biological; humanized IL-6R antibody; immunosuppressive; not first line but potential blockbuster
2	dalfampridine/fampridine (Ampyra/Fampyra)	Acorda Therapeutics	multiple sclerosis (walking difficulties)	priority review small (old) molecule; potassium channel blocker 4-AP; orphan drug
3	polidocanol (Asclera)	Merz/Chemische Fabrik Kreussler	sclerotherapy (varicose veins)	small (old) molecule; local anesthetic and antipruritic (also found in ointments and bath additives)
4	carglumic acid (Carbaglu)	Orphan Europe	N-acetylglutamate synthase (NAGS) deficiency	priority review small molecule; orphan drug
5	tesamorelin (Egrifta)	Theratechnologies	lipodystrophy in HIV patients	biological; orally active modified polypeptide growth hormone secretagogue
6	levonorgestrel (EllaOne, etc.)	HRA Pharma/Watson	emergency contraception (morning after pill)	biological; 2nd generation synthetic progestogen
7	fingolimod (Gilenya)	Novartis	multiple sclerosis	priority review natural product; first oral drug for MS; sphingosine 1-phosphate receptor modulator; potential blockbuster

(continued on next page)

	INN (trade name)	Marketed by	Indication(s)	Notes
8	eribulin mesylate (Halaven)	Eisai	breast cancer	priority review natural product; antimitotic macrocyclic ketone analog of the marine sponge's halichondrin B—a triumph of synthesis
9	cabazitaxel (Jevtana)	Sanofi-Aventis	hormone refractory metastatic prostate cancer	priority review small molecule; semisynthetic derivative of natural taxoid; second-line treatment
10	pegloticase (Krystexxa)	Savient Pharmaceuticals	gout	priority review biological; enzyme solution of recombinant porcine-like 4*300-AA tetrameric peptide uricase; orphan drug
11	alcaftadine (Lastacaft)	J&J/Allergan/Visaton Pharmaceuticals	allergic pinkeye	small molecule; histamine H1 receptor antagonist
12	lurasidone HCl (Latuda)	Dainippon Sumitomo	schizophrenia	small molecule; multireceptor antagonist and 5-HT_{1A} receptor agonist
13	alglucosidase alfa (Lumizyme/Myozyme)	Genzyme (Sanofi)	Pompe disease (First available treatment for this glycogen storage disease type II)	priority review biological; alpha-glucosidase analog; enzyme replacement therapy (ERT); orphan drug $300,000/year

14	dienogest (Natazia)	Bayer Healthcare Pharmaceuticals	birth control	small molecule; anti-androgenic orally active synthetic progesterone
15	dabigatran etexilate (Pradaxa)	Boehringer Ingelheim	stroke and blood clots ("blood thinner"; warfarin alternative therapy)	priority review small molecule; direct thrombin inhibitor; potential blockbuster
16	denosumab (Prolia/ Xgeva)	Amgen	osteoporosis/prevention of skeleton-related events in patients with bone metastases from solid tumors	biological; human antibody; targets bone removal protein RANK ligand
17	ceftaroline fosamil (Teflaro)	Forest Labs	MRSA, skin infections and pneumonia	derived from natural product; advanced-generation cephalosporin antibiotic; i.v.
18	liraglutide (Victoza)[1]	Novo Nordisk	type 2 diabetes	biological; long-acting glucagon-like peptide-1 (GLP-1) analog; potential blockbuster
19	velaglucerase alfa (VPRIV)	Shire Pharmaceuticals	type 1 Gaucher's disease	priority review biological; identical AA sequence to natural product; hydrolytic lysosomal; glucocerebroside-specific enzyme; orphan drug $200,000/yr;

(continued on next page)

	INN (trade name)	Marketed by	Indication(s)	Notes
20	incobotulinumtoxinA (Xeomin)[2]	Merz Pharmaceuticals	cervical dystonia and blepharospasm	biological; natural product toxin; blocks neuromuscular transmission by decreasing ACh release
21	collagenase Clostridium histolycitum (Xiaflex)	Auxil	Dupuytren's contracture	priority review biological; natural product; collagenase; orphan drug

Table 3.6: FDA approvals in 2010

No pharma company in 2010 had more than four drugs approved. No more than one new drug approved. No more than four drugs (Actemra, Gilenya, Pradaxa, and Victoza) are expected to reach peak sales of $1 billion per year. Ten, including the six orphan drugs, were approved with priority review. There were 10 biologicals, 4 natural products, and 7 small molecule drugs. Some biologicals, such as Myozyme, are very expensive and need to be administered throughout a lifetime. It is not in our FDA approval list from 2010 as we did not list vaccines, but this biological cell, vaccine cancer therapy is worth mentioning: sipuleucel-T (Dendreon's Provenge) is a personalized (autologous) active immune therapy—a vaccine of sorts from the patient's own cells—for treatment of metastatic prostate cancer; it is an example of the ultimate personalized medicine.[3] This first such therapy was approved in 2010. Dendreon has built several huge facilities and awaits orders to start to earn back the R&D expenditures. Many in biotech accuse the management of tremendous overreach that made investments even harder to find for biotech projects; in June 2012 it closed one of the three factories.

1 Approved by EMA in 2009.
2 See also Dysport in Table 3.5 for 2009.
3 See Chapters 08 and 09.

	INN (trade name)	Marketed by	Indication(s)	Notes
1	brentuximab vedotin (Adcetris)	Seattle Genetics	Hodgkin lymphoma and anaplastic large-cell lymphoma (ALCL)	priority review biological; chimeric antibody with antitumor agent; orphan drug
2	Centruroides (scorpion) immune F(ab') 2 (Anascorp)	Rare Diseases Therapeutics	scorpion bites	biological; equine-derived antivenom
3	indacaterol (Arcapta Neohaler/Onbrez)	Novartis	airflow obstruction for chronic obstructive pulmonary disease (COPD)	small molecule; ultra long-acting beta-adrenoceptor agonist
4	adenovirus types 4, 7 vaccine (Ardovax)	Teva Women's Health	prevention of febrile acute respiratory disease from adenovirus infection	biological; live oral vaccine
5	belimumab (Benlysta)	Human Genome Sciences/GSK	autoantibody-positive systemic lupus erythematosus (SLE)	priority review biological; human monoclonal antibody; inhibits B-cell activating factor (BAFF)
6	ticagrelor (Brilinta)	AstraZeneca	prevention of thrombotic events in patients with acute coronary syndromes (ACS)	small molecule; platelet aggregation inhibitor
7	vandetanib (Caprelsa)	AstraZeneca	metastatic medullary thyroid cancer	priority review small molecule; vascular endothelial growth factor receptor (VEGFR) antagonist; orphan drug

(continued on next page)

	INN (trade name)	Marketed by	Indication(s)	Notes
8	Factor XIII concentrate (Corifact)	CSL Behring	Factor XIII replacement in rare bleeding disorder	biological
9	roflumilast (Daliresp/Daxas)	Forest Labs/Nycomed	reducing COPD exacerbations	small molecule; long-acting inhibitor of the enzyme PDE-4
10	ioflupane i-123 (DaTscan)	GE Healthcare	imaging in Parkinson's disease	priority review small molecule; phenyltropane; radiopharmaceutical
11	fidaxomicin (Dificid)	Optimer Pharmaceuticals	*Clostridium difficile*-associated diarrhea (CDAD)	priority review small molecule; RNA polymerase inhibiting antibiotic; natural (fermentation) product
12	azilsartan medoxomil (Edarbi)	Takeda Pharmaceuticals	hypertension	small molecule; angiotensin II receptor antagonist
13	rilpivirine (Edurant)	Tibotec Therapeutics/Centocor	treatment-naive HIV1 patients	small molecule; non-nucleoside reverse transcriptase inhibitor (NNRTI)
14	icatibant (Firazyr)	Shire Human Genetic Therapies	hereditary angioedema (HAE)	priority review small molecule; peptidomimetic; bradykinin B2 receptor antagonist; orphan drug
15	gadobutrol (Gadavist)	Bayer Pharmaceuticals	MRI contrast agent for detecting CNS lesions in patients	small molecule; gadolinium-based MRI contrast agent (GBCA)

16	gabapentin enacarbil (Horizant)	GSK/Xenoport	restless leg syndrome	small molecule gabapentin prodrug
17	telaprevir (Incivek)	J&J/Vertex Pharmaceuticals	hepatitis C	priority review small molecule; protease inhibitor antiviral
18	azficel-T (LaViv)	Fibrocell Science	smoothing nasolabial fold wrinkles in adults	biological (cell therapy); patient's own cultured, collagen-producing fibroblast cells injected into smile line wrinkles
19	spinosad (Natroba)	ParaPRO Pharmaceuticals	head lice	natural product small molecule; new use for larval and adult insecticide
20	belatacept (Nulojix)	Bristol-Myers Squibb	renal transplant organ rejection prevention	biological; T-cell activation blocking fusion protein; orphan drug
21	ezogabine/retigabine (Potiga/Trobalt)	GSK/Valeant	epilepsy	small molecule; anticonvulsant with novel action: voltage-gated potassium channel opener
22	*Coccidioides immitis* spherule-derived skin test antigen (Spherusol)	AllerMed Laboratories	detection of delayed type hypersensitivity to *C. immitis*	biological

(continued on next page)

	INN (trade name)	Marketed by	Indication(s)	Notes
23	linagliptin (Tradjenta)	Boehringer Ingelheim/Eli Lilly	type 2 diabetes	small molecule; DPP-4 enzyme inhibitor
24	boceprevir (Victrelis)	Merck	hepatitis C	priority review small molecule; protease inhibitor antiviral
25	vilazodone HCl (Viibryd)	Cinical Data, Trovis, Forest	major depression (MDD)	small molecule; a serotonin reuptake inhibitor and 5-HT$_{1A}$ receptor partial agonist
26	crizotinib (Xalkori) w/ companion genetic test	Pfizer w/Abbott Molecular	non-small cell lung cancers	priority review small molecule; ALK and ROS1 enzymes inhibitor; orphan drug
27	rivaroxaban (Xarelto)	Bayer Pharmaceuticals/J&J	prevention of blood clots	small molecule; factor Xa inhibitor
28	ipilimumab (Yervoy)	Bristol-Myers Squibb	advanced melanoma	priority review biological; antibody for metastatic melanoma; orphan drug
29	vemurafenib (Zelboraf) w/companion diagnostic mutation test	Genentech/Daiichi Sankyo w/Roche Molecular Systems	metastatic or unresected melanoma with expression of gene mutation BRAF V600E-together	priority review small molecule; B-Raf enzyme inhibitor; orphan drug
30	abiraterone acetate (Zytiga)	J&J	metastatic castration-resistant prostate cancer	priority review small molecule; inhibits enzyme 17 α-hydroxylase/C17,20 lyase (CYP17A1)

31	aflibercept (Eylea)	Regeneron/Sanofi-Aventis	wet (neovascular) age-related macular degeneration (AMD)	priority review biological; VEGF inhibitor
32	crisantaspase/asparaginase Erwinia chrysanthemi (Erwinaze)	EUSA Pharma	acute lymphoblastic leukemia in patients with allergy	priority review biological; enzyme replacement; orphan drug
33	deferiprone (Ferriprox)	ApoPharma	iron overload due to blood transfusions in patients with thalassemia	small molecule; iron chelator; orphan drug
34	ruxolitinib (Jakafi)	Incyte Pharmaceuticals/ Novartis	myelofibrosis	priority review small molecule; JAK-1 enzyme inhibitor; orphan drug; potential blockbuster
35	clobazam (Onfi)	Catalent/Lundbeck	seizures associated with Lennox-Gastaut syndrome	small molecule; old benzodiazepine derivative for new indication; orphan drug

Table 3.7: FDA approvals in 2011
Two drugs were approved together with their companion diagnostics; in oncology, this means that the patients carrying the mutation will be the only ones treated, with correspondingly higher response rates. This is another way our drugs become better: they are better focused. The list includes 15 approvals with priority review, including 8 of the 11 orphan drugs. Eleven are biologicals and 24 are small molecule drugs, of which two are natural products. Only four are expected to earn over $1 billion per year.

Chapter 04: Which diseases do we want to treat?

How many diseases are there?

The Food and Drug Administration (FDA), the European Medical Agency (EMA), and other regulatory agencies have a long list covering more than 500 conditions that they recognize as individual disease entities. The (U.S.) National Organization for Rare Disorders (NORD)[57] recognizes 1,200 rare diseases affecting 1 in 10 Americans in its Rare Disease Database. Many of the 7 billion people in this planet suffer or will suffer from more than one disease in their lifetimes, and most suffer from many diseases simultaneously.

If we counted every human microbial infection caused by a different bacteria or virus as a separate disease, then this list would be as long as the number of bacteria and viruses known and unknown to us. Thus, the list of 500 diseases is a short list since it lumps together all the Gram-positive bacteria, which are still mostly penicillin sensitive, and then all the Gram-negative bacteria as they often can be treated successfully with broad spectrum antibiotics.

Then there are those patients who are not diagnosed although they are clearly sick, sometimes even after seeing several specialists over a number of years, because we simply do not yet have a name for their disease.

So, there is no shortage of diseases, yet the pharmaceutical industry is aiming at producing therapeutic agents and vaccines to prevent and to treat approximately 60 large, prevalent, and, for them, predictably profitable diseases. Biotechs add to this list another 100 conditions, preferably those with orphan drug status. They may also aim at the 60 big diseases targeted by Big Pharma. Biotechs might need or even want to be acquired or have a partnering deal with Big Pharma in order successfully

---

57   http://www.rarediseases.org/

The Future of Drug Discovery. http://dx.doi.org/10.1016/B978-0-12-407180-3.00004-0

to develop a drug candidate for a disease it considers too small. The diseases may be too small for Big Pharma to develop drugs in their own large and expensive operations, but the resulting drugs may not be too small to own.

How pharma companies have selected which diseases to treat
To understand how the drugs available were developed and the new ones are selected, we need to answer the following questions:
- How are these diseases selected?
- Who selected them in the companies?
- What happens to patients who suffer from diseases that nobody in the industry has an interest in treating?
- Why is it seldom discussed?

The next to last question is unfortunately easy to answer. These patients will be treated by the physicians who diagnosed them and with drugs not specifically developed and approved to treat their disease or with a combination of such drugs. This "mixture" might hopefully help these patients with many of their symptoms. But there is no industrial effort to produce drugs that are focused on the specific properties, that is, the cellular and molecular hallmarks of their pathological process or on the pathological organism involved. It matters not a jot how well scientists understand the pathology. Scientists have often elucidated the pathogens or mechanisms behind these often smaller diseases, the pursuit of which would bring patients tremendous relief, if someone only worked on treatment.

If these patients belong to a group that is very small (e.g., less than 200,000 cases in the United States), then this disease will be declared an "orphan disease." *Developing drugs to treat these diseases has many financial advantages.*

However, if the patient is unfortunate and suffers from a disease that, in terms of prevalence and incidence, lies between the large diseases and the orphan diseases, then no matter how much good science exists around this disease, and no matter how clear the path is to try to address the pathology with a drug, it is unlikely that anybody in the industry will devote effort and funds to produce such a drug. This is because drug company decisions on which projects to work are all made by the marketers. They could not care less about what new scientific evidence would make the design of a rational drug therapy relatively easy and straightforward; in all major pharma the business unit weighs in on the project portfolio proposed by their scientists. They may be more influenced by profit, stock price goals, internal politics, and personalities than science.[58]

In the absence of strong government and interest group pressure—such as was the case with HIV—nobody will use any new strong scientific evidence to start a drug-development program. That is, of course, if no one can convince biotech investors that, within this disease, there lay a new therapy that will be so effective that relatively small and potentially short trials will be able to show efficacy. In such a case, a biotech could go "all the way" and pay not only for phase 1 and 2a but also for the expensive phase 3 clinical trials and own the drug at the end. This scenario is the absolute exception. Long-term investors who are not required to retrieve, with profit, their limited partners' money after 5 years are rare. The financial outlook for small companies is further worsened by the initial public offering (IPO) market in biotech being, for all intents and purposes, closed since 2009. In the absence of public stockholder funds, the successful phase 2 drug of biotech can today be left on the shelf unless some major pharma buys it, often at a "fire sale" price. There are several dozen cases of this happening. The Big Pharma business unit says: "it is a not a strategic match for us; we would not market it to earn $200-300 million [per annum]," and passes on it.

The often "almighty" marketers of Big Pharma will make the following point: the costs to develop a drug are roughly the same, whether the sales

---

58   See Bartfai T and Lees, GV (2006) *Drug Discovery: from Bedside to Wall Street*. Elsevier/Academic Press: Amsterdam, p. 58.

will be $300 million per year or $3 billion dollars per year. Therefore, from the stockholders' and the management's point of view, one should attempt to develop 10 drugs that each might bring in $3 billion a year rather than 10 drugs that would each bring in only $300 million a year. This logic will not change unless the R&D people can prevail within the company and show that better science may lead to lower risk of development failure. In addition, it is often mentioned by the industry managers that competition will take care of these problems since:

> We in the industry do the best drug discovery, and we will eventually move to new diseases because of competition. However, we would rather see the number of drugs—and mostly "me-too" drugs—increase than address new diseases with the inherent risk of expensive failures in drug development. (See Table 4.1.)

In fact, the decisions in 2009-2011 have amounted to an industry-wide retreat from many important therapeutic areas like pain, Alzheimer's disease (AD), antibiotics, urology, and so forth. The industry worked on these areas earlier, and enjoyed some success, but significant medical need remains. Drug development has been concluded to be too difficult and too risky. It may also take too long to have anything approved and to generate sales.

It is hoped that physicians who try to find drugs to treat their patients use their right for *off-label prescribing* among the drugs already registered. By doing this, they may make a discovery that enables them to use one or several existing drugs to treat people with diseases that are of no interest today to the pharma industry. The physician's disclosure of a successful treatment, by publication of the patient's case study in a specialist journal, may be the best hope for other patients with the same disease.

The funding & direction of biomedical research

Since the early 1960s, our society has put together a fantastic research enterprise in life sciences; it is mostly government sponsored everywhere.

Indication	Prevalence (millions)	Medical needs	No. of projects (PHrMA)
Group 1. "Gap": under-pursued diseases			
Alzheimer's disease (AD)	5.3 (42)	9	79
COPD	17	8	35
Schizophrenia	2.2	7	54
Neuropathic pain	18	8	56*
Stroke	5.8	9	27
New antibiotics	240 (4,000 worldwide)	4	88
Malaria	0.002 (2,600 worldwide)	9	6
Epilepsy	2.3	6	16
Group 2. "Balance": adequately pursued diseases			
Rheumatoid arthritis (RA)	3.1	4	86
Hypertension	84	2	27
Hypercholesterolemia	112	3	43
Major depression (MD)	22.3	4	71
Multiple sclerosis	0.4	4	39
Group 3. "Industry's choice": diseases pursued after R&D cuts			
Type 2 diabetes	25.8	4	234
Cancer overall	11.7	6	887
Breast	2.7	5	
Ovarian	1.2	9	
Prostate	2.5	7	
Lung	0.4	8	
Colorectal	1.8	8	
Leukemia	0.25	3	
Melanoma	0.7	8	

(continued on next page)

Indication	Prevalence (millions)	Medical needs	No. of projects (PHrMA)
Orphan diseases			460
Huntington's disease	0.03	9	
Cystic fibrosis	0.03	9	
Gaucher's disease	0.005	2	

Table 4.1: The gap between our greatest medical needs & the number of projects pursued to cover these with new therapeutics
"We have more or less a gap of five years without research into new antibiotics," Thomas Lönngren, then-Executive Director of the EMA, said in December 2010. "It's an issue where commercial consideration doesn't really match the public health need." His American counterpart, FDA commissioner Margaret Hamburg, said the same thing in October 2010. "We need new and better drugs—and we need them now," she stated at an event at the National Press Club. "Yet the pipeline is distressingly low." This table shows diseases divided into three groups based upon the matching of the medical need and the number of projects being undertaken by the industry. Group 1 contains the diseases where the medical need is much greater than the number of projects being pursued, that is, where there is a big "gap" between need and activity. Increased activity may only come with government intervention. Group 2 contains diseases where the medical need is more "balanced," with need being likely matched by activity. Group 3 indicates diseases that are receiving almost an inordinate amount of attention. They are pharma's choice rather than a reflection of absolute medical need. This is not to say that these diseases are not extremely important, but the underlying problem is that companies are striving to compete with others' successes with me-toos and are not trying to innovate with truly new drugs and take the risks of expensive failures.

In the first column, the prevalence is given for the United States. We have added worldwide estimates for infectious disease (new antibiotics), but the number in parentheses for Alzheimer's disease is a projection. Column 2 is expressed on the authors' arbitrary scale, nominally from 1-9; it does not take into account prevalence, just the need for treatment for each condition. This number would be 1 when we can cure the disease, 4-5 when we can successfully slow disease progression or stop it and treat the symptoms, and 9 when we are poor in slowing disease progression and treating symptoms in most of the patients where the disease is diagnosed and an intent to treat exists. The third column lists the number of projects being pursued as listed by PHrMA as of May 2011. We draw attention (*) to the number of projects under neuropathic pain, since many of the drugs being tested are antidepressants. Instead of 56, the more accurate number is around 30. PHrMA: American Pharmaceutical Manufacturers Association; all the major European companies are members, although Roche recently left to join the biotech equivalent.

In life sciences today, governments and other private funds[59] outspend the pharmaceutical industry when it comes to basic research. It was not always like this (see Figure 4.1 for how this ratio of pharma vs. government spending on basic research has changed over the last five decades).

The greatest life science research budget is that of the U.S. government. The National Institutes of Health (NIH) budget has grown since 1938 from $464,000 to $31 billion and the life science efforts from the National Science Foundation (NSF) currently contribute a further $3.4 billion.

The rest of the developed world adds to this significantly, with the European Union (EU) contributing both with a slice from member countries' contributions to the general EU research budget and from the national research budgets of the individual member countries. If one added to the list the significant research expenditures from China and Japan, Switzerland, South Korea, Singapore, and at least two of the largest nongovernmental organizations (NGOs), the next most significant contributors in descending order[60] would be Germany, China, Japan, Switzerland, France, the Wellcome Trust, the UK, the Howard Hughes Medical Institute (HHMI), Australia, and Canada. The United States and Switzerland, followed by Germany, expend a higher proportion of their GDP than most, as do the Scandinavians. Most of the developed or otherwise rich economies only spend a small fraction (~0.02-0.03%) of their GDPs on life science research. The NIH budget is a whopping 50% of the total global life science research expenditure, showing the resolve and commitment of successive U.S. administrations. Yet, the NIH and NSF budgets are less than 0.25% of the U.S. GDP. Surely the world could afford more biomedical science research if the health of the human inhabitants of the planet were at stake?

---

59 Such as the UK's Wellcome Trust (investing approximately £600 million annually) and the U.S.'s Howard Hughes Foundation (investing approximately $850 million annually).
60 A caveat to this statement is the fact that the actual destination of funds is hard to unravel, with different countries including different types of funding under life sciences. For example, Germany's "life sciences" includes medical technology, and China and Japan are somewhat "opaque," but we believe our list is an effective indicator.

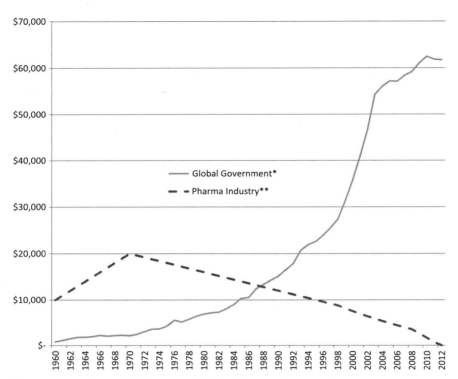

Figure 4.1: Financial Sources of Life Science Research

Research, forming the basis of development of drugs, vaccines, and diagnostics, has been carried out in academia, government, drug companies, and biotech companies, using funds from taxpayers, investors, and nonprofit organizations, who sponsor the research. During the past 50 years the size of research expenditure has grown dramatically and now is stabilizing or slightly shrinking in the past years. The source of basic life science research results for the pharmaceutical industry was, until about 1980, overwhelmingly the industry itself; only by the mid-1980s did results from public sources, academic and government institutes, become important for pharma companies. Today, the Big Pharma companies have dispensed with basic research (almost) completely, saying that it is too slow, too unfocused, and is done better by academia and government. We have made a complete transition from the industry hiring the best scientists to work in its own laboratories in the 1960s to the industry closing all non-strictly drug development-related activity and relying entirely on basic research produced and financed by governments and private foundations. This leads to critical remarks about the patents, such as those voiced by Joseph Stiglitz, *the 2001 Nobel Laureate in Economics, who pointed out that new drugs are based on public data and, since society is also the purchaser, why permit such strong ownership for private pharma? He believes this slows the discovery of new drugs. *Global government research expenditures are estimated as being about twice the annual NIH budget. **Pharma industry expenditures are estimated from identified trends and policies from within the industry; these numbers are the authors' estimates, not from verifiable data points. Estimated expenditures are given in billions of dollars.*

The governmental agencies and ministries involved in healthcare and education financing have these sums invested in research, which includes the education of medical researchers and thus their stipends, salaries, and, sometimes, the whole budget of the university.[61]

A major message of our book is that basic biomedical research over the past five decades, such as that on the cell biology of normal and transformed cells (i.e., cancer cells), is the basis of all the breakthrough medicines of the past decade for different cancer forms, and has been almost exclusively pursued in government-sponsored laboratories worldwide. Pharmaceutical companies have steered clear of basic research since the late 1970s, having closed many of their highly successful academic research institutes[62] between 1980 and 1996. Industry-sponsored research in institute form, with researcher autonomy, is perceived as too slow and erratic in producing data directly leading to novel drugs. Thus, for new drugs, especially in the areas of pain, AD, schizophrenia, chronic obstructive pulmonary disease (COPD), and so forth, the drug targets almost exclusively have to come from government-sponsored research, if

---

61   Budgets for epidemic control at the World Health Organization (WHO) and at national agencies such as the U.S. Centers for Disease Control and Prevention (CDC) near Atlanta, are also substantial and relevant for vaccines, which are largely outside the scope of this book. Stockpiling antibiotics and antivirals, in case of influenza, is an important part of preparedness for catastrophes, and the sales of these drugs are important for the very few pharma companies still involved in antibiotics and antivirals. Hepatitis C and HIV are still regarded as profitable and well-attended diseases by pharma's drug-development programs.
62   A few remain open including the Novartis Research Foundation Friedrich Miescher Institute for Biomedical Research in Basel.

society wants pharmaceutical companies to work on developing drugs in these therapeutic areas.

Conversely, when looking at who pays for most clinical trials, the pharma industry outspends the governments grossly (see Table 7.1), although one should note that some of the high-quality, long-duration, and large government-sponsored clinical trials in the UK (from NICE, the National Institute for Health and Clinical Excellence) and in the United States (from the NIH) are having a huge impact on the practice of medicine.[63]

The trend is clear: pharma is not ever going to spend on basic research in disease areas it altogether abandons for drug development.

The increase from nearly no translational research to an emphasis on translational medicine research is a pronounced trend of governmental research organizations worldwide. This policy shift may not have been fully thought through: governments' clinical research budgets are so low compared to those of the pharmaceutical industry that it will not have meaningful results, compared to industry-sponsored clinical trials, unless it is substantially increased by at least fivefold. However, with an increased focus on translational research in governmental research, the risk is that it will be achieved only at the cost of basic research, and then no one will spend sufficiently on basic research. Funding for translational research must be additional to the funding of increased basic research.[64]

If this funding is achieved by new appropriations by the U.S. government, it would have to be an extra 0.05–0.1% of the U.S. GDP, that is, $7.5–15 billion to compete in selected therapeutic areas. Presently pharma is spending approximately $85 billion on clinical research, that is, 0.56% of U.S. GDP, or ~0.3% of the GDP of the developed world's pharmaceutical-delivering

---

63   See Chapters 03 and 10.
64   It should be noted that the 2012 NIH budget request includes about $6 billion for cancer research across several institutes "to facilitate 30 new drug trials and double the number of therapies and vaccines in clinical trials by 2016." The NIH is trying to compete with pharma in areas they are already avidly pursuing (see Figure 7.1). But even in this area, which is grossly over-represented in industry and government in terms of the number of projects, the industry's expenditures on clinical trials is far greater than the government funds.

countries.[65] One would not have to match pharma's clinical research investment to create a competitive environment, since pharma is competing with itself to produce drugs for the same conditions. However, it is unrealistic in the present economical climate to expect a huge injection of funds even if other countries contributed. Future prospects do not look brighter.

If this is the route society follows, then we will have created government-sponsored medical research where the proportions of expenditures and the power over decisions will be dominated by clinical rather than, as today, by basic researchers; this may ultimately have unintended consequences for the basic research funding and direction. It will not be as bad for society as the present dominance of economists over all decisions in big pharmaceutical companies, but it might lead to the weakening of basic research when we need it focused on those areas abandoned by pharma. Basic research would have to provide the drug targets and the deep understanding of disease mechanism to lower the risk of failure in clinical trials. Without such development we cannot hope and cannot expect drugs to be developed in areas of large medical need.

Greed and speed of return on investment were not the only things that led pharmaceutical companies to drop basic research; the recognition that government-sponsored academic research in universities and research institutes was just far better. Let's not reverse this situation, let's make the best of it.

While we do not suggest the establishment of government-owned pharma industries and, indeed, other larger pharmaceutical companies and not governments take over weaker pharma companies at an astonishing rate and at prices of $40-50 billion, we do suggest openly and in a focused manner to embrace and to utilize the presently existing distribution of roles: the governmental predominance of funding and pursuit of basic research, and the industry domination of drug development using the published data from government-supported research in academia and

---

65 i.e., the United States, Switzerland, Germany, Japan, France, and Sweden.

governmental research institutes. We suggest a combination of focused investment in basic research and inducements for the industry.[66] We should exploit these finely tuned roles that are now working well, for example, in oncology and HIV/AIDS, to work in discovering drugs for AD, other neurodegenerative diseases, neuropathic pain, and so forth.

It is sobering to think that U.S. investment in basic cancer research, which started in 1938 with the National Cancer Institute (NCI), has now been over $100 billion, mostly in the last decade (see Figure 4.2). Worldwide, the investment has probably been much more than $200 billion. HIV/AIDS research, which was accelerated in 1995 with the investment in the Office for AIDS Research (OAR), has topped $37 billion via the NIH alone. The U.S. government has also appropriated funds for AIDS via the CDC, the Department of Health and Human Services (DHHS), and so forth.[67] Of course, other countries have also invested heavily; the virus was first isolated and characterized in France.[68] How much needs to be spent to work on AD more aggressively?

The scientific basis of disease treatment

Life sciences research is in an explosive phase that was turbocharged with the completion of the Human Genome Project in 2001, and the result of this and of hundreds of other projects is creating a deeper understanding of many diseases, and not only of genetic or inherited diseases.

In literally hundreds of diseases this provides a new scientific basis for developing drugs that may treat several hundred thousand to several million sufferers in each disease. The scientific results are accumulating at an unfortunate time point, and the years from 2008 to 2012 may go down in history as the period when large pharmaceutical companies

---

66   See especially Chapters 11 and 12.
67   See National Institutes of Health: History of Congressional Appropriations, Fiscal Years 2000-2012, http://officeofbudget.od.nih.gov/approp_hist.html
68   Françoise Barré-Sinoussi and Luc Montagnier first presented their data in September 1983; they were jointly awarded the Nobel Prize in Physiology or Medicine 2008 for "discovery of human immunodeficiency virus" (shared with Harald zur Hausen for "discovery of human papilloma viruses causing cervical cancer").

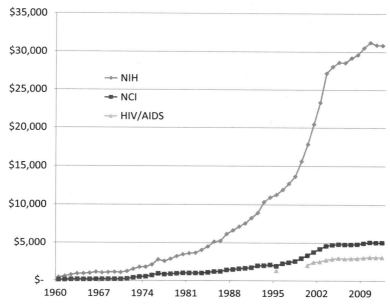

Figure 4.2: The U.S. Government's Investment in Biomedical, Medical, Cancer, & HIV/AIDS Research

The NIH budget has more than doubled every decade over the last 40 years, but growth appears to be slowing, even with the NIH's increasing emphasis on translational research. The basic research needed to begin to control difficult diseases is considerable. The NCI, by no means the only funder of research into cancer, has spent over $100 billion over the decades, with over $50 billion being invested in the last decade. HIV/AIDS research in the United States has topped $37 billion, mostly in the last decade. Basic research is costly, but more has to be invested to address the problem of the neglected diseases, both larger such as AD, schizophrenia, and antibiotic-resistant bacterial infections and smaller, such as Huntington's disease and Parkinson's disease.

took a short-term view and only wanted to develop drugs for very large indications. They think they need millions of patients with diseases, where clinical trials will be relatively short and the likelihood of success is higher than what they have recently experienced. This sudden and abrupt change in Big Pharma's willingness to test new science encompasses the entire industry and has cut R&D personnel by approximately 40,000 in a recent 24-month period. Indeed, it now embarks on large stock buyback strategies with its cash reserves in order to preserve its stock price, while closing whole clinical research areas. This change could not have come at a worse time.

The gap between the diseases for which we have the scientific basis to try to cure and those the industry judges from the private companies' economical point of view is increasing since 2009, and this increase is accelerating (see Figure 4.3).

At the same time we face new epidemics such as AD, obesity-linked type 2 diabetes, and the ever-present specter of new viral and bacterial epidemics hanging over our heads as microbes show no understanding of economic cycles and continue to develop resistance to our drugs.

It is worth understanding how pharma selects which diseases it believes it can work on profitably and in the short term—a new attribute for this industry. This chapter is devoted to these considerations and to how society can change the list of diseases that are pursued by using the best scientific data available based on the timely opportunity these data give us and not only on pre-estimated high profitability for the industry.

In 1980, Big Pharma, a more fragmented industry with smaller companies, believed that one needs to work in 10-15 therapeutic areas. In 1990, it was reduced to eight or nine areas. In 2009-2011, most of the large companies, three times bigger than those in the 1980s, worked upon a lowly four or five areas (see Table 4.2).

A wave of acquisition-led growth started long ago in 1994 when Roche bought, for $5.4 billion, Syntex, still the largest pharma in Mexico. In 1995, Glaxo engineered the takeover of Burroughs Wellcome and the subsequent merger with the conglomerate SmithKline-Beecham in 2000.[69] The largest pharmaceutical company, Pfizer, has, through its acquisitions, incorporated therapeutic areas, know-how, and drugs from Warner-Lambert (including Parke-Davis and Auguron), Pharmacia (including UpJohn, Searle, and SUGEN), and Wyeth, which has had a long, checkered history of acquisitions and ownership. As well as causing a

---

69   See also Chapter 07.

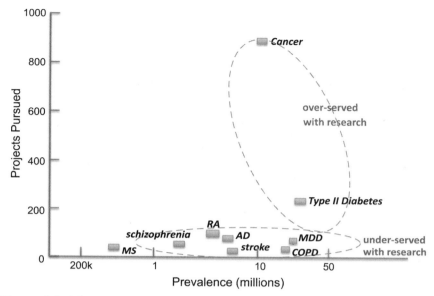

Figure 4.3: **The Number of Projects being Pursued by Pharma Compared to the Disease Prevalence**

The number of projects being pursued for any given indication is a hard number to obtain. Expensive competitor landscape studies are commissioned by Big Pharma on specific diseases and the results are not publicized. On the other hand, the official lobbyist for the industry in the United States makes a point of publishing a table each year from the sources of their member organizations in the United States to show how many conditions the industry works on "selflessly." The data in this figure and Table 4.1 count the same project more than once in some cases where a given drug candidate is being tested in multiple conditions (e.g., the inflammatory diseases RA, psoriasis, and Crohn's disease, or in neuropathic pain and depression). Still these data cover, according to financial analysts, the major trends in the United States and also Western Europe, and match data from other sources on which projects are being pursued, especially information to analysts and stockholders about the pipelines of major pharma; active clinical trials as listed on ClinicalTrials·gov. For none of these listings are the companies obliged to keep the data up to date, and they are not legally binding. We feel that this figure, despite its limitations, shows a deeply worrying trend, as noted by, for example, the FDA and EMA commissioners, who, from their different vantage points, see which projects come for approval and note the "gaps" between medical need and pharma projects in, for example, antibiotics' development.

Number of top 20 companies designating selected therapeutic areas as "core" or "additional" areas of research—1997		
Therapeutic area	Core	Additional
CNS	20	—
Cancer	20	—
Anti-infectives	18	1
Cardiovascular	18	0
Respiratory/allergy	15	1
Metabolic	14	2
Osteoporosis	10	1
Rheumatologic/arthritis	7	3
Gastroenterology	7	2
Dermatological	5	4
Urological	4	2
Anesthesiology	3	0
Ophthalmological	2	0
Vaccines	2	0
Transplantation	2	0

Table 4.2: The 15 core therapeutic areas of the top 20 companies in 1997
Now there are only 7 of these 20 companies left; others grew to make it to the top 10. Together they now focus on five to six therapeutic areas (cf. Table 2.6).

reduction of employees at all levels and disruption of local communities when sites are closed, these acquisitions are arguably of questionable benefit even to shareholders. A very large amount of shareholder wealth in the other companies has evaporated without significant benefit to Pfizer's shareholders. Having acquired all this "intellectual real-estate," Pfizer publicly announced in February 2011 its dramatically reduced interest in many therapeutic areas (Table 4.3). When will Wall Street realize that these headline-grabbing mergers and acquisitions are not good for society?

The medical needs in the areas that are now missing from the industry's list did not disappear; only smallpox has been eradicated. Diseases in

2009	2011
Cardiovascular, metabolic and endocrine diseases	Cardiovascular, metabolic and endocrine diseases
Internal medicine	
Urology	
Neuroscience	Neuroscience
Oncology	Oncology
Pain and sensory disorders	
Regenerative medicine	
Inflammation and immunology	Inflammation and immunology
Orphan and genetic diseases	
Vaccines	Vaccines
Antibacterials	

Table 4.3: Pfizer's reduction in therapeutic breadth
Pfizer has dropped over half of the therapeutic areas it was working on just 2 years ago. Welcomed by Wall Street, maybe, horrific for those working and developing the abandoned areas, and not really appreciated by society or government, it seems. See text for details, but this information resonates throughout the book.

the now neglected areas, including some newly diagnosed ones, both treatable, such as attention deficit hyperactivity disorder (ADHD), and untreatable, are still very much with us. We still do not have efficacious, safe proprietary or generic drugs to treat all of them, which might have explained the reduction of therapeutic areas by Pfizer and pharma in general. Since setting up these successful pharma companies took over a hundred years, it would be clever to find a way to use the drug discovery machines these companies represent in a broader set of diseases. But how do we do this? To approach this problem we need to understand the prevailing ideas within pharma about which diseases to treat.

New avenues of research & the emergence of biosimilars
Orphan diseases became everybody's darlings. This is best illustrated by the fortunes of one of the first companies that addressed genetic

diseases. The company is called Genzyme and quite recently was in an $18 billion hostile takeover battle by one of the giants of the industry, Sanofi-Aventis. After a long fight Genzyme was finally bought for $20 billion. Surely, Genzyme was, and is, an interesting company. They recognized early on that for several "storage diseases," where the patients lack a specific active enzyme owing to genetic defects, one could recombinantly manufacture these enzymes and use them in replacement therapy much like insulin or growth hormone (GH). Even though these enzymes are often lacking in the brain, they gambled that by injecting the enzyme into the peripheral circulation a small amount will make its way into the brain, and this amount might be sufficient to make a large therapeutic difference and change disease progression and reduce mortality. No large pharma company would have permitted such a speculative "phony" project to go ahead, since there is no objective reference to know whether a sufficient amount of enzyme will enter the brain to make a therapeutic difference. Patients may report improvement, but will this be sufficient evidence? These projects would have been killed at once, or would have been transformed into a project: "let's make a small molecule, i.e., an activator of the mutated enzyme, which surely enters the brain, and which may affect the mutated enzyme in such a manner that it exhibits some activity." Indeed the novel approach used to find such small molecules is now becoming a reality some 30 years after Genzyme's initial enzyme therapy. Over these 30 years, Genzyme has made some $50 billion by selling enzymes, only a few percent of which reaches the brain. Genzyme's strategy, approach, and products were embraced; society paid; and a huge therapeutic difference was made.

In short, Genzyme has become the producer of a few human enzymes using recombinant protein production in the same way we use it to produce insulin, GH, tissue plasminogen activator (tPA), or therapeutic antibodies. Genzyme and its many latecomer competitors produce these missing enzymes for replacement therapy in a very few, very ill patients. The clear diagnosis of a genetic disease guarantees a high response rate, which is the key for charging the extremely high prices. They have very small marketing costs because the specialist physicians who treat this very small group of patients are well known to them, and because the patients are all well organized by both their parents and by professional organizations dedicated to the diseases. The real issue was to develop unequivocal diagnostics. The science of these diseases and the enzyme activity deficits were far ahead of drug development and recombinant technology. For several of these diseases testing for genetic carriers in New York City was already, for some groups, "mandatory." For example, Ashkenazy Jews have Gaucher's disease at a ~50-fold higher frequency than some other groups and it was made "obligatory" for them to be tested for the carrier gene when applying for a marriage license in New York City.[70] Hence, Genzyme became one of the companies interested in this captive market, and for a long while it was the only producer of these enzymes and also the only producer of the genetic tests. When Genzyme became subject to a hostile takeover effort, it cleverly separated and sold its genetic disease-focused diagnostic business, which is one of the best examples of *companion diagnostics* (see Chapter 08). These companion diagnostics are needed to establish the case for the use of a specific drug or set of drugs on particular individuals. Thus, the enzymes Genzyme is producing to replace the faulty or absent enzymes of patients are given to those who clearly need them. This is the secret of high responder rates, which all other companion diagnostics promise. The "number to treat" to elicit an effect is 1, that is, targeting the right patient group is maximally efficient. After selling off the diagnostics part, the now mostly orphan drug company is still worth $20 billion. Now, one may wonder why the Genzyme management was so shaken that Sanofi-Aventis' hostile attempt to buy the company succeeded.

---

70 This screening is confidential and provides information to couples who might be at risk for transmitting a severe disorder to their children.

Genzyme had a virtual monopoly to treat patients in four orphan diseases, based on its early bold initiative to go after the seemingly "unlikely-to-function" enzyme replacement, but their patents are now expiring. In addition, Genzyme had production problems. It is unacceptable when one company is the sole producer of a drug that sustains the lives of its patients, and regulators, by rapid approval procedures, moved to permit competitors to produce Genzyme's medicines and save these lives. So, rapidly, companies like Teva (see the section "Generic drug makers"), and Protalix Biotherapeutics stepped in and effectively said: we are ready to produce a *biosimilar* to be ready as soon as the patent expires and are, therefore, working on the process of making these enzymes such that the FDA can approve our preparation. When there is a production problem, a biosimilar, which could be legally approved within a few months to a year, should be given rapid approval so that patients are not without these essential lifesaving replacement enzymes. Because of this, Genzyme no longer has a monopoly on enzyme replacements.

Two very serious, large, and well-capitalized companies (Merck and Teva) have made credible public announcements of their plans that within 6 months from a major biological coming off patent protection, they plan to present a biosimilar to the FDA for approval, and thereby challenge the market dominance of the company that had originally brought a well-selling biological to the market. These credible promises created hope that prices would come down from the existing $25,000–250,000 per year, but it now seems that biosimilars will only sell for 15% less than the original biologicals.

Generic drug makers

To make generic drugs that are small molecules is not trivial, but several dozen companies (see Table 4.4) have mastered the chemical synthesis and the formulation problems of small molecules and are ready on the day that patents expire to seek approvals. Every successful molecule with a known expiring patent has at least 2–6 generic producers; competition is fierce.

1.	Teva Pharmaceutical—Israel-United States, generic and proprietary
2.	Mylan—United States, generic
3.	Sandoz—Switzerland, generic, but, as part of Novartis, proprietary is in the same concern
4.	Watson Pharmaceuticals—United States, generic
5.	Greenstone—United States, generic
6.	Par Pharma—United States, generic and proprietary
7.	Hospira—United States, injectable drugs
8.	Apotex—Canada, generic
9.	Mallinckrodt—United States, generic
10.	Dr. Reddy's—India, generic and proprietary

Table 4.4: The top 10 generic drug companies: location & direction[1]
Large Chinese generic drug makers are not listed as data are hard to obtain even though they manufacture drugs for hundreds of millions of patients through contracts with large municipalities. Certainly, the largest of these companies can decide to apply for registration of their generics in the United States, when they are willing to subject themselves to FDA inspections and start to compete with the companies listed in this table. The price competition in generic drugs is tremendous, and profit margins are much smaller than for proprietary drugs, but, of course, the need for capital and the financial risks are also much smaller. When success breeds its own capital, some generic companies reason that entering proprietary drug development is the next logical step in increasing the value of the company. This has so far been done by purchasing companies with proprietary drugs, for example, when Teva purchased Cephalon for $6.8 billion in cash in May 2011; companies also start their own research. Most generic companies have found the process of discovery and approval for proprietary drugs to be painfully slow and erratic compared to efficient and rapid copying of drugs that took others 10-15 years to develop. Teva has its own proprietary multiple sclerosis drug in Copaxone (glatiramer acetate).

1   http://www.fiercepharma.com/special-reports/top-10-generic-drug-companies-2010 #ixzz1M9SykLp8.

The generic companies include Canadian, Indian, and Israeli companies, as well as the more expected U.S., German, and Swiss entities. What Table 4.4 does not say is that almost all the major pharma in the top 15 by capitalization (see Table 1.2), which are primarily all selling and developing proprietary drugs, also make generic drugs. They often just continue to manufacture their own compound that has lost patent protection and drop the price somewhat, but many times they register to make generic drugs. This was done when GSK picked the Roche weight-loss drug Xenical (orlistat) when it lost patent protection and registered as a generic manufacturer of orlistat (as Alli). Thus, there are many very competent and well-capitalized companies that make generic drugs. Should one expect huge drops in the price of drugs? This will be discussed in Chapter 10.

Biosimilars

To make biosimilars is much more complicated than making generic, small molecule nonbiological drugs. The public promise from Merck and Teva, who have demonstrated that they are able to do this, has made planning for future costs of biologicals somewhat easier for all healthcare and insurance companies, especially during the discussions of "affordable healthcare" reform in the United States.

However, the knowledge-base requirement and the investments for producing biosimilars are much higher than for generic small molecules. There has not been a credible entry into the biosimilar market that promises real cost relief for insurers. The high cost of biologicals is similar to that of therapeutic antibodies to treat different cancers, at approximately $25,000–75,000 a year.

Merck now owns Schering-Plough and thus has a very serious arm with history and ability to produce original biologicals and, therefore, also has the credibility to produce biosimilars.

The FDA guidelines for biosimilars were much anticipated and were published in spring 2012. The FDA has a "totality of the evidence" approach to approve a biosimilar as having the same efficacy and safety as the biological it copies. Most observers see that biosimilars will have only a small price advantage and will have a hard time capturing market share from the original biological. However, in sales of insulin and GH, there is great price competition, so maybe these observers will be proven wrong.

"Firsts in class," "me-toos," & "best in class": marketers' dreams

To understand which drugs are being selected to be developed, one has to restate that large companies are completely driven by their marketing decisions. The number of people involved in marketing drugs in each large pharma is counted in the thousands and thousands. Their most important weapon is their annotated list of physicians with whom they visit regularly to inform them about their company's new drug(s). They will try to convince these physicians about the advantages of this or that new drug. Their work, of course, is easiest when that company succeeds to produce the first in class drug; that is to say, if the company were to produce a drug to treat a disease for which previously no other drug was available. In this case, the marketers' task is relatively simple. Of course, they are supported by numerous publications and company-sponsored meetings or symposia at large meetings of medical societies specifically devoted to the specialty. The first drug to treat the disease represents a significant breakthrough. Incidentally, it is not inherently immoral for pharma companies to inform physicians about their products in this way, despite what you may have read in more sensational publications. Of course, if the marketers exaggerate or distort the evidence or claim it treats disorders for which the treatment has not been approved (no matter if it is proven later to be effective), it is extremely immoral. Significant fines should and do follow, as GSK, Pfizer, and Merck will testify.

In portfolio meetings, the marketer will point out, over and over again, that there is less interest in the company to produce a given drug candidate when there are already (established) drugs to treat this disease; it makes their job infinitely more complicated. However, when there are already approved drugs to treat the disease, but those drugs have a different mechanism of action, a new entrant can be very successful, and is initially usually aimed at the patients who are nonresponders to the earlier approved drugs. An easy example is found in the treatment of the very common, easy to self-diagnose disease, heartburn. Over the counter (OTC) inexpensive antacids are still widely taken, whether drinkable or chewable. When heartburn was first treated with drugs that were not antacids in the late 1970s and early 1980s, there were two giant UK companies producing histamine H_2-receptor antagonists. Their drugs cimetidine (Smith Kline & French's first in class Tagamet) and ranitidine (Glaxo's Zantac) were roughly equivalent in their ability to reduce heartburn. Incidentally, both were designed by so-called *rational drug design* through a refined model of the H_2-histamine receptor and so-called *quantitative structure–activity relationships* (QSAR).[71] While they were expensive, but not overly expensive, they were and remain safe. They are so safe that today they are both available as OTC products. After a succession of mergers, Glaxo Wellcome and SmithKline Beecham merged and so the resultant GlaxoSmithKline (GSK) owns and produces both Zantac and Tagamet and sells them as OTC products for roughly $0.50–1 a day as needed.

A drug with a new mechanism of action was approved to treat the exact same condition of heartburn, namely omeprazole (Losec) from the then tiny Swedish company Astra. This drug addressed the very source of the problem of heartburn: the production of acid and the production of protons. Comparisons with H_2-histamine receptor antagonists were not so easy anymore. Omeprazole was the first in class among the proton-pump inhibitors, a whole class after the strongly marketed me-too H_2-histamine receptor antagonists. When there is a new first in class drug in terms of its mechanism of action rather than the targeted disease, then the marketers' job is to explain that this drug is likely to be effective in patients who do not respond very well to the earlier drug. This new mechanism of action promises to be useful for nonresponding patients. As well as having a more robust effect in dyspepsia, the proton-pump inhibitors are indicated for the treatment of ulcers, hypersecretory conditions, gastroesophageal

---

71 The "third in class" was famotidine from Yamanouchi Pharmaceutical, marketed, among others, by Merck and Johnson & Johnson in the mid-1980s and trademarked under various names globally including Pepcid. It has an advantage in that its metabolism does not utilize the cytochrome P450 enzyme system and therefore may be used without interfering with certain drugs that are metabolized through that commonly used pathway. It is also available OTC. It should be noted that the H_2-receptor, a G-protein-coupled receptor (GPCR), has not yet been crystallized. But, having been already so well exploited as a drug target, not much effort is being made to study it. Other human GPCRs have been crystallized since 2007.

reflux disease, and for maintenance of healing of erosive esophagitis. They have reduced ulcer surgeries by over 80% (and these were among the most common surgeries). This shows that a good drug can change medical practice.

To sell a drug that is first in class or has a new mechanism of action in a large disease to physicians is relatively easy according to most marketers. To keep it as a market leader, however, may be difficult and require expensive post-approval studies that further and further differentiate it. Neurologists are a major exception according to the experience of marketers. They do not easily switch one medication for a new one, with or without a new mechanism of action. In particular, they are hesitant to switch anti-epileptic medication because the risks of seizures and other problems are such that they have learned that only patients who have serious problems with their existing medication, or do not respond at all (i.e., have *refractory epilepsy*), are being put on new medicines.

Unfortunately, for the patients who suffer from a not so large and potentially profitable disease, and despite the efforts of everybody in R&D, every major company's marketers often settle on the same large disease as a market opportunity. They want a very prevalent disease that would be able to support a drug with sales of several billion dollars a year, no matter—almost—how many drugs are in that market, as long as they are expensive. Therefore, within a 6-18 month period, several so called me-too drugs will be approved. These drugs are by definition aimed at treating the same disease through the same mechanism. These drugs can be separately developed because they are protected by individual patents. They can be protected by individual patents because they represent a slight, or sometimes not so slight, variation of a chemical structure. But their mechanism of action, the protein they target, and the disease in which this protein plays a role is the same. So in this case, when there is no real exclusivity, the physician can choose in the first 18 months between three or four drugs. The marketers have invented the concept of *best in class*. Best in class is a drug that admittedly may do the same as two or three other drugs, but may, for example, have easier administration. Thus, if the other drugs are all administered with injection and this one is orally available, then that is a huge advantage and marketers will embrace it. Or, if all the others in the same class have to be taken twice a day and this one has to be taken once a day, then it clearly is going to be easier to sell. If the others require a laboratory test of liver enzyme activation that will delay treatment for maybe a week and the new one does not, then this drug will have a competitive advantage, even if its efficacy is just the same.

This is the job of marketing departments. They require the researchers and developers to find any small "differentiating" advantage between any two, three, or four drugs that are devoted to the treatment of the same disease using the same mechanism, but which are still somewhat different. This difference will be the basis of the marketing. The job of marketers is admittedly not easy when one thinks that presently over 250 type 2 diabetes drugs are in development, and there are already over 50 approved drugs, many being both generic and effective for many, but not all, patients.

While the time period of exclusivity for a novel drug is now very short, the value of being first in class or best in class is similar in terms of advantage. In many companies, however, they believe that best in class is going to be more profitable. At the clinic, this is probably true: no great value is given for innovation. Physicians do not reward the pioneer: they want efficacy and few complaints about side effects, and little noncompliance with the treatment course. Today, rather unfortunately, many companies will choose to make a fifth or sixth me-too within a new class, in hopes that it will be best in class for the treatment of, say, type 2 diabetes, where the number of patients is in the hundreds of millions and expected to grow in the following decades. Rather than make a completely new first in class drug in a less prevalent disease, they are safer making a me-too drug from a profit expectation point of view. It is easier and less risky than trying to treat society's greater needs such as neuropathic pain, epilepsy, schizophrenia, and AD. This is a very sad state of affairs for patients and, thus, for society.

It is clear that as long as marketing drives the choice of which diseases to treat, society is in trouble. The logic of the development costs of a drug being the same whether it will sell for millions or billions of dollars is simplistic. New drugs that would address society's needs may also sell for billions of dollars. Admittedly they are harder to develop, with both greater cost and risk, but we have to try. Company leaders today are not as tolerated by stockholders and analysts as they were in the 1970-1980s at, for example, Merck and BMS, whose focus was on medical need and the scientific basis to address it. In the past, once the scientific basis for treatment had been elucidated, drug companies pushed ahead to fulfill the medical need. And companies were, ironically, more profitable.

Table 4.5 is far from complete. Approximately 65% of approved drugs are me-too type drugs and one must wonder how it is possible that the maxim of capitalism that competition will bring down the prices works in a very limited manner here. Me-too drugs are not cheaper than first in class drugs. There have been many discussions, all blocked by the industry with appropriate expert help from famous academic researchers, about whether the regulatory agencies should stop approval of the fourth, fifth, and sixth me-too drugs[72] using the same drug target and the same mechanism of action. The largely valid arguments for approval of the first three or four drugs are that their different side effect profiles may account for different tolerability and different possibilities for combination treatments. Most clinicians like that there are two to three drugs of the same mechanisms of action to choose from. This we mostly agree on, but the 5th-10th me-too drugs are being approved and their approval shielded from discussion by political and ideological, not clinical and scientific, arguments. The defenders of the unrestricted me-toos argue that the regulatory agencies should not start to make policy decisions, even those with which, incidentally, most objective observers agree. They argue that when one company starts a drug-development program it is unclear how

---

72 Maybe we should coin the term "me-too—too" drugs for the later entrants than third in class.

	Examples of me-too drugs in selected diseases
1	Major Depression. SSRIs: fluoxetine (Prozac, Sarafem, and Fontex), sertraline (Zoloft and Lustral), paroxetine (Aropax, Paxil, Seroxat, and Sereupin), citalopram (Celexa and Cipramil), escitalopram (Lexapro, Cipralex, Seroplex, Lexamil, Lexam, Entact, and Anxiset E), and fluvoxamine (Luvox)
2a	Hypertension. ACE inhibitors: captopril (Capoten), enalapril/enalaprilat (Vasotec oral/injectable), lisinopril (Prinivil or Tensopril and Zestril), benazepril (Lotensin), fosinopril (Monopril), moexipril (Univasc and Perdix), perindopril (Coversyl and Aceon), quinapril (Accupril), ramipril (Prilace, Ramipro, Tritace, and Altace), and trandolapril (Mavik)
2b	Hypertension. Beta-blockers: acebutolol (Sectral and Prent), atenolol (Tenormin), bisoprolol (Zebeta), metoprolol (Lopressor or Lopressor LA and Toprol XL), nadolol (Corgard), and timolol (Blocadren)
2c	Hypertension, edema. Loop diuretics: furosemide (Lasix), bumetanide (Bumex or Burinex), ethacrynic acid (Edecrin), and torsemide/ torasemide (Demadex and Diuver)
3	Cholesterol-lowering drugs, hypercholesterolemia treatments. HMG-CoA reductase[1] inhibitors: lovastatin (Mevacor), simvastatin (Zocor), atorvastatin (Lipitor), pravastatin (Pravachol or Selektine), pitavastatin (Livalo), and rosuvastatin (Crestor)
4	Schizophrenia. Atypical antipsychotics: clozapine (Clozaril, Azaleptin, Leponex, Fazaclo, Froidir, Denzapine, Zaponex, Klozapol, and Clopine), risperidone (Risperdal), quetiapine (Seroquel and Ketipinor), and olanzapine[2] (Zyprexa, Zalasta, Zolafren, Olzapin, Oferta, and Zypadhera)
5a	Type 2 diabetes. Dipeptidyl peptidase-4 (DPP-4) inhibitors: sitagliptin (Januvia), vildagliptin (Zomelis and Galvus), saxagliptin (Onglyza), linagliptin (Tradjenta and Trajenta), and alogliptin, dutogliptin, and gemigliptin[3]
5b	Type 2 diabetes. Glucagon-like peptide-1 (GLP-1) receptor agonists: exenatide (Byetta) and liraglutide (Victoza)
6	Oncology. Epidermal growth factor receptor (EGFR) blockers: cetuximab (Erbitux) and panitumumab (Vectibix)
7	Rheumatoid arthritis. Tumor necrosis factor-α (TNF-α) inhibitors: etanercept (Enbrel), infliximab (Remicade), and adalimumab (Humira)
8a	Heartburn and peptic ulcers. Histamine H_2-receptor antagonists: cimetidine (Tagamet) and ranitidine (Zantac)

Examples of me-too drugs in selected diseases
8b	Heartburn and peptic ulcers. Proton-pump inhibitors: omeprazole (Losec, Prilosec, Zegerid, Ocid, Lomac, Omepral, and Omez), lansoprazole (Prevacid, Zoton, Monolitum, Inhibitol, Levant, and Lupizole), dexlansoprazole (Kapidex and Dexilant), esomeprazole (Nexium, Esotrex, and Esso), pantoprazole (Protonix, Somac, Pantoloc, Pantozol, Zurcal, Zentro, Pan, and Controloc), and rabeprazole (Erraz, Zechin, Rabecid, Nzole-D, AcipHex, Pariet, and Rabeloc)

Table 4.5: Me-too drugs in selected diseases
Most of the drugs listed in this table are blockbusters and sell for more than a billion dollars per year. Not all trade names have been listed, but hopefully enough to give a flavor of international marketing elaborations throughout the industry. The six SSRIs have at least 19 trade names. The 11 ACE inhibitors have at least 17 trade names. Lansoprazole alone has over 40 trade names according to various countries' name tastes.

---

1 *HMG-CoA reductase is 3-hydroxy-3-methylglutaryl-CoA reductase or HMGCR, the target of the statins. The first statin, compactin/mevastatin, discovered in Japan from the mold* Penicillium citrinum, *was never marketed, and so lovastatin, from Merck via the oyster mushroom* Pleurotus ostreatus, *was first in class. Simvastatin, a synthetic derivative from the mold* Aspergillus terreus, *was Merck's more powerful second in class and, temporarily at least, best in class, until Lipitor from "Parke-Davis-Warner-Lambert-Pfizer" was released. Lipitor was the best selling drug of all time with annual sales of over $12 billion. Pfizer allegedly delayed the launch of a generic once its patent had expired in June 2011 to give it an extra 5 months or so. Lipitor was probably the main reason Pfizer bought Parke-Davis-Warner-Lambert.*
2 *Olanzapine is also combined with fluoxetine (an SSRI, see under 1) and marketed for treatment of resistant depression and depressive episodes of bipolar disorder by Eli Lilly as Symbyax.*
3 *At the time of writing, alogliptin (fromTakeda Pharmaceutical Company) was under review, dutogliptin (from Phenomix, which has gone out of business) was in phase 3 clinical trials, and gemigliptin (from LG Life Sciences) was in development.*

many of the competitor programs will make it to approval. This is also true, but it is hard to understand why business considerations do not take care of the innumerable me-toos. The relentless use of research and development resources in therapeutic areas and in indications already covered over and over again is hard to justify when we have so many outstanding medical needs with no drugs or with no adequate drugs. One must also emphasize that the huge marketing costs are a direct consequence of the policy of having many me-too drugs. Pharma beats almost all industries in advertising costs: much of this could go toward research.

Some hope in limiting the number of me-toos is coming from the German practice that grants approval for me-toos, as do the EMA and FDA, but which requires that after 2 years of use, when sufficient clinical data are accumulated, companies must prove that their me-toos are better than the earlier drugs or the price will have to be dropped. If this becomes a generally used mechanism worldwide it may limit the eagerness for making me-toos (see also Chapter 10).

Rescuing successful phase 2 candidates from oblivion

This me-too drug-favoring strategy of Big Pharma leaves smaller companies like biotech companies and really small pharma to try to develop first in class drugs for smaller indications. However, the problem is that when they reach a successful phase 2, they are unable to finance the development of the much more expensive phase 3, that is, go through the very necessary clinical trials. Therefore, there are phase 2 trials in small indications that were successfully finished but will not continue to lead to a drug in clinical practice. Three years ago, business developers from pharma combed the globe for companies with a successful phase 2 compound, and they often bought the whole company rather than negotiate over a project that was often the only or certainly most advanced project of the smaller company. These projects determined most of the value of the biotech, with the projects that did not yet reach phase 2 accounting for almost nothing of the companies' value. But today, in 2012, Big Pharma has closed hundreds of their own projects with positive phase 2 data, arguing that even the largest companies like Pfizer and Merck can only afford three or four expensive, large and long phase 3 trials. Meanwhile, most of the small companies with phase 2 data are valueless, and have already closed or will likely close. Thus, the few (~10 %) that might have had successful phase 3s will now never find out. The patients will never know benefit from these potential new drugs. The patents will continue to block some potentially useful R&D avenues for some time; as a response, we start to see that drug patents, not necessarily the drug candidates, are being bought for very low prices by big companies.

These are places in the drug discovery process where some creative governmental intervention, with tax breaks or other tools, could help patients suffering from smaller diseases to have their medical needs met. It is unlikely that free enterprise will rapidly invent organizations with a better ability to research and develop drugs than today's large pharma. The Big Pharma comprise tens of thousands of people (approximately 690,000 in the United States alone, after the large layoffs) who not only have different competencies, but who have worked together, know each other, and understand each other's comments regarding the disposition of a drug, its toxicities, and its expected storage properties. If one starts to create a new drug research organization from scratch, one is going to go through a lot of trials and errors in drug development with, inevitably, years and years and billions of dollars wasted. Even the government-sponsored powerhouse of basic and clinical research in the United States, the NIH, has not yet been very successful in producing drugs. Its translational medicine program is underfinanced and has no real track record. Its $700 million per year budget would not buy a decent phase 3 study in a large disease. Yet, the clinical studies sponsored by the UK and U.S. governments have been very important in establishing today's standards of medicine.

Now, tens of thousands of professional drug developers with decades of experience have at the same time been laid off by pharma and remain mostly unemployed. Many are located at the largest and more famous R&D sites now closed or reduced, such as Sandwich, Kent, in the UK, and Kalamazoo and Ann Arbor, Michigan, and Groton, Connecticut, in the United States. These towns do not have many alternatives for scientists with such long and specialized education and experience. So the best strategy for society would be to use the existing pharma and biotechs that have several projects. They will need to be presented with incentives and pushed gently, or not so gently, to fill the gap of clearly recognized medical need in diseases, which do not represent huge markets, but for which the medical need is great. The starting points should be where we have the scientific basis of how to move ahead and to develop effective drugs. The U.S. Small Business Administration agency and many other state programs are active in this area, but are underpowered.

This type of program to keep Big Pharma's big research engine proceeding with society-selected indications must go hand in hand with some phase 3 trial program support that is initiated by governments. It would take successful, original, and not me-too, drugs from biotech in phase 2, and would provide some perspective for the innovative work of biotech in areas abandoned—or in areas never worked on by Big Pharma—but with a clear medical need (see Table 4.6).

At the level of governments in North America and Europe, we have in the past 20 years already washed our hands of large diseases like malaria and tuberculosis affecting tens of millions in Africa and other presently poor markets. The governments proudly point to the contributions of the Wellcome Trust, the Rockefeller Foundation, the HHMI, the Calouste Gulbenkian Foundation, and so forth, and to the rising importance and generosity of NGOs financed by billionaires such as Bill Gates, Warren Buffet, and George Soros, or run by former politicians like Bill Clinton and Kofi Annan. If we are not careful we now may be taking the even more hypocritical step and assigning finding drugs for treatment of AD and neuropathic pain to NGOs. But these diseases are common in areas such as Detroit's poor and rich parts that present no exotic photo opportunities in Africa with pop stars such as Bono. How would this work? In small genetic diseases there is a rising trend to meet the indifference by patient groups (see also the section "NGOs"). This is not an excuse for lack of government support, however.

Una¢¢ounted ue of $afe drug$

Experience shows that when we develop a safe and efficacious drug, it finds many other uses in other indications than initially intended. This common "upside" is seldom taken into account by the marketing departments;

Alzheimer's disease (AD)
Chronic obstructive pulmonary disease (COPD)
Schizophrenia—treatment-resistant cases and antipsychotics without metabolic syndrome
Neuropathic pain
Antibiotics—in particular for treatment of Gram-positive hospital infections
Tuberculosis—the largest killer in Africa, especially as a consequence of HIV/AIDS
Malaria—left to academics and NGOs
Stroke
Asthma
Liver fibrosis

Table 4.6: Diseases where society badly needs drugs
Society badly needs drugs for these diseases, whether they are easy to find or not. They are all Group 1 diseases with millions of patients. Type 2 diabetes (metformin-resistant patients) is a group 1 indication that is being pursued by the industry. There is still some activity to find drugs to treat or prevent Alzheimer's disease, although this is rapidly declining. The cancer indications that would fall in Group 2 are being worked on diligently by industry, such as ovarian cancer, melanoma, pancreatic cancer, and hepatic carcinoma.

they are likely underestimating the utility of safe drugs.[73] One cannot be sure that if Big Pharma could be nudged or forced to develop drugs for small- or medium-sized indications that these drugs would not also find other uses and, in the end, sell for billions of dollars. Good examples of this process over the years are plentiful.

When Novartis developed Gleevec, approved in 2001, it was thought that it would be a small drug selling for $200-300 million/year. It was shown to be so selective for the soluble tyrosine kinase in a rare cancer form,

---

73 This is, of course, totally reasonable. How can one predict and project the secondary uses of a drug? Of course, some drugs are premeditatedly launched for a smaller indication when the scientists and marketers both know that there is a bigger "prize" in mind. But, the note of caution to marketers is clear: Do not reflexively block the development of drugs for smaller indications as a matter of course or "business school mantra." Underlying mechanisms of diseases may be shared; a safe drug will find an indication with astonishing reliability. Therefore, the fewer safe drugs in your portfolio, the less chance of finding secondary indications. As one of our mentors said: "Beware about wasting a good 'No'."

chronic myelogenous leukemia (CML), that it was likely only to be useful in this one very special leukemia. Since this pronouncement, Gleevec has become an extremely successful drug clinically and financially, because it turns out to be useful in the treatment of many more leukemias than CML and for treatment of gastrointestinal stromal tumors, an indication where there was almost nothing available. Sales of Gleevec are currently $3.7 billion annually and Novartis has developed its successor drug, which is in clinical trials. As part of Novartis' growing oncology portfolio, it also entered the cancer diagnostics field by purchasing Genoptix. Genoptix has a very large number of tumors stored for comparative purposes. This allows new biopsies to be compared with potentially many thousands of tumors of this kind, with information on which combination of drugs they responded to best. Novartis' main goal is, of course, companion diagnostics to go with its treatments.

When omeprazole (Losec) was developed it was thought that it would sell $300 million annually because it was not expected to force out drugs that were already well established in the market. In addition, Tagamet and Zantac were supported by such large companies as Glaxo and SKB. Losec ended up selling $5–12 billion annually in the competent hands of Merck in the United States.

One cannot claim that marketing departments have been very successful in determining the final income of a drug. It would be good for all of us as a society, but also for a drug company, its employees and its stockholders, if we returned partially or fully to the 1960s and 1970s mindset when a scientific breakthrough at the molecular or cellular level enabled the development of a new drug for a disease. A scientific seminar over a new discovery, and subsequent discussions within the company's R&D departments, were the driving force to develop a novel, first in class drug rather than the estimates of the marketing department about how much revenue a drug will generate. Such estimates are, of course, important for a profit-making organization, but making drugs is a special human effort that hopefully is more ethical than the average industry—or at least it should be. If necessary, the ethics should be an emphasis reinforced by government involvement.

NGOs

The last 20 years have seen the rise of NGOs. Charitable organizations are mostly interest groups formed by patients or their relatives. They not only act to apply public pressure but also, sometimes, put the funds forward to sponsor preclinical and early clinical research to produce drugs that could help their patient community. Sometimes a celebrity is in the focus of such an effort. Michael J. Fox's Foundation is now a sponsor of several Parkinson's disease research and clinical projects. For spinal cord injury research, actor Christopher Reeve was a lightning rod. Sometimes these organizations are without a celebrity: the Hereditary Disease Foundation, the Huntington's Disease Assistance Foundation, the Alzheimer's Association, and so on. Their importance is high in our diversified society. Their financial ability is limited, but they might bring drugs to successful phase 2. There will be at least a clinical proof of concept showing that these new drug candidates are effective in the treatment in a smaller group of patients of specific great interest to this group. If this is the case, then there is the hope that one can mobilize the financial means required to complete a more extensive, larger, and therefore more decisive, phase 3 trial. If successful, this leads to registration of a new drug without the profit-making organizations that did not want to invest their resources. The patient organizations play an immensely important role by keeping patient data about those who may benefit from a drug in a rare disease. Otherwise, to identify and locate the patients for a trial would be a difficult task for a company or Contract Research Organization (CRO). They also shield patients from repetitive and unlikely to succeed drugs; with the help of medical expertise, the parents of children with Down's syndrome have become very selective in permitting enrollment.

Creating indications in the clinic or at the FDA?

In this context, one should also say a few words about the cases when pharma tries to define or invent an indication, not being obviously satisfied with the more than 500 already defined disease entities. The most quoted example is probably the case of Novartis with methylphenidate (Ritalin), which is used to treat ADHD in children and adults. For more than a decade a fight raged in which some child psychologists and child psychiatrists were accusing Novartis of inventing a disease in order to sell their drug. Today there are several other drugs, amphetamine analogs and others (e.g., Adderall, Concerta, Dexedrine, etc.), that are used alongside Ritalin to treat ADHD. The disorder is now well recognized, the number of prescriptions is in the millions, and it is now regarded as an example of a disease where a relatively specific pharmacological tool, a drug, is used to help, together with extensive psychological testing, to define the diagnosis. Those who respond to this drug with proper behavioral changes are at least operationally defined as ADHD patients and can be usefully treated with these drugs. Many U.S. high schools now insist that, once diagnosed, the students take these medications or leave the school.

In other cases, drug companies are not being reimbursed by insurance companies when a drug is used for a disease for which it has not been specifically approved. Yet physicians may use their discretion, which permits off-label use of approved drugs, to prescribe any drug for their patients for any of their diseases. These patients may benefit from these physicians showing that the drug has some efficacy in their disease. A good example is the use of antidepressants, tricyclics, selective serotonin reuptake inhibitors (SSRIs), and serotonin-norepinephrine reuptake inhibitors (SNRIs) in the treatment of patients who are not only depressed but present with lower back pain. Sometimes they are not depressed at all but have lower back pain and physicians have found that the antidepressants, mostly the old tricyclics, are useful in reducing their symptoms, so they prescribe it. However, lower back pain is not a specific disease indication recognized by the FDA or EMA. Companies like Lilly with its SNRI duloxetine (Cymbalta) would like the FDA to create an indication in which the SNRI would be an approved drug. Lilly, and others, would like to influence positively the FDA so that they can charge for their already available drug in this other indication. A decision by the FDA would change the profitability of an already existing and introduced drug. This is important because it changes drug company strategies, but it is not decisive in the discussion about which diseases from the long list of untreated diseases pharma chooses or ought to choose to address. This possibility of additional "indications" is, of course, being discussed but is never a sufficient argument for a drug-development program to be financed in a big company unless the primary indication is attractive to the marketers.

Off-label use definitely enables approved drugs to treat additional diseases, but is it a desired tactic?

Sometimes the company-promoted off-label use can only be avoided when governments step in and sponsor large, long clinical trials, which companies would or could never do. These long, through their design and duration, highly significant clinical practice trials can illuminate the efficacy, or the lack of efficacy, and, more importantly, the safety issues of long-term use of some drugs. A particular example is the numerous studies in the United States, Sweden, the UK, Canada, and the EU that established low-dose aspirin, a 100-year old generic drug, as efficacious in prevention of myocardial infarcts and transient ischemic attacks.[74] We will talk about this issue in other chapters, but it is clear that it is in the best interest of physicians and patients to find drugs, independent of the indication for which they were approved, as long as they are efficacious and safe doses are known. Safety is paramount and physicians should continue to have the right to prescribe any drug to any of their patients as long as this drug is approved and safe doses are known. They also should be able to explore whether it is efficacious for their patient, alone or in combination with other drugs. We have to find other ways than billion dollar fines, which obviously do not work, to force pharma actually to use the thousands and tens of thousands of patients who receive their drug for an off-label indication as a good enough indicator that this is worth doing a serious clinical trial dedicated to the indication, in which the "signal of

---

74 See for further information under Second International Study of Infarct Survival (ISIS-2), Swedish Aspirin Low-Dose Trial (SALT), United Kingdom transient ischemic attack (UK-TIA), etc.

efficacy" was seen by patients and physicians. Maybe this way we would find out more about how properly to use this drug without pharma losing the large income. One can understand why pharma may be reluctant to fund a trial that may not only stop off-label use but also adversely affect its on-label use income. Similarly, pharma is reluctant to conduct superiority trials whenever it can avoid it; it wants its drug to be approved as better than placebo whenever possible. Many remember when Merck spent a huge sum to prove that Zocor was superior to Lipitor as a cholesterol-lowering agent, only to show that the opposite was the case. Soccer fans might call it a most expensive own goal.

How can society affect the selection of indications by Big Pharma & by biotech?

The case of oncology, after neglect from the 1950s to late-1980s, is today the darling of all pharma. For many companies, it is the largest profit-producing therapeutic area. A whole 60% of Roche-Genentech's profits came from oncology drugs. This shows that government-sponsored long-term research that creates the scientific understanding of the disease mechanisms and identifies drug targets for pharma, which no longer spends funds and time on basic research, at least not in-house, is a powerful long-term way to influence for which diseases drugs will be developed by pharma.

The decades-long government investment in cell biology and fundamental cancer research[75] stimulates private enterprise, especially when coupled, as in the case with cancer treatment, with acceptance of high prices on an almost "guaranteed" market. These are the components of a recipe that can make Big Pharma work in an indication. The likelihood of being able to achieve approval after not so long and not so large clinical trials (an average cancer trial is 1/50th as large as an average cardiovascular trial and only one-third as long) is another important element of this selection process in for-profit companies.

---

75   See Figure 4.2.

Cancer is not associated with stigma such as, for example, HIV. It is regarded so terrible a disease that when any drug is approved, the market is guaranteed; it is hard or impossible for governmental or private insurance schemes to deny cancer treatment once an FDA-approved drug is available, no matter how high the price.

Forever escalating prices will probably not be possible in the long term and some of the oncology drugs that might provide only 4-6 weeks longer survival than placebo and cost $30,000-100,000, will come under pressure. But here we look at oncology as a successful area where society as a whole, through research investment and market guarantee of sorts, has made the indication, which was previously regarded as hopelessly fragmented, attractive for the industry. The small molecule synthetic toxins used as chemotherapy agents, which from 1960 to 1990 were the main oncology drugs, used to provide only a relatively trivial income compared to the investment of around $3,000 per year. They are still used as the basis of cancer therapy, in combination with radiation of solid tumors, and the more focused, biological-based, and thus much more expensive, modern therapies. Oncology is now a preferred therapeutic area to which pharma brings its talent and experience and where new drugs are coming, not only the very expensive biologicals of 1990-2010 but also recently some successful small, orally available molecules, for example, for melanoma, and non-small cell lung cancer (see Table 3.7).

We close this chapter with a news item extracted from the *Wall Street Journal* from February 1, 2011, applauded by Wall Street and investors since a stock buyback was matched with over 5,000 staff reduction and the dropping of some potentially risky research projects. This is a report on the largest pharma company in the world, and thus as such is a bellwether of the industry. It should also be noted that other giants like GSK, Merck, and Sanofi have outlined and carried out similar plans slightly before or after this announcement from Pfizer.

Wall Street applauds bad news

Pfizer Inc.'s new CEO on Tuesday outlined plans to reduce the company's spending and work force and focus more sharply on promising drugs as it faces slowing sales of some of its blockbuster medicines ... Ian Read announced a $5 billion stock buyback and an ambitious overhaul of operations that will cut jobs and research spending while aiming to boost research productivity and emerging market sales. Pfizer will cut its 110,600-person work force by up to 5 percent [... "only" c. 5,000 well-qualified are suddenly "surplus to requirements", with still more to come, but at least stock price went up or, rather, "soared" ...] *Pfizer shares soared $1, or 5.5 percent, to $19.22, their highest closing price in a year.*

The company said it is still on track to cut annual spending by $4 billion to $5 billion by the end of 2012, compared with 2008 levels, as it continues to shed nearly 20,000 jobs and close numerous factories and research sites since buying Wyeth.

For all of 2010, Pfizer reported a 4 percent decline in net income, to $8.26 billion, or $1.02 per share. Revenue totaled $67.81 billion, up 36 percent, thanks to $18.1 billion from sales of Wyeth products.

Erik Gordon, an analyst and professor at University of Michigan's Ross School of Business, questioned Pfizer's prospects, asking, "Is Pfizer in a death spiral?" ... [We would add how extraordinary it is that companies buy companies that they don't seemingly want given that they decimate them] ... *"We'll maintain earnings by cutting R&D, so our pipeline probably will be emptier, so sales will drop some more until we do another expensive acquisition," he wrote sarcastically.*

Pfizer reduced its prior 2012 revenue forecast for 2012 by $2.2 billion, to about $64.25 billion. That year is key because Lipitor, with nearly $12 billion in annual sales, loses U.S. patent protection Nov.

30. Because Pfizer plans to cut 2012 research spending by $1.5 billion, to about $8.25 billion, it still expects adjusted earnings per share of $2.25 to $2.35.

We could have chosen any number of press releases from the other top 10 pharma companies and found all of the same steps outlined: focus on existing products, cut R&D costs, and meet patent erosion by savings. We also found that all of these companies report large incomes and healthy profits and yet their stock prices are way down compared to 5-10 years ago because they do not fulfill investor expectation. Something is fundamentally wrong with Wall Street and investor expectation of pharma stocks. We are not the first to point this out, of course, but society's needs are not being met by Wall Street's short-term self-interest, and we believe this requires intervention by governments, NGOs, and the public.

Chapter 05: Therapeutic areas: strategically important diseases of the future

Diverging views of society & industry

There are a few especially important diseases and therapeutic areas from the viewpoint of society, as well as from the viewpoint of the industry. These are especially important because these diseases affect a very large number of patients, have high prevalence, and thus, they affect the economic output of society and the distribution of expenditures within healthcare and, in a broader sense, within the whole society.

Some of these diseases are able to disrupt the workings of our society. Most countries recognize that epidemics are politically and legally highly destabilizing and cause huge economic losses. Even before modern globalization brought enormous and rapid flows of goods and people from all corners of the world together, epidemics of the plague, cholera, polio, and so forth showed the difficulties in isolating microbes, stopping outbreaks, and halting the spread of disease. Recently avian influenza (bird flu), severe acute respiratory syndrome (SARS), and the fights to restrict methicillin-resistant *Staphylococcus aureus*, and multidrug-resistant tuberculosis (MDR-TB), have confirmed modern vulnerability to outbreaks. The response to microbial epidemics needs to transcend national borders and ignore differences in the payer systems of national healthcare. This is clearly recognized, with the cooperation within the World Health Organization, with the setting up and use of the Global Fund,[76] but it is not sufficient just to share diagnostics and epidemiological data: we need vaccines and drugs developed for the whole world. Even with multinational cooperation, friendly countries such as the UK and the United States can be enveloped in arguments about delivery of paid-for flu vaccines.

---

76   The Global Fund to Fight AIDS, Tuberculosis, and Malaria.

The Future of Drug Discovery. http://dx.doi.org/10.1016/B978-0-12-407180-3.00005-2

Two large epidemics are slowly encompassing the whole world, not only Africa: obesity/type 2 diabetes and Alzheimer's disease (AD). These epidemics threaten abrupt and almost unstoppable reorganization of the economy and societal structures unless we bring them under medical and pharmacological control. The obesity/diabetes epidemic is going to affect countries like China and India dramatically, while countries with an aging population like Japan, Germany, and the UK will be hit by the consequences of AD the hardest. Models of the consequences show that up to 15% of the work force will be involved in the 24/7 care of AD patients. These trends should be shaking governments into action.

The health economics that deal with the economic effects of disease burden and the effects of healthcare cost in society is, together with the study of public health, becoming increasingly important in political discourse in all countries; there are superb books on the topic from different political viewpoints. We will only deal with aspects of these important branches of the economy and of medicine that affect the choices of pharmaceutical companies.

Companies try to look forward 10-12 years and to foresee not only the biology and epidemiology, but also the economic and political landscape at the time when any new drug would enter clinical practice, would be paid for, and should start to produce revenue.

The development of drugs to prevent, or at least to treat, these strategically important diseases constitutes from society's view the most important task for the industry, yet today in all countries' pharmaceutical industry even vaccine production is in strictly private hands and the decisions are privately made. Governmental organizations weigh in on the safety of what is produced and, in cases of vaccines (and insulin and antipsychotics), about who should pay for the goods if proven safe and effective. Governments, by recognizing the societal importance of vaccine development and vaccination programs, have also influenced outcomes by limiting the liabilities of the private vaccine producers. Active involvement of nongovernmental organizations (NGOs) and governments in what drugs to develop is restricted to the trickle of funds devoted as charity to organizations working on diseases predominantly afflicting poor populations, such as malaria, leishmaniasis, sleeping sickness, and MDR-TB, which is now shared by all of Asia and prevalent in countries like Russia, China, and India.

The drugs that will treat these large diseases also potentially represent the largest incomes. Yet, because some of the diseases represent large drug development risks, even over the unusually high risk the whole industry carries, the big companies are abandoning work in some of these disease areas. The declining interest in AD and pain are examples. This does not bode well for our society.

The understanding and willingness of governments to step in as a partner and financier or limiter of liabilities is not apparent when it comes to the several large and potentially very profitable diseases we are discussing. Governments have always been involved as regulators and distributors, and have previously been involved in the development of some pediatric vaccines and drugs, for example, to control outbreaks or treat epidemics of infectious diseases. These increasingly neglected diseases are just as important for our society as are the infectious diseases.

The human & economic cost of major diseases

Among these large strategically important therapeutic areas/diseases that affect very large numbers of patients and have large human and economic costs are the following:

1. New antibiotics, especially for treatment-resistant *Pseudomonas*, *Staphylococcus*, and tuberculosis
2. AD
3. Obesity and type 2 diabetes, and associated kidney and retinal complications
4. Neuropathic pain
5. Schizophrenia
6. Ovarian, prostate, lung, and gastric cancer, and glioblastoma

7. Hundreds of neurological diseases that collectively affect approximately 10 million patients, that are chronic, and where the scientific understanding of the pathophysiology is good but the market size is judged by the industry's present standards as too small

Data are available in widespread sources for the estimated economic costs of these diseases. For example, the American Diabetes Association published[77] these data in 2008:

The total estimated cost of diabetes in 2007 is $174 billion, including $116 billion in excess medical expenditures and $58 billion in reduced national productivity. Medical costs attributed to diabetes include $27 billion for care to directly treat diabetes, $58 billion to treat the portion of diabetes-related chronic complications that are attributed to diabetes, and $31 billon in excess general medical costs

Table 4.1 and Figure 4.3 describe the gap between the number of pharma-supported projects and the existing medical need. The list above is just a summary of the position in 2012. Most diseases are under-researched. Even though research is broad for many, it is just that it is not proportional to the need.

Of the diseases listed, only type 2 diabetes is being adequately addressed by resources of the industry. For the rest, we are not doing very well. While progress in the treatment of cancers, especially leukemias and breast cancer and in the past 2 years melanoma and non-small cell lung cancer, has been substantial, it is thanks to government-funded basic research since the 1960s.[78] Because of this large long-term investment, scientists are aware of many drug targets and thus the industry, which largely dropped its own basic research by the end of the 1990s, makes steady progress.

---

77 American Diabetes Association (2008) Economic costs of diabetes in the U.S. in 2007. *Diabetes Care*. Mar; 31(3):596-615.
78 See Figure 4.2.

Each of these areas will be discussed in purely economic terms because, along with having disease-specific aspects, they also provide some very general points of view about the development of pharmaceuticals, about the interplay between government and private industry, and about the importance of government investment in basic research when industry does not want to or cannot anymore afford it.

AD: the most loomingly threatening disease

The most important example is AD. This neurodegenerative disease, which leads to cognitive decline, loss of memory, and inability to recognize faces or names, is, in short, one of the most horrible diseases in many senses. Many argue that all our humanity depends on our memories, and our memories determine who we are. When we lose these we are losing ourselves.

Although Alois Alzheimer diagnosed the first patient more than 100 years ago, AD has not been an important issue of research or of healthcare discussions, and certainly was not discussed in terms of a major threat to society as it is recognized today. The reason for this is that the major risk factor for AD is age. When the average life span of the population was 50-60 years, the frequency of AD was relatively low. Since definitive diagnosis still requires postmortem neuropathological examination of the brain, not many cases were identified. In contrast, the prediction for the United States is that in 2030 every second person aged 80 or above will have AD. The proportion of these people in Japan and the whole Western world is rapidly increasing.

What it really means is that up to 10% or more of the 2030 population in Japan, North America, and Europe may suffer from AD, and this is now being modeled by think tanks and insurers everywhere. Taking care of an Alzheimer patient, if they are taken care of individually, requires three full-time working persons each working 8 hours per day. This translates to a very large proportion of the productive labor force being devoted to taking care of patients with advanced AD, who cannot themselves be relied upon for the most elementary of functions. This is only the economic consideration. The societal implication is huge; there is currently a shortage of care givers.[79]

The 2011 estimate is that $600 billion is being spent on taking care of AD patients. Yet there is no drug available that prevents or cures the disease, or even significantly modifies the rate of progression of the disease. The only drugs today approved are giving a relatively small—although in large trials statistically significant—slowing of the loss of cognitive function in mild to moderate AD and in one case are approved to treat moderate to severe AD. Memantine (Namenda from Forest Laboratories) is a 30-year-old German drug (from Merz) originally used for neuropathic pain treatment. It produces very small changes in the rate of decline in already seriously demented patients. It is liked because of its relative safety, not its efficacy. The total number of approved, available drugs is five and none of them can be used to prevent, cure, or even significantly slow the progression of this disease.

The number of diagnosed Alzheimer patients in 2011 in the United States was 5.3 million, and a similar number applies to Western Europe, but, including the nondiagnosed patients, the total is estimated at some 30% higher. Where do we stand with the development of drugs to be used in the therapy of AD patients? The scientific background is such that in this disease there are both sporadic forms, accounting for 99.8% of cases, and clear familial (or inherited) forms, which is to say, cases that have an early onset of disease at about 40 to 45 years based on a genetic predisposition; these account for 0.2% of cases. There are several other genetic vulnerabilities identified. A very frequently occurring vulnerability is being a carrier of a protein isoform called ApoE4. One can carry two of these gene copies when one is homozygotic. One can carry one *ApoE4* and one *ApoE3*, which is more common in the population, when one is heterozygotic. But, the vulnerability for AD is significantly higher in the *ApoE4* homozygotes, who make up 2% of the U.S. population.[80]

---

79   See also Chapter 11.
80   See also Chapter 09.

Incidentally, in 2007-2008, the first two full-genome sequences of notable individuals were published: those of Craig Venter,[81] who published "The Sequence of the Human Genome"[82] coincidently with the Human Genome Project's parallel study,[83] and Jim Watson,[84] the co-discoverer of double helix.[85] In the first case, Venter's sequence showed increased risk of AD[86] and in the second case the *ApoE3/4* encoding sequence was omitted from Watson's data at the specific request of Dr. Watson. He did not want to know if he were susceptible to an incurable disease to which a grandmother had succumbed.[87] Interestingly, the cost of the Human Genome Project was $3 billion over 13 years, Venter's sequence cost some $100 million, and Watson's was variously reported at $1-2 million in 2-4 months.[88] The costs are dropping in a dramatic manner: Complete Genomics, Life Technologies, and Illumina have disclosed that from January 2012 they will provide a full genome sequence for anyone for $1,000. We have yet to start a discussion about what cognitively happens to individuals carrying both the ApoE3 and ApoE4 genes—one from each parent—as their age increases.

There are more serious, but luckily less frequent, genetic causes of AD, such as the "Swedish" and "Dutch" mutations in the amyloid precursor protein. These mutations and mutations in another associated protein, presenilin, and a combination of these mutations lead, in a small group of people, to very early onset (about 40 years of age) rapid progression AD. These patients, who will have "familial forms of AD," make up a small

---

81   Levy S et al. (2007) The diploid genome sequence of an individual human. *PLoS Biol.* Sep 4; 5(10):e254.
82   Venter JC et al. (2001) The sequence of the human genome. *Science.* Feb 16; 291(5507):1304-1351.
83   International Human Genome Sequencing Consortium; Lander, ES *et al.* (2001) Initial sequencing and analysis of the human genome. *Nature.* Feb 15; 409(6822):860-921.
84   Wheeler DA et al. (2008) The complete genome of an individual by massively parallel DNA sequencing. *Nature.* Apr 17; 452(7189):872-876.
85   Watson JD and Crick FHC (1953) A structure for deoxyribose nucleic acid. *Nature.* Apr 25; 171, 737-738.
86   In addition to antisocial behavior, cardiovascular disease, and wet ear wax (see http://en.wikipedia.org/wiki/Craig_Venter).
87   See http://www.nature.com/news/2007/070528/full/news070528-10.html
88   See http://www.nature.com/news/2008/080416/full/452788b.html

portion, 0.1–0.2%, of all AD patients. Most of the AD patients endure the sporadic form, yet *the discovery of patients with familial AD suggests the possibility of highly focused trials for AD preventive medicines in a group whose risk is very high.* Almost 100% will develop the disease unless we succeed in finding a preventive therapy.

It is worth explaining that in diseases where there is a large sporadic group of patients yet a small "familial group" or "genetically determined group" the understanding of the familial forms had great importance, in almost all cases, for finding treatments for the sporadic cases. This is because when people with familial disease are treated, we are fairly sure of the causative mechanism. It may be compared to the increasing introduction of companion diagnostics in oncology: treating those who have a genetic cause of the tumor improves responder rates from 5% to over 60%.[89] Yet we have great difficulties in finding any (preventive AD) trials involving family members of patients who have or have died from familial AD. The patient associations that "organize" these individuals have good lists of who would be eligible, but basic research and pharma have failed these people and missed this opportunity for two reasons. One is pure greed: "Why wait 4–5 years to show in familial cases that a therapy works, and then do another 4-5-year study in the real market representing sporadic patients?" goes the argument. It is added that "it is hard to recruit for familial case clinical trial," which does not seem to be true, or it has to do with the second factor: the drugs we so far have put into trial are associated with such bad side effects that it is hard to convince people presently fully healthy, even if they know that they are likely to have early AD, to endure the side effects for an uncertain delay of the onset or for the prevention of the disease. We need to improve science and pharmacy, and we need governments, not NGOs, to pay for the more focused trials.[90]

---

89   See Chapter 08.
90   See also Chapter 11, where we may reveal that our argument is vindicated: one trial, designed in the way we recommend, is now being conducted. For those readers who wish to "fast forward" you should look, for example, at http://www.multivu.com/mnr/56128-banner-alzheimer-s-institute-genentech-nih-prevention-trial-genetics

It is important that in the new healthcare legislation in the United States, upheld by the Supreme Court in June 2012, one cannot be excluded or penalized for a pre-existing condition or a genetic predisposition. This will become more and more important, especially as genome sequences are becoming affordable as part of diagnostics, not just as a research tool.

In general, the presence of genetic forms of the disease accelerates the understanding of the disease and indirectly accelerates the development of drugs to treat the disease. This is also the case with AD. The early onset disease has been linked to mutations in the metabolism of the amyloid precursor protein leading to the appearance of amyloid plaques. These are amorphous aggregates formed from several proteins. The major component is a fragment of the amyloid precursor protein. Research directed toward the proteolytic enzymes that produce this fragment of amyloid protein, the amyloid beta (or Aβ or Abeta) peptide, led to an investigation to dismantle the plaques formed from this peptide. The last 15 years have seen a tremendous effort by the industry to develop inhibitors for the two major APP-hydrolyzing proteases. Beta-secretase and gamma-secretase produce the amyloidogenic Abeta 1-40 or 1-42 peptides, but, so far, no peptidase inhibitor has reached clinical use. A gamma-secretase inhibitor (semagacestat or LY450139) from Lilly came closest; it reached phase 3 trials and then was withdrawn in 2010 because of toxicities. This additionally shook the confidence of large pharma in Alzheimer therapies.[91] It is worth examining which companies try to develop AD drugs, the intensity of their effort, and the major issues that affect the intellectual and economic investment in the development of Alzheimer drugs.

Early diagnostic imperatives

The start of each treatment is diagnosis of the disease. Today, AD diagnosis heavily relies on neuropsychology test batteries, which have

---

91   Confidence has not been improved by the poor results from Lilly's therapeutic antibody trial of solanezumab (see Chapter 06).

become better and better. They are now able to detect mild cognitive impairments and early AD. But nobody really knows how much damage has already occurred in the brain when cognitive impairment becomes obvious to relatives, friends, and colleagues. It is, therefore, very important that 2011 has seen the clinical entry of several imaging agents.[92] When working well, these permit the visualization of amyloid plaques in the living brain, and might, therefore, be important in establishing whether a drug aimed at inhibiting the production of amyloid peptide is really successful in reducing the plaque load. It is, however, evident that nobody is bothered by carrying amyloid plaques. When it is conclusively shown that the amyloid plaque load predicts cognitive impairment, we will then be able to convince people who exhibit no cognitive evidence of AD to take drugs that prevent the formation of amyloid peptide and amyloid plaques. But then these drugs will have to be very, very "clean" with no or a very low incidence of serious side effects or even annoying side effects.

If we had succeeded in producing a drug candidate with a strong scientific rationale suggesting it would prevent AD, without major and minor side effects, then which people would be convinced to take it? Firstly, those with a very high risk of developing familial AD would take it, preferably before showing any symptoms. Later, those who, through aging and some first signs of mild cognitive impairment, appear to have the risk of developing AD in a few years would take it. Some of these candidates would have to be prepared to test this drug in trials that will take 3-5 years. The principle is very similar to the way we have convinced millions and millions of people to take the cholesterol-lowering statins. High cholesterol *per se* is not a disease, but it is a harbinger of many cardiovascular diseases. If amyloid peptide and amyloid plaques can be detected and shown more rigorously to be a harbinger of AD, then volunteers would be easier to find. But for this to happen one will need much cleaner and much safer Alzheimer drugs than those we presently have.

---

92   The approval for the imaging agent florbetapir (Amyvid) to image amyloid plaques from Avid-Lilly was, however, delayed over procedures of evaluation.

Based on earlier neuropsychological diagnosis, patients are selected for the clinical trials of proposed Alzheimer drugs. These trials are becoming longer and longer. The reason for this is that we are entering into these trials based on the success of neuropsychological assessment that now captures early Alzheimer patients, in ever milder forms of the disease.

The first Alzheimer drug clinical trials in moderate to severe patients could show that the first class of drugs, the acetylcholine esterase inhibitors (AChEls), could slow the decline of cognitive abilities significantly after a 6-12 month treatment (trial) period. The latest trials with AChEls have, however, taken 18 months to show a significant difference in cognitive decline between drug-treated and placebo patients. The milder, and earlier the AD cases enrolled into the trials, the longer we have to dose the drug to show a significant difference in the cognitive performance between drug-treated and placebo patients. This is a clear recognition by pharma that, in order to show efficacy, they will need longer trials. These are a major expenditure, but, more importantly, the results are further and further away from what affects the stock price in the 2-3-year period upon which present pharma executives focus or are obliged to focus.

Another issue regarding Alzheimer patients and clinical trials is that the average age of these persons is above 65 and they suffer from a great number of other diseases, for which they are also being treated. This means that the drugs to be used in Alzheimer therapy have to be devoid of interactions with a very, very large number of drugs. It also means that because of age and other diseases, a relatively large number of these people will drop out of the trial or may die during the 18- or 24-month length of the trial. This means that these trials, at least at phase 3, will have to be very long and very large. The industry has conducted such long and large trials in cardiovascular disease and in type 2 diabetes. However, most large and long trials—usually post marketing, i.e., post approval, phase 4 trials—are carried out by governmental agencies in the UK, United States, and so forth. But the repeated failure of Alzheimer drugs over the last 10 years is making more and more companies silently withdraw from the effort to develop therapeutic agents for the treatment of AD, which would slow disease progression, prevent the disease, or cure the disease.

This is understandable from the point of view of profit within organizations, but it is not acceptable for our society. As we recognize AD as a serious risk for our society, we cannot afford to give up trying to make drugs that achieve effective treatment. Today, there are no seriously capable organizations except the pharma industry to develop such a drug. So, when they withdraw, openly or silently, and are permitted so to do, we will end up with the horrific prospect of every second over 80-year-old citizen suffering from AD, but not being offered any kind of treatment that would help the patient, the family, and society as a whole.

Translational research

When we say that the only seriously capable complex, sophisticated large organizations to develop therapeutics are the pharmaceutical companies, we are not disregarding the expensive efforts government-supported institutions, such as the National Institutes of Health (NIH) and corresponding European institutions, put into what they call *translational research*, that is, research that is directed toward affecting medical practice.

Translational research, which is the modern equivalent of applied research, is an increasingly important part of their task. However, in retrospect, one can today clearly state that these organizations have not discovered any major drugs in the past 40 years. They have, during these last 40 years, been the major contributors to the basic science breakthroughs that are the scientific basis of drug development in the world's private pharmaceutical companies, which all abandoned in-house basic research from 1980 to 2000. The government-sponsored research institutions, together with some major NGO-sponsored research entities (e.g., the Wellcome Trust, the Howard Hughes Medical Institute, and the Bill and Melinda Gates Foundation), have introduced a multitude of extremely important tools to preclinical and clinical research. These permit the regulatory agencies and the industry to measure and improve the success of drug discovery, drug development, and the drug approval processes. Starting in 2012 the NIH collaborated officially with the Food and Drug Administration (FDA); in principle they are both government sponsored. This will assist the FDA, which has so far relied on *ad hoc* panels of academics for scientific advice, to lean more on scientists in government pay. NIH scientists have a much stronger set of rules to keep them from receiving payments from the industries that apply for drug approval. This will help dilute the requirement of Congressional Committees periodically to uncover high-profile examples of the FDA receiving advice from academics with a conflict of interest. Conflict of interest is a serious matter that can undermine all public trust in the impartiality of FDA decisions regarding drug approvals, no matter if the decision itself was impartial.

Thus, the recent, long-awaited official agreement, pushed by the Obama Administration, to improve the quality and image of FDA decisions by having two U.S. tax-payer financed organizations, the NIH and the FDA, sharing scientific competence, bodes well. The NIH is the world's powerhouse for preclinical discoveries through its intramural and extramural programs, and it is important in academic medicine in small proof-of-concept trials; however, as a clinical research organization, it is small to medium sized. The roughly $5 billion spent by the NIH on clinical projects and the $700 million proposed for translational research in 2011–2012 is dwarfed by the estimated $92 billion research budgets of major pharma and major biotech spent in the same year on R&D, over 85% of which is translational research (see Tables 5.1 and 5.2). The effort is also dwarfed by the collective experience that exists in these companies in the development and testing of clinically useful drugs.

It is clear that the NIH and its international counterparts bear huge responsibility for the "real" science in AD. When one compares funds poured into HIV/AIDS and cancer research to those put into AD, one is shocked. It is clear that funding initiatives can bring large numbers of scientists to work on a problem, and that it is what we badly need. Instead, AD research is conducted by a small club; this we cannot afford.

1.	Roche $8.7B	9.	AstraZeneca $4.23B
2.	Pfizer $7.40B	10.	Eli Lilly $4.13B
3.	Novartis $7.06B	11.	Bristol-Myers Squibb (BMS) $3.48B
4.	Johnson & Johnson (J&J) $6.66B	12.	Boehringer Ingelheim $3.03B
5.	Sanofi-Aventis $6.25B	13.	Abbott Laboratories $2.61B
6.	GlaxoSmithKline (GSK) $5.59B	14.	Daiichi Sankyo $1.89B
7.	Merck $5.58B	15.	Astellas Pharma $1.63B
8.	Takeda Pharmaceuticals $4.64B		**Total $72.88B**

Table 5.1: Top 15 R&D budgets of the major pharma companies in 2009
Compare to the NIH budget of $29.5 billion in 2009.[1] Around 70% ($22B) of the NIH budget and 20% ($20B overall) of the companies' budget is for preclinical research. This is not basic research per se, but research to select the drug candidate to enter into clinical trials. Almost all basic research is now left to government and NGO financing. Internationally, governments fund more than 60% of basic research in large national institutes and universities; the rest is from private sources to universities. NGOs fund 2% and industry the remaining approximately 30%. Eighty percent of all private investment is for translational research in the hope of developing diagnostics and drugs that will generate profit. We do not have precise figures, but the indications are that the budgets would have fallen by a collective 15% in the two subsequent years (2010 and 2011).

1　See also Figures 4.2 and 7.1.

Therefore, it is not a promising route to let private industry back out of trying to develop Alzheimer drugs, saying: "it's too hard; it's too risky; it's too slow; it's too expensive," and assume that governments will step in to the vacancy. There has to be a serious effort to find a formula by which governments, gently or not so gently, force the industry to continue its effort in developing Alzheimer drugs. Intervention can come from tax breaks or other incentives, as well as somewhat punitive legislation for pharma to release data from programs they have dropped, in order to support this highly risky activity *because it is so important*. We have seen how U.S. and other governments can enhance and semi-force the development and production of antidotes

1.	Amgen $2.72B	9.	CSL[1] $267M
2.	Biogen Idec $1.2B	10.	Amylin Pharmaceuticals $172M
3.	Gilead Sciences $849M	11.	Genmab $123M
4.	Genzyme $805M	12.	Cubist Pharmaceuticals $119M
5.	Celgene $745M	13.	Merial Animal Health $115M
6.	Kyowa Hakko Kirin $478M	14.	MannKind $109M
7.	Vertex Pharmaceuticals $454M	15.	Abraxis Biosciences $107M
8.	Life Technologies $320M		**Total $8.58B**

Table 5.2: Top 15 R&D budgets of the major biotech companies in 2009
Around 80-90% of biotech budgets ($6.9B from the above) is allocated to translational research.

1 Originally Commonwealth Serum Laboratories.

to biological weapons, and how it can incentivize and encourage the production of vaccines.

AD is not as acute as bird flu or the risk of a bioterrorist attack, but it is as, or more, threatening for the individual and for our society.

Obesity & type 2 diabetes

The first biological to be used on a large scale was insulin, albeit preceded by some vaccines and antidotes to snake toxins, and so forth. The first clinical trial of insulin involved one patient: a child. We often forget this. As discussed earlier, production of insulin is now made with recombinant technology in bacteria or yeast. The three major producers, Novo Nordisk, Lilly, and Sanofi-Aventis, are producing both acutely active and delayed, slowly, or long-acting depot or retard insulin preparations.

One may think that insulin-dependent diabetes is, therefore, a well-treated disease and needs no further diagnostic and drug development efforts. This could not be further from the truth: up to 30% of patients are resistant to the most widely prescribed diabetes drug, metformin (see below); most patients are becoming increasingly resistant to insulin; and we have ongoing exacerbations with the patients who are not becoming resistant to either of these two drugs.

Even with well-controlled diabetic patients who, by judicious use of insulin, do not let their blood glucose rise, the development of renal illness, blindness resulting from retinal vascularization problems, diabetes-induced neuropathies, and pain in the extremities is very high. On top of this comes the world's increasing obesity, the most obvious risk factor for type 2 diabetes. Thanks to a rising standard of living and global flows of food staples, fewer and fewer people in the world are starving, or, rather, more and more people are not starving. Obesity growth is linked with the change of diet in Asia. In India and China, where more bountiful food, coupled with wealth, is added to some genetic predisposition in these two huge countries, there has been a dramatic increase in obesity and in type 2 diabetes. It should be noted that not all obese people will develop type 2 diabetes, only about 20% do, but the cost of treatment for these people and the cost of treatment of the complications from diabetes is staggering and comparable to that of AD.

It is clear that it is in the interest of patients, society, and the pharmaceutical industry to find drugs that prevent the rapid increase in the number of obese people and, therefore, reduce the risk that 20% of these will develop type 2 diabetes. It is also clear that we have to develop better treatments for this very large group, which is estimated to include close to 300 million people by 2030, all of whom will have type 2 diabetes. Unfortunately, it is very difficult to develop safe drugs that prevent or cure obesity when the patients are unwilling or unable to switch diet and to exercise. Diet control and exercise are both becoming increasingly difficult in the stressful world of rising standards and rising expectations of work and other achievements.

The pharmaceutical industry has seen some spectacular successes in this area. Unfortunately, these then turned into spectacular failures, sometimes taking with them the entire company, no matter how big it was. Most in the industry clearly remember the successful development of Fen-Phen (fenfluramine + phentermine), a very active (amphetamine-like) mixture of appetite control drugs that has shown clearly visible, tangible results of large rapid weight loss. The beauty of trials on obesity drugs is that the patients can, by checking their waistlines or stepping on to a balance, see for themselves whether the drug is efficacious. The fallacies of these trials are many, however. While it is relatively easy to achieve a 5-10% weight loss in the first 6-8 weeks, it is very hard to keep it over 12 months. This is why the FDA now insists that drugs that might be approved achieve and maintain a 5% or higher weight loss over a 12-month treatment because less than that is not clinically meaningful. Also, drug treatment is not comparable to other ways of achieving dramatic weight loss such as bariatric surgery, itself not without dangers. Surgery is, however, very expensive and not acceptable or appropriate for every patient, but bariatric surgery can produce a 30% or higher weight loss that remains after 12 months.

Fen-Phen had been a spectacular success for the company American Home Products until it turned out that a large number of patients develop valvulopathy—changes in the heart valve—as a result of taking this drug. As this is an irreversible disease state leading to death in many cases, the subsequent lawsuits brought down this very large pharmaceutical conglomerate. History should record that Fen-Phen as a combined drug was never approved by the FDA and was the result of an off-label development at some U.S. academic institutions.

Similar amphetamine-based weight loss drugs by Servier were questioned and were recently withdrawn in France. Other weight-loss drugs have fallen on other safety issues. Some of the few approved and "safe" ones have very unpleasant side effects. For example, orlistat (Xenical) blocks uptake of fat by the intestine, which causes hard to control diarrhea with almost inevitable soiling. Despite this, GlaxoSmithKline entered the generic drug market with orlistat (Alli) as its first generic (see Chapter 04).

The development of weight loss drugs is very attractive but very difficult; the last 3 years have seen the industry bringing forward compounds or combinations of compounds that showed efficacy of 6-

10% weight loss over 12 months, but which contributed to an increase in social isolation, suicidal ideation, and suicides. It forced the FDA to demand that companies specifically examine these side effects, and it finally asked its outside academic–clinical experts whether obesity is such a life-threatening condition that we should permit the taking of drugs that might significantly increase suicidality. The answer was no; we have to be able to find drugs that achieve the same weight loss without these serious side effects.

Other weight loss drugs have shown large increases in blood pressure and heart rate, and were deemed not safe. Presently, the industry is wondering if it is possible to make a truly safe obesity drug, while several biotechs are hampered by their financial inability to afford the long cardiovascular safety study rightly requested by the FDA.

But, unlike in the case of AD, the industry is not abandoning the area because it seems that the development of these drugs is easier in the sense that the scientific basis to fight obesity is better understood, and that the chance of proving that one has an efficacious safe drug is better than achieving the same in AD. In particular, the efficacy of the drug is shown and seen by the patients themselves within weeks. The other problem is maintaining this efficacy. It is so clear that there is a great desire in our world to achieve the ideal body weight determined by fashion and by health advisories of a body mass index (BMI) around 22-24. Despite a period of 3 years of efficacious drugs not being approved because they were not safe enough, it is less likely that the industry will abandon its search for obesity drugs.

When it comes to diabetes drugs, we start to recognize that the control of blood glucose can be further improved. The biggest contribution to improved control is not by drugs, but by continuous, daily, or repeated daily self-diagnosis of high blood glucose levels. These levels can be measured at home using the glucose meters developed in the last 30 years, which have become so cheap and reliable that all patients can use them. This so-called *point of care device*, of which we will see many in other indications, enables patients to control their own therapy, which in this case is of great importance. The first glucose meter developed by Boehringer Mannheim was as big as a refrigerator and required 2-4 ml blood. Today's machines use just a drop of blood, are pocket-sized, and, in most countries, given free of charge. This locks the patients into buying the measuring strips, much like Kodak practically gave away the instamatic camera so you would buy its film. That this marketing works shows how widespread self-monitoring of blood glucose has become.

Secondly, we realize that there are drugs like the GLP-1 (glucagon-like peptide-1) analogs and inhibitors of the GLP-1 degrading enzyme DPP-4 (dipeptidyl peptidase-4), which can fine-tune glucose control and will postpone some of the diabetic complications.

The problem for those who are developing diabetes drugs is that we have a very large number of relatively efficacious, cheap, generic drugs such as metformin,[93] which have side effects but work quite well. For the largest number of patients these drugs will remain the mainstay of their diabetes treatment because they are well known and because they are cheap. The new drugs have to demonstrate significant improvements over the presently available insulin releasers, insulin sensitizers, and so on. In this quest for better control of blood glucose, we have also learned metabolic disease patients are accepting of injection, not only of insulin but also of other drugs. This opens the route for the use of biologicals in an area where this was not widely foreseen. Today, the GLP-1 analog exenatide (Amylin/Lilly's Byetta—a synthetic version of exendin-4) and its competitor liraglutide (Novo Nordisk's Victoza) are injectable biologicals generating revenues of more than a billion dollars each per annum. Together with insulin, we have now accepted in clinical practice other injectables to control blood glucose. In contrast, the inhibitors of DPP-4 are oral drugs: sitagliptin (Merck's Januvia) and saxagliptin (BMS's Onglyza).

---

93 Metformin has had a long history. First synthesized in 1920, then trialled by a French physician in 1957, it was introduced in the UK in 1958 but not until 1995 in the United States. In 2010, 48 million generic prescriptions were filled. See http://en.wikipedia.org/wiki/Metformin.

In summary, it has to be said that the impact of the fight against obesity as a major risk factor for type 2 diabetes cannot be overstated. The problems of finding efficacious and safe obesity drugs are great, both practically and theoretically, because eating is so deeply and intricately programmed in our brain. So many processes of mental well-being are controlled by parts of the neuronal circuits that control repeated, pleasurable activities such as eating. Nevertheless, it is clear that here the industry continues to stand at the gates of the FDA with new drugs and drug combinations that can achieve significant weight loss.

Surgical versus drug interventions

A comparison of surgical procedures such as bariatric surgery to drug treatment is an important one. Those who work for insurance companies and major health plans calculate the risk-benefit ratios of major surgeries. One often finds that bariatric surgery is only recommended for those who are relatively young and who are enormously difficult to treat with drugs, diet, and exercise. Whether this will change with improvements in surgical procedures or not is hard to foresee. But it is clear that many patients will prefer any available oral or injectable drug if it comes close to the efficacy of the weight loss produced by a surgery where today mortality is over 1%.

Neuropathic pain

Morphine is one of our oldest drugs. The ancient Egyptians called it "God's own medicine." This was not because of its marvelous pain-killing properties, but because it effectively stops diarrhea, which is one of the great killers in the world. The existence and knowledge of how to dose morphine and other opiates has been the basis for the effective treatment of pain for a long time. Many thought that opiates could be useful in the treatment of all pain states. Neither the patients nor the anesthesiologists held this view and it is manifestly not the case. There is a very large group of pain syndromes—neuropathic pain resulting from neuronal injury and cancer pain—which are often not responsive to opiate painkillers. On top of this, opiates have huge safety problems that include constipation, alcohol interaction, and so forth, as well as their well-documented addiction potential. Relieving pain is one of the great dreams and aspirations of mankind. Yet the introduction of new efficacious pain medications is very, very slow. The inadequacy of all pain treatments is best illustrated by the following:

> Most clinical trials for pain killers evaluate the efficacy of the medication using a visual analog scale. Patients judge for themselves the intensity of the pain on a linear analogue scale from "0" = no pain to "10" = excruciating pain. The gold standard of non-opiate, non-morphine-type pain drugs is gabapentin. Gabapentin is a more than $2 billion-selling drug that in its clinical trial reduced pain from an average of somewhat above "7" to an average of "4," not to zero. The FDA suggests that patients may be recruited for pain trials if they assess their own pain to be above "4." This means that even after having taken the best available drug many patients would still be eligible to enroll in a new trial for a painkiller.

Current practical treatment of pain may use multiple drugs. Physicians and patients learn to use several drugs to achieve some pain relief. The biggest problem is not that our basic pain research is lacking in effort, but that the animal models, in which we try to assess the efficacy of new pain medications, are not very reliable. Therefore, many clinical trials that were initiated after successful animal experiments have failed. There are additional big problems with developing new pain medications. This includes the potential for misuse of painkillers. People take them recreationally rather than because they have pain. Often these drugs, which were made for oral use, are being ground up and injected intravenously when their effect is much faster and much more robust in the brain, sometimes causing deadly accidents. So, whoever tries to introduce a novel serious painkiller has to prove or has to safeguard against abuse potential. This is difficult.

Painkillers are also the most often overdosed drugs. Patients in pain start taking the recommended dose then readily take more or more often when the pain does not abate. Therefore, these drugs have to be very safe even at 5 to 10 times the recommended dose. Another problem of many painkillers is their interaction with alcohol.

Despite these inherent difficulties, we cannot stop trying. In many ways painkiller development is ideal for the pharma companies as the trials are short: dental pain, 72 hours; postoperative pain, 3–7 days; and post-herpetic neuralgic pain, 7–14 days. It is just that what works in *all* the animal models consistently fails in patients, explaining why the industry has openly stopped trying in some very notable cases. Some of the largest pharmaceutical companies, such as Roche—the most profitable pharma company today—Novartis, Astra-Zeneca, and others, have openly closed their pain research units, saying that it is too difficult. This leaves the field to small companies or to companies such as Merck and Pfizer (previously active in COX-2 inhibitors, see Chapter 03) that are mostly only interested in one type of pain, inflammatory pain, for which we already have relatively good medication, as everybody who has been given ibuprofen by the dentist knows.

Pain is an example of an area of disease where the number of people affected is tremendous. The suffering is chronic. The economic opportunity therefore exists, yet the companies openly withdraw from competing in this area. This is calling for serious governmental entry into the field at the level of both basic and clinical research, which would help to define more valid, more reliable, and more translatable models, so that the existing argument of "whatever works in animals may or may not work in humans, and we will only know it $500 million dollars and 3 years later" will no longer be valid. Directive research by governments could change the situation and would, therefore, change the daily lives of tens of millions of people with chronic pain.

The huge medical need and market opportunity in neuropathic pain is thus dominated by gabapentin, a drug developed as the anti-epileptic Neurontin by Parke-Davis (now Pfizer), which is now more than 18 years old. It was approved in 1994 and has spawned many generic forms such as Fanatrex, Gabarone, Gralise, Nupentin, and so forth. Those who work in pain clinics are using a mixture of dedicated painkillers, anti-inflammatory drugs, tricyclic antidepressants, and anti-epileptic drugs to treat neuropathic pain, but their success is very limited.

Cancer

In the 1970s and 1980s, the 20 large pharma companies, of which today exist less than 10 because of mergers and acquisitions, were not very interested in the area of oncology. The argument was that cancer, leukemias and solid tumors, are often discovered too late to do anything and that many cancers will not be treated easily because breast cancer, prostate cancer, lung cancer, renal carcinoma, pancreatic cancer, and so on, are clearly different diseases of different organs that will require completely different medications; therefore, the market is very fragmented. So, not only are the patients diagnosed late but there are also too few patients for each cancer form, maybe with the exception of some leukemias and lymphomas (see Table 5.3). However, it turns out we knew too little about some of the underlying cellular pathways and that certain controls of the cell division that runs amok in cancer are general in many cell types; thus, there will be carry over from developing a drug for one cancer indication (see the section "Effective governmental & societal intervention"). We were too organ focused, and not focused on cellular pathways.

In any clinical trial, the industry would not want to use, as the comparison, the most commonly used chemotherapy: the cytotoxic agents. These nucleotide analogs are still among the most efficacious cancer drugs, but with terrible side effects like hair loss, nausea, and weight loss. They are still used frequently, and these are drugs that are very cheap to make and very cheap to buy.

Big companies are not leaving the therapeutic area of oncology, although 2010-2011 was full of great disappointments when it came to clinical trials. This has shaken some of the best-selling cancer drugs such as bevacizumab (Roche-Genentech's Avastin), which has been approved for treatment of

All invasive cancer sites	All	Males	Females
Brain and nervous system	126,000	67,000	60,000
Breast	2,605,000	13,000	2,592,000
Cervix	247,000	0	247,000
Colon and rectum	1,112,000	541,000	572,000
Endometrial cancer and uterine sarcoma	575,000	0	575,000
Esophagus	29,000	22,000	7,000
Hodgkin's disease	165,000	85,000	80,000
Kidney and renal pelvis	281,000	165,000	117,000
Larynx	90,000	72,000	18,000
Leukemias	244,000	137,000	107,000
Liver and bile duct	28,000	19,000	9,000
Lung and bronchus	371,000	173,000	198,000
Melanoma of skin	793,000	385,000	408,000
Multiple myeloma	62,000	34,000	28,000
Non-Hodgkin's lymphoma	438,000	227,000	211,000
Oral cavity and pharynx	249,000	161,000	88,000
Ovary	177,000	0	177,000
Pancreas	33,000	16,000	17,000
Prostate	2,276,000	2,276,000	0
Stomach	66,000	37,000	28,000
Testis	196,000	196,000	0
Thyroid	434,000	96,000	338,000
Urinary bladder	535,000	395,000	140,000
Totals	11,715,000	5,353,000	6,361,000

Table 5.3: Estimated cancer prevalence in the United States in 2007
Data include the 23 most prevalent cancers; totals include other less prevalent cancers, of which there are many.

non-small cell lung carcinoma and for colorectal cancer, but which has failed to show efficacy in breast cancer. This also may be initiating a possible re-evaluation of the original approval in non-small cell carcinoma, thereby endangering one of the best-selling cancer drugs from Roche.

Drug name	Company	Indication
Dimebon	Pfizer	Alzheimer's disease
Ocrelizumab	Roche-Genentech Biogen Idec	multiple sclerosis
Taspoglutide	Roche	type 2 diabetes
Semagacestat	Lilly	Alzheimer's disease
ASA404	Novartis	lung cancer
NOV-002	Novelos	lung cancer
Zibotentan	AstraZeneca	prostate cancer
Vicriviroc	Merck	HIV
Recentin	AstraZeneca	colon cancer
NV1FGF	Sanofi-Aventis	critical limb ischemia

Table 5.4: The top 10 phase 3 failures of 2010
Drug list is as reported by FierceBiotech.[1] The average phase 3 trial costs $400-750 million. All major pharma are present on the list. These companies have extensive drug development and clinical trial experience. The only small and new company is Novelos Therapeutics, Inc. of Madison, WI.

1 http://www.fiercebiotech.com/special-reports/top-10-phase-iii-failures-2010

Several of the spectacular clinical trial failures of 2010 were in oncology (Table 5.4), but so were three of the most spectacular successes (Table 5.5). Oncology remains a highly successful area, both medically and economically, for pharmaceutical companies. We also saw the first new therapeutic modalities such as the antibody-drug conjugate (ADC) brentuximab vedotin (Seattle Genetics' Adcetris), approved in August 2011 for anaplastic large cell lymphoma (ALCL) and Hodgkin's lymphoma; many others are in trials.

Effective governmental & societal intervention
There are 40 times as many drugs being tested for cancers than for schizophrenia. Why? In short, the explanation is government-sponsored basic research. Today oncology[94] is the most drug target-rich area,

94 Perhaps together with inflammation.

Drug name	Company	Modality	Indication
carfilzomib (PX-171-007)	Onyx	proteasome inhibitor	multiple myeloma
crizotinib (Xalkori)	Pfizer	anaplastic lymphoma kinase (ALK) and ROS-1 inhibitor	lung cancer with companion diagnostics
vismodegib (Erivedge)	Roche	small molecule antagonist	basal cell carcinoma
vemurafenib (Zelboraf)	Plexicon-Daiichi (Roche Group)	protein kinase inhibitor	melanoma with companion diagnostics
brentuximab vedotin (Adcetris)	Seattle Genetics	antibody-drug conjugate	Hodgkin's lymphoma, anaplastic large cell lymphomas
trastuzumab emtansine/(T-DM1)[1]	Roche	antibody-drug conjugate	breast cancer

Table 5.5: Advances in cancer therapies: new approvals 2009-2011
New drugs, new antibody-drug conjugates, and new orphan drug strategies by both small and large companies; phase 3; and approvals in 2009-2011. It is important to note three trends in this table: (1) companion diagnostics appearing and improving responder rate from 5-10% to 60%; (2) we have become—after 10 years and dozens of failures—good at designing protein kinase inhibitors that are less toxic than the first ones were (by not binding to the ATP-binding site of the enzyme), and we can often design a selective compound for the mutated protein kinase that leaves the non-mutated, non-cancer-related form free from inhibition; and (3) the therapeutic antibodies are coming in different formats and armed with different cell-killing mechanisms on top of selectively recognizing some marker of the cancer cell. Most of the entries in this table are first in class drugs, proving that we can, when we put the resources into it, innovate with cancer drugs. Why can we not in AD or pain?

---

1 Antibody drug conjugate of the antibody trastuzumab (Herceptin) linked to the cytotoxic mertansine.

whereas large chronic diseases, which affect up to 1-2% of the population over their entire lifetime, like schizophrenia, are extremely poor in drug targets.

The reason for the richness of drug targets in oncology is twofold. One is the decision by governments and NGOs, such as cancer societies, to engage large-scale sponsoring of basic research over several decades starting in the 1960s. Firstly, this research has shown that many molecular mechanisms are common in very different cancer forms. Therefore, even though on the surface prostate and ovarian cancer are clearly different and occurring in different genders, there are molecular pathway similarities. Effective drugs may affect basic underlying mechanisms of the repair of DNA, or the formation of vasculature, which is needed to supply the tumor with blood, and so on. These putative drugs might be used to treat more than one cancer form. Secondly, the discoveries of drug targets in leukemias and then in solid tumors have accelerated as a result of major public spending. When considering the importance of this, one has to remember that until the 1960s the pharma industry had been responsible for the basic research in most areas of life sciences (except embryology), which was the foundation for most of the drug developments. Since the 1960s, government-sponsored research in physical and life sciences in the United States and Western Europe has increased (the "Sputnik effect") and has almost completely replaced the basic research efforts of big pharmaceutical companies. It is true that pharma spent $92 billion on research and development in 2009, but a very small portion, maybe $10 billion, of this was considered basic research. This is to be compared with the more than $60 billion spent annually on basic research by public and other sources. The NIH alone in the United States has a budget of over $30 billion.

The example of oncology shows that when politicians recognize the need either for popular or other reasons to support research, then they can initiate sustained and large-scale efforts that eventually produce scientific breakthroughs. HIV treatment is another area serving as a good example of the joint forces of patient interest groups, relatives of patients, celebrities, and governments to put pressure on a pharma industry that had not been in general very successful in developing antiviral agents. Yet, in the relatively short period of 20 years, HIV has switched from being a 100% deadly disease to a chronic disease that can be managed at several levels. This is one model, in which society can influence pharma by spending on basic research (to provide basic functional understanding and drug targets). Society would then rely on different sized companies, small ones first and bigger ones later, to pick up the scientific breakthroughs and apply them in the development of novel drugs. This is a very long-term, indirect way to find new drugs, but it has worked and it does not rely on specifying the commercial entities that will use the scientific results; instead it hopes that several will, and that they will do it in competition with one another.

There is also post-drug development encouragement and incentive by allocating NGO budgets to guarantee the purchase of a very large number of doses for developing countries. They exert a push–pull mechanism: the push on development and pull on production.

The examples of oncology and HIV cannot be underestimated. They are extremely important if we are not to give up work on Alzheimer therapies and on finding drugs against neuropathic pain and, for example, against schizophrenia, where the present drugs have relatively low response rates and are associated with severe metabolic side effects in many cases leading to early type 2 diabetes in young schizophrenics.

There are many good reasons to protect the freedom of researchers and not to direct all research, mostly because we really are not that good at predicting the truly innovative breakthroughs, many achieved through studying systems such as *Escherichia coli*, yeast, nematode worms, sea slugs, and fruit flies, and leading to cancer drugs. Nevertheless, one must not shy away from directing a much larger portion of the research budget to AD and antibiotics resistance than is happening presently. NIH and European research agencies already have large directed programs, but they are not large enough. Biotechs would be most helped if phase 2 and phase 3 clinical trials in AD were made possible with the partnership of government as an alternative to partnering to Big Pharma, which is currently not interested in these trials.

Chapter 06: Blockbuster proprietary drugs versus generic drugs

What happened to the blockbuster drug pipeline?

Big pharma comprises a collection of industries that were enormously successful over the past four decades. They became used to double-digit growth and double-digit returns. The heart of this spectacular showing were the "blockbuster drugs"; that is, drugs that have generated a revenue of a billion dollars a year or more for many years.

All of the major indications and diseases for which efficient drug treatment exists have their share of blockbusters (see Table 4.5). They were wonderful for their owners because they continue(d) to bring in billions of dollars a year long after the R&D expenditures had been paid. They require a focused marketing force, but their utility for the companies is unbelievable. Their income pays for many failed drug-development projects and for most of the shareholder dividends. It is easy to understand why companies became attached to the model of trying to work on drug-development projects that can produce blockbusters; it is easy to understand the addiction of companies to the blockbuster model. The R&D costs of a blockbuster drug and those of a drug that will sell only for $300 million per year is likely to be similar because the most expensive part, the phase 3 trials, can be comparably long, and may require similar numbers of enrolled patients. Certainly, the development of blockbusters is not that many times more expensive than the multiple they bring in, such as the up to $11 billion annual revenue from Lipitor or the current $7 billion for Humira, and so forth. Thus, the companies crowd the diseases where several blockbusters are, or were, possible. These are chronic diseases, with many millions of patients who could be diagnosed relatively easily and where the efficacy of the blockbuster candidate could be shown relatively easily. But, Big Pharma is running out of blockbusters with patent protection; the big companies are largely unable to replace their blockbusters as these lose

The Future of Drug Discovery. http://dx.doi.org/10.1016/B978-0-12-407180-3.00006-4

patent protection with other blockbusters. They are thus in a "crisis" of investor confidence, as reflected in the steady drop in share prices. Lilly lost patent protection in 2011 for most of its large profit-making blockbuster drugs; Pfizer's share price has been suffering because it has been unable to replace Lipitor, whose patent expired November 2011, with one or several blockbusters.

Where can the industry find new blockbusters?

Why such a crisis, when the drug-development process is becoming more and more sophisticated, there is deeper better science on which to base new treatment, and diagnostic techniques are improving rapidly?

The answer is that the blockbusters epitomized the first large successes of drug therapies in almost all large diseases and the blockbusters were approved often in trials against placebo, because that was the standard of care when they were introduced. One may say that for the modern pharma industry they were also the "low-hanging fruit": the diseases and drugs that were relatively easy to identify as a business opportunity. They were not easy to research and develop—in itself a tremendous achievement—but it was possible to predict that if a drug with this profile of efficacy were launched, the company would be able to sell 5-50 million doses a month. The big companies of the pharma industry are very even in terms of talent, technical force, and capital. Thus, wherever a blockbuster were found, other companies would follow with their own versions in rapid succession. Exclusivity in an indication with blockbuster potential might only be 6-12 months, indicating, indeed, that most of our Big Pharma companies have the same skills (and the same weaknesses). For example, when the first ACE[95] inhibitor became a blockbuster, the second was only 12 months behind. When the first selective serotonin reuptake inhibitor (SSRI) became a blockbuster, then the second, third, and fourth—all still making more than a billion dollars—followed within 10-12 months. The second and third drugs in their class could also become blockbusters

---

95 Angiotensin-converting enzyme.

because the diseases they address are so large that there is commercial space for several billion-dollar-a-year drugs.

Today there are very few large indications waiting for their first blockbuster: indications for which we have no current symptom treatment that is fairly efficacious, has a response rate of ~60% or higher, and where there is no generic drug yet, or no drug that will soon become generic. The success of the industry producing these first relatively efficacious, relatively safe drugs occurred at the time when increasing welfare in the post-WWII United States and Western Europe created a large market for medicines through employer or government-paid insurance schemes. Now, by virtue of this success in the first 40 years of modern drug development, the bar to make a blockbuster drug has been raised. Comparison against only placebo is insufficient when already approved treatments exist that are truly the new standard of care. As previously indicated,[96] all rheumatoid arthritis (RA) drugs have to produce significant symptom relief and slowing of joint degradation on the top of methotrexate. Similarly, all diabetes drugs have to work on top of metformin; all hypertension drugs have to run against propranolol, which has a great efficacy and safety record, and so forth. It is not the fault of the regulatory agencies that they must insist on running a new candidate against, or in addition to, the "standard of care," or that the standard of care is indeed much higher now than in 1960. The regulatory agencies have developed, during the golden decades of producing dozens of blockbuster drugs, as much as the industry itself.

The purchasing power for medicines is still increasing in the world, as we add billions of new patients in China, India, Russia, and Latin America to those of the Western European and North American markets. It is possible to discover new drugs in areas where we have no treatment at all, such as certain cancer forms. These new drugs almost certainly would become blockbusters such as Plexicon-Daiichi-Roche's new, and thereby probably the world's first efficacious, melanoma treatment. Similarly, a successful drug for pancreatic carcinoma, and so forth, would become a blockbuster.

---

96   See Chapter 02.

Thus, new blockbusters can be found for diseases where the existing standard of treatment is low or so low that there is effectively no existing care. In addition, blockbusters emerge where the market created by the first in class drug is huge, for example, the GLP-1[97] analogs for treatment of type 2 diabetes. These drugs showed that an efficacious "injectable" with a new mechanism of action is accepted by patients with a metabolic disease.[98] Not only the first but also the second and probably the third in class will also be blockbusters as the market created is so large and the advantages are so significant. It is hard to lose weight while on insulin, whereas diabetic patients on GLP-1 analogs can and do lose weight while controlling their blood glucose.

It is also true that we await new blockbusters in large underserved diseases like Alzheimer's disease (AD), schizophrenia, neuropathic pain, and so on, large indications where surely efficacious and safe drugs will become blockbusters. Every industry manager knows this. Hence, all companies in the pharma industry have been active in these diseases for the past 15 years.

More science here, please
The recent post-recession rethinking reduced the portfolio of research projects. But, it is certainly worth repeating that the cut projects are in the very same diseases where the scientific understanding is not very deep, where the reliability of animal models is poor in predicting efficacy in humans, and where we need especially safe drugs as the treatments will be life-long. So the industry experienced a large number of expensive and, in a certain sense, embarrassing phase 3 failures (see Table 5.4) in the past 4 years. This sent the more feeble-hearted and already very rich, large companies to abandon these diseases openly, as in the case of pain where Roche, Novartis, and AstraZeneca have closed their research, or in AD where companies are becoming very careful and the number of clinical

---

97   Glucagon-like peptide-1
98   Since the 1930s insulin has, of course, been a widespread injectable, and continues to be as the new nasal formulations struggle to establish a foothold.

trial entries is very limited, although the medical need is enormous and growing. Telling was Myriad Genetics' abandonment of the Alzheimer drug tarenflurbil (Flurizan) in 2008. This failure of the proclaimed first selective amyloid beta-42-lowering agents in an extensive 3,000-patient phase 3 study, after promising phase 2 results against mild AD in 2005, is one reason companies are being put off. It is indeed unfortunate that when focusing on science's best target to date, no benefit results.

Other larger companies, such as Lilly with its gamma secretase inhibitor semagacestat (LY451039)[99] and Pfizer with latrepirdine (Dimebon), have recently experienced painful failure in phase 3 trials of AD. It is not to be forgotten that all these efforts are focused on one disease mechanism in AD: the formation of the peptide amyloid beta (Abeta 1–40/42), which is neurotoxic, kills neurons on its own, and can rapidly aggregate and form amyloid plaques that enclose several other proteins, but are predominantly aggregates of Abeta 1–40/42. The serious narrowing of the AD research field is a very dangerous thing, as we may soon find out when the two most advanced antibody programs, solanezumab (Lilly) and bapineuzumab (backed by J&J and Pfizer[100]), which have the same antigen, fail due to lack of efficacy. They "work" by extracting Abeta 1–40/42 peptide from the brain to the cerebrospinal fluid. It is hoped that they lower the brain amyloid plaque load as imaged, but if they fail to slow significantly the cognitive decline in the treated patients then that would undermine the heavy investment into this mode of action by major pharma players. If these therapeutic antibodies show statistically significant effects on cognitive parameters, then we will find ways to live with their serious side effects, including small cerebral hemorrhages that caused the Food and Drug Administration (FDA) to halt the trials temporarily. In addition, we will then be seeing many other ways to lower Abeta 1–40/42 tried by these same companies, but mostly by other companies that missed the AD market with an antibody.

---

99 Originally being co-developed by Elan and Eli Lilly.
100 Originally being co-developed by Elan and Wyeth, whose assets became J&J's and Pfizer's, respectively.

If these two antibodies fail, we will deeply regret that we permitted a tremendous narrowing of a research field by loud and well-organized cliques of scientists who focused on discrediting others researching alternative possible mechanisms of AD, and who have monopolized the research grant distribution between themselves. This is not an uncommon outcome of the peer-review system and of "friendly corruption," where one believes that all smart researchers have understood that this is the *only* way forward, and those who do not see the light cannot be so smart and hence it would be a waste to support them when resources are limited. Peer review is still the best system, but in the case of such mounting epidemics as the AD epidemic, one should be more judiciously providing space and funds for smaller, less loud yet more original and, at the beginning probably more fantastic, ideas to avoid missing the real possibility to provide some treatment.

It was indeed subsequently confirmed in late August 2012 that Lilly's solanezumab failed to show a significant improvement both in cognition and function in the two "EXPEDITION" trials for mild to moderate AD. After pooling the two datasets there was a slight indication that there was a slowing of cognitive decline, and this is argued by Lilly to show that the data support the amyloid hypothesis. Providing the data show that it is safe, Lilly may decide to take the drug candidate further with another trial with a different end point, as agreed with the FDA, but it will take at least another 18 expensive months or more if milder cases are included. Whether Lilly can or should afford this is a matter for its board.

The results from this line of investigation are largely very disappointing and point again to the problem of having insufficient drug targets in AD.[101]

The new blockbusters

It is not impossible to bring out new blockbusters, but it is certainly much harder than it was during 1960-1980 when every decent drug with

---

101 The recently released (September 2012) data from the public research consortium ENCODE is hoped to provide further drug targets, but that would be a long way off (see Chapter 09).

efficacy and safety had a good shot at becoming a blockbuster. Several oncology drugs (Gleevec, Avastin, Herceptin), RA drugs (Enbrel, Remicaid, Humira), and multiple sclerosis (MS) drugs (beta-interferon, Copaxone, Tysabri, Gilenya) have become blockbusters in the past 10 years. But the frequency with which we find them and the predictability of finding them is not sufficient to maintain the model that the big companies should sustain their income by bringing out new blockbusters. Lilly has been trying its best for 10 years to repeat its major breakthrough of the SSRI fluoxetine (Prozac) in treating major depression. However, Prozac is a very safe and highly efficacious drug with an ~60% response rate, so the task is much tougher than it was when Prozac was introduced. The introduction of a serotonin-norepinephrine reuptake inhibitor (SNRI), duloxetine (Cymbalta) or venlafaxine (Effexor), nowhere approaches or replaces the sales and success of Prozac. Lilly also tried to replace its atypical antipsychotic blockbuster olanzapine (Zyprexa), which came out of patent protection in 2011. Zyprexa has a response rate of ~50-60%, but it has plenty of weaknesses on the safety side. Even with a huge space for improvement, Lilly has not succeeded.

Of course, all other companies are also trying to bring out better antidepressants, but now those have to stand against the generic fluoxetine, generic citalopram (Forest Laboratories' Celexa), and generic paroxetine (GSK's Paxil), and better antipsychotics without the metabolic side effects that have led to type 2 diabetes and ketosis in some olanzapine patients. So far none have succeeded. The best efforts for antipsychotics are aimed at a new mechanism of action, such as Lilly's non-dopaminergic metabotropic glutamate 2/3 (mGluR2/3) agonist LY2140023. After a successful phase 2, it could not be shown to have efficacy in phase 3, thus pushing Lilly stocks down.

Schizophrenia is one of the poorest researched lifelong diseases, with manifold increased risk of suicide and with symptom treatments that are old, yet the research investment and research successes are very low. It is not uncommon that the poor animal models of this highly human thought disorder are not well translated into small phase 2 clinical trials. Thus, trials are not followed by successful phase 3 trials, which would be short at 6-8 weeks, sometimes even 2 weeks, and also relatively small with 400-500 patients using an active, approved antipsychotic comparator. These trials are thus relatively cheap because of limited enrollment and duration, but could lead to a new $2-4 billion drug. Yet, there are so few of them because we do not have the scientific efforts to provide a serious base for drug development, and we continue to spend only a small fraction of the sum we spend on cancer research.

Pfizer and others are trying to find a safer, better cholesterol-lowering drug that can compete with simvastatin (Merck's Zocor), which has been generic since 2004 in the UK and 2006 in the United States; atorvastatin (Pfizer's Lipitor), which became generic in November 2011; and AstraZeneca's rosuvastatin (Crestor), whose main patent will expire in 2016.[102] Again, so far no success; it will come, but the bar is now higher—much higher. So far, the safe paths are used such as combinations of two well-proven, patent-expired drugs such as Merck's Vytorin, which is a fixed dose combination of simvastatin and ezetimibe (Zetia), two well-proven drugs to lower cholesterol and triglycerides in blood.

However, there are plenty of indications where blockbusters will come; it is just that companies no longer have a flow of these year after year.

Double-digit growth becomes an unreasonable expectation

Thus, the painful admission will have to come to the pharma companies and their stockholders that these specialized companies should make drugs that have reasonable profit because they fulfill a medical need, but may no longer be relied upon to serve double-digit growth to Wall Street. Now pharma has chosen the merger and acquisition and cost-cutting business model, rather than the change in selection of drug-development projects model, for company development and growth. This change to a model of more restrained expectations, however, will inevitably come as

---

102   In anticipation of losing 50% of its revenue in 2016, AstraZeneca, despite having currently $33 billion in sales, cut its R&D workforce by 23% and spent $4 billion buying back its own stock.

the industry is soon—if not already—so consolidated there are therapeutic areas where a single company has 10-20% market share, and mergers will bring no large cost savings. The loss of patent protection for blockbusters is inevitably hitting the sales and profits, and this cannot be avoided. New drugs will have to be made, and the industry is good at that. Now that one of the leading companies, Merck, admits it cannot provide double-digit growth, the others will follow suit. It is likely the investors will remain, because it is still most likely a safer and better bet[103] than, say, steel, paper, oil, or information technology, but, of course, the stock may not recover. The value of these companies fell despite the steady, reliable dividends.

Big Pharma attaches a generic arm

As well as having a research-based arm to discover, register, and sell proprietary drugs, many large drug companies today have an arm to produce and sell generic drugs. The proprietary arms are largely shrinking (e.g., GSK has, reportedly, only ~25% of its income from proprietary drug sales), but they are still spending 14-18% of their income on R&D, which clearly makes pharma one of the most research-intensive industries.

The very existence of generic drugs is a testimony to the past successes of drug discovery. Pharma tries to reduce the impact of impending patent expiry. All is tried to prolong the term and value of proprietary status. Efforts include making the drug easier to administer, from, say, twice daily to a once a day, through an extended release formulation; extending it to a pediatric formulation; even to delaying the launch of the generics through legal and possibly not so legal deals; and old-fashioned lower pricing. They can even launch their generics before competitors in order to be first to the generic market. They can also more inventively construct a new formulation by separating the originally patented drug's racemic mixture and seeking approval of the more active enantiomer (e.g., esomeprazole

---

103 This is the authors' perspective with reference to the present potential growth and is in no way a recommendation for potential or existing investors.

and omeprazole, and citalopram and escitalopram).[104] The patent extension process has critics and has been termed "evergreening."[105] When the patent time irrevocably expires the generic competitors have already been working for a year to have their generic forms approved so that they hit the pharmacies as soon as legally possible.

The equation is simple. If a generic manufacturer has good pharmaco-economists and follows how prescriptions of the proprietary drug are distributed between countries, areas, and indications, via the many companies that are specialized in providing these types of data on prescription drugs, then it will know which drugs are making significant profit for their inventors. A generic company needs to have built good medicinal chemistry, process chemistry, and analytical chemistry departments and distribution chains. If it has the production volume to negotiate the distribution of many generic products at once with the large purchasers, then it will have to feed this large machine with new products, that is, with new generics to make and to sell. In competition with the other large generic makers it must offer its products promptly and cheaply. It is now reduced to a competition at the same level as between competing toothpastes. The intellectual and the clinical trial parts of the industry are absent, together with the huge risks of failure and loss of investment. The generic drugs are tested for chemical equivalence with careful analytical methods to show that the proprietary drug maker's original tablet and the generic maker's tablet contain the same chemical and in the same quantity. Differences in formulation that may affect some patients, and smaller differences in packaging, and so forth, may occur, but substantially the same effective medicine is now available for a fraction (5–20%) of the cost. When will this process end?

There is every incentive for the generic companies to make generics of every drug that is selling at any profit; that is, where manufacturing and distribution costs are less than the market price. Once they have built their

---

104   Many proteins are exquisitely good at distinguishing stereoisomers and if you show that one enantiomer is more than seven times active than the other, you can have it patented.
105   See, for example, http://en.wikipedia.org/wiki/Evergreening

copycat machine and have competed with each other, acquired or merged with each other so that only a few generic companies remain standing, which appears to be approaching, they have to think of other ways to make money. One popular way is to cut a potentially allegedly illegal deal (such as in the delay of generic Lipitor; cf. the case of Plavix where BMS had their patent extended) so that the generic company delays its entry into the market. The originator of the drug continues to sell the drug at the higher price, despite the expired patent, for a while. It is easy to imagine coming to a financial agreement with the waiting generic competition that has at this time limited production and approval-seeking costs. Luckily for patients and insurers, these deals do not last and are deemed illegal in some countries that are keener than others on permitting earlier access to cheaper generic drugs, for example, Canada. In other countries like India, home to large generic manufacturers, the Indian Patent Office (IPO) and the courts can become involved in pricing of still proprietary drugs and have now lifted the patent protection on Bayer's kidney and liver cancer drug sorafenib (Nexavar), such that a local generic manufacturer, in this case Natco Pharma, can produce it at much lower prices for the Indian market than Bayer's $5,500 per month. The IPO has thus issued its first ever compulsory license and effectively ended Bayer's monopoly. The Indian Patents Act allows for such licenses after 3 years of a patent for drugs deemed as too expensive. Gleevec became the latest case of the IPO finding against, in this case, Novartis. Large pharma fight these rulings.

It is now clear to most large pharmaceutical company managements that, in order to maintain a steady level of income in the face of erratic performance of R&D, they have to diversify. Now they make generic drugs of their own portfolio, where the process is already established. If they create a sufficiently large generic arm, they can also pick up successful drugs from other Big Pharma. GSK competes with other generic makers of the former Roche drug, Xenical. It does so successfully, but, of course, the margins are much, much smaller for generic drugs than for original drugs. The risks of losses in product investment are tremendously smaller. Of all proprietary research-based projects, 1 in 100 will become a drug, yet for generic drug projects, all will be drugs at the top 10–20 generic drug makers. The only question is how low will be the margin. Companies like GSK and J&J have less than 30% of their income coming from proprietary drugs that they discovered or bought while these drugs were patent protected. The rest of the income is from generic, over-the-counter devices, cosmetic and household products, and so forth. The greater stability of this type of composite income is paid for partly by lower margins, but it is clear that all major pharma are going toward this model.

Purely research-based pharmaceutical companies are becoming a relative rarity.

Generics attach an R&D arm

These mechanisms drive the expansion of generic drug makers until consolidation and equilibrium is achieved among them. Typically, the really successful generic companies want more *value-added products.* They are in the same position as the dye industry at the end of the nineteenth century that moved on to make higher value-added products, in this case drugs.

Thus, large generics are very active in in-licensing and in starting their own research to produce higher margin proprietary products. Their problems with R&D productivity will naturally be the same as those of the older, larger pharma. Efficacy in copying drugs does not guarantee any success per se in discovering drugs.

Will all drugs become generic?

Are there any drugs that will not become generic? The answer is probably no.

The patent-protected drugs that are useful in the clinic, and thus have sales, are all sold at margins that permit the future generic makers to yield a profit while selling them cheaper. The patent that protected the drug guarantees that the procedure to synthesize the drug is described, as well as the analytical methods to check it. The inventors are guaranteed protection in exchange for disclosing the methods of the invention such that those skilled in the art can repeat the invention. When it becomes legal, others cannot only repeat it but can also sell the product of this repetition.

For more complex small molecules with difficult formulations, the threshold is somewhat higher to become generic, but it is definitely not impossible. For complex biologicals expressed in bacteria, yeast, and human cells, the investment costs to produce these proteins are significant, but once the generic company is producing a few "biosimilars"[106] then it will desire to have a pipeline of new biosimilars to fill its expensive fermenters and occupy its expensive protein analytical, quality control. The clinical trial departments show safety, but do not have to demonstrate the biosimilar's efficacy, since the latter is assumed from the clinical trials of the original biological and from the clinical experience of 20 years with this biological. There was a period about 10-15 years ago when analysts explained to us that there will be no price competition in biologicals. They were negligent of history and wrong about the future. They forgot that our first biological was insulin, and there is continuing fierce competition to sell insulin both by differentiating the same peptide hormone preparations through formulations, preparations, and pure price competition. Similarly, the early biological entries of growth hormone products and beta-interferon have seen price competition, although beta-interferon prices remain high, despite there being several producers and despite the large expansion of use of the drug to treat MS.

Regulating biosimilars

The reason for the bigger threshold for biosimilar generics than for small molecule generics is that the manufacturing process is poorly documented and disclosed today. Even if the amino acid sequence in rituximab (Rituxan or MabThera)[107] is identical to the sequence of its biosimilar

---

106   Common abbreviation for "similar biological medicinal products"; they have been also called "subsequent entry biologics (SEBs)."

107   Rituxan or MabThera, the second largest earner for Roche (currently ~$6.3 billion per year), is approved in oncology for treatment of non-Hodgkin's lymphoma and also used in the treatment of RA.

competitors,[108] the glycosylation patterns are different. There is no one to say with certainty whether this matters in terms of efficacy and safety, and so on. More practically, while the biosimilar producer is building a file from the results of the large 200-patient trial, the proprietary drug has data on tens of thousands of treated patients and a patent fortress built around it for different indications. This makes it likely that the time it will take to exert significant price pressure on biologicals through the biosimilar mechanism will be longer than for generic small molecules; the price drops will be likely smaller.

The U.S. efforts to cap healthcare costs focused on the most expensive drugs in the Biologics Price Competition and Innovation Act of 2009. Following the political lead, the regulatory bodies requested studies and data on biosimilars to cover all areas, as they do for small molecule generics. But, in addition, they rightly demand immunogenicity testing in humans, and some of the efficacy tests are much more time-consuming and expensive than for generic small molecules. The European Medicines Agency (EMA) and the FDA produced guidelines for biosimilars. These guidelines focus on safety of the biosimilar, that is, mostly lack of immunogenicity so that it does not induce antibody production, and some of the easier to measure surrogates of efficacy, such as pharmacokinetic and pharmacodynamic parameters.[109] But no real efficacy is needed to be demonstrated, as in the sometimes long trials the original biological has undergone. Despite all of this "easing" of the process of approval, the FDA spokesman said that the agency expects no more than 3-4 applications for approval of biosimilars per year. If one adds to this that the analysts believe that these will be only 10-15% cheaper, then it does not seem that this will contribute in a major way to reducing healthcare costs.

The analysts also point out that the expected lower price is not sufficiently lower to change the presently hard barrier biosimilars find in replacing

---

108   From Teva, Sandoz, and GSK.
109   See, for example, Shea, TJ (2011) EMA releases long-awaited guidelines for biosimilar antibodies, http://www.mondaq.com/unitedstates/article.asp?articleid=122376&login=true&newsub=1 4 March 2011.

more expensive biologicals; namely, that patients and physicians do not trust them sufficiently. If governments want to accelerate the approval process of biosimilar entries to reduce medicine prices, then companies need to demand a much more standardized production and a much better documentation of the production steps—from fermentation conditions and the organism, through to purification—than is the case today. This would help the biosimilar entries with their most important problem, which is to have physicians and patients believe that it is truly equivalent to the original biological. The generic drug maker Teva's trials of their biosimilar compared with Rituxan uses the protocol of giving two injections of each to the patient; thus, the same person can compare results. The belief is that equivalence is more important than the U.S. government's suggested shortening of the patent time, although both will improve the chances of reducing the cost of biologicals through biosimilar mechanisms.

Generics and biosimilars will be around in increasing numbers. It is, thus, unlikely that any drug that is being sold under patent protection and is useful clinically will not have a few generic equivalents. Many major insurers like the national health plans in Europe already ask physicians to use the generic drug whenever possible to reduce pressure on their drug budget. Thereby, expensive non-generic drugs for, say, oncological treatment could be offered to those who need them within the limited drug purchase budget.

The future of R&D
What will happen to the R&D organizations about 5-10 years from now when for many of our large disease indications there will be reasonable, efficacious, and safe generic drugs available?

This is already true for drugs that regulate high blood pressure, with 5-6 classes of drugs, such as beta blockers, ACE inhibitors, central alpha-adrenergic agonists, angiotensin-receptor blockers, and diuretics, and with each class having 5-15 members. The answer is that there will be very few new entrées like the renin inhibitor aliskiren (Novartis' Tekturna) in 2007 that was run against ACE inhibitors and was somewhat more efficacious.

It should also be noted that the area of cardiovascular medicine is far from saturated with drugs. While we treat high blood pressure reasonably well, we observe very low patient compliance. This tells all of us that these drugs are far from satisfactory if people do not take them while they know that their likelihood of suffering a stroke or heart attack is increasing dramatically when they do not control their blood pressure.

Cardiovascular medicine departments are now working on blood thinners and stroke and congestive heart failure medicines. The development of these drugs appears to be having their specific sizeable problems, yet the number of potential patients is very large. The new blood thinners are competing against generic warfarin, an efficacious but not very safe drug that requires frequent laboratory tests and often causes bleedings. The latest entries are apixaban (Pfizer-BMS's Eliquis), dabigatran (Boehringer Ingelheim's Pradaxa), and rivaroxaban (Bayer-Janssen-J&J's Xarelto), showing that the biggest companies share risk but do not give up cardiovascular medicine.

Similar to the antihypertensive agents, for depression we have five fairly successful classes of drugs to choose from, such as MAO inhibitors, tricyclic antidepressants, SSRIs, SNRIs, 5-HT1a receptor blockers, and generics in each class. While during the previous decade there were no new drugs registered, in January 2011 vilazodone (Forest's[110] Viibyrd) was approved. Will there be new antidepressant drugs developed given this saturated field? Yes. Drugs will come because there is unmet medical need on a large scale.

- We do not have any drugs that cure depression; all are symptom treatments and let the disease recur several times
- All of the approved drugs have a 50–60% response rate

None of them have so rapid an onset of therapeutic effects that they would provide effective protection against suicide in the first 7–21 days. None of the existing antidepressant drugs is without some side effects.

---

110   Vilazodone was originally developed by Merck KGaA, the part of Merck that remained in Germany after World War I. It was presented to the FDA by Clinical Data and is now marketed by Forest Laboratories. Merck KGaA is the oldest operating pharma company.

Clearly there is room for novel antidepressants that can be priced highly even when many fairly efficacious and fairly safe antidepressants are generic. In fact, an antidepressant that would be faster acting and would thus reduce suicide risk would be necessarily a first-line medication, and it would be unethical to start treatment with another one were such a drug available. Thus, even in every indication we presently can treat, there is a place for better drugs.

We are convinced that even with generic drugs present for all major indications there will be new drugs developed and approved. The new entries will reflect new scientific understanding, will use a different mechanism of action, and will mostly be second line therapy for those who failed the cheap generic and for the majority of efficacious first-line generics. How small does a nonresponding population have to be still to develop a drug for it? The answer is that the orphan drug status—unless its current 200,000 patient limit in the United States is changed—sets the most desirable small population for pharma companies.

The genetic, genomic, and companion diagnostic-provided information will continue to be cheaper than failing a trial, so the new entries will reflect better enriched patient populations with fewer failed trials, and thus a lower average development cost. Again, the degree of enrichment of a trial population works two ways: it increases responder rate and approval likelihood, but limits the use in the clinic to those who are proved to belong to the diagnostically established smaller category. Nevertheless, the trend is clear: the new proprietary drugs will have a higher responder rate and will often be approved together with their companion diagnostics.

There are still huge, unmet medical needs

In general one must say that almost all of our present drugs will become generic. Even with indications saturated with generics there are huge, unmet medical needs apparent for all to see and address in, for example, stroke, COPD, and so on. The bar, however, is higher for these new drugs, but the patients are there, and thus the market is there. Entry of new drugs into the generic-rich areas will be slower but will not stop.

Chapter 07: Why is pharma a special industry?

It would be hard to identify an industry that competes in terms of complexity and scope. It grapples with finding a safe means of preventing or easing human suffering. It is held to extremely high ethical standards. Profit alone should not and cannot determine its product choices, quality, and safety. The industry starts with high-grade raw materials and adds a tremendous amount of value. Medicines and vaccines are an extraordinarily special class of products. The products are consumed daily and globally in millions of doses for many years. There is a global market with large numbers of customers. It is controlled by national and international regulation.

Pharma is a very high-tech industry that employs the largest portion of university graduates of all large industries, that is, those that have over 1,000 employees. The confluence of many technologies has now enabled the modern drug discovery process to be broken down with many specialist tasks outsourced, primarily for cost savings. There is a very long new product development cycle of 10-12 years coupled with the potential of high risk and high return. It is relatively safe from economic cycles. Because demand is relatively stable—even the major epidemics such as influenza recur regularly—and the shelf-life of the products is mostly measured in years, demand can be usually met.

It has enjoyed historically enthusiastic stock market investors; the decline in stock prices since 2008 is the first such experience for this industry, which continues to pay medium to high dividends.

How do companies introduce novel drugs into clinical practice? The yin-yang of the industry wants to play it safe and create a new entry of known classes of drugs, yet still find a novel niche through innovation, which is inherently riskier and cannot, at the beginning, be as safe. Competition forces companies to do both: improve drugs in a class and open new markets by novel classes of drugs that treat as yet untreated

The Future of Drug Discovery. http://dx.doi.org/10.1016/B978-0-12-407180-3.00007-6

diseases or treat diseases by utilizing a novel mechanism of action, that is, being "first in class." Biotech and small pharma are under extreme pressure to be innovative as they will not be able to achieve many sales of me-too drugs when faced with superior and overwhelming marketing of Big Pharma, no matter how strongly they promote their being "best in class."

Drug discovery is the most regulated human activity

It is based on the need of humans to cure illness and reduce suffering, in combination with the strong profit motives of the investors in drug development. This huge, science-based activity of developing, marketing, and selling drugs, which patients take, now accounts for ~2% of the GDP of the developed nations and for ~14-18% of the healthcare budgets that occupy 10-16% of national budgets. No one can ignore this activity, which provides vaccines for our newborn and young, and medicines for all of us throughout our lifetimes. The dependence on drugs and new drugs is worldwide, and is increasing as our world becomes more tightly connected and new microbial diseases spread within days around the globe. The vaccines, antibacterials, and antivirals need to follow the microbes around the globe, which causes serious problems with distribution and payment within this global market. These issues are being tackled by governments and intergovernmental institutions such as the World Health Organization (WHO) "because, there is simply no other choice."

Drug development is also one of the most knowledge-based and capital-intensive human endeavors. Government and nonprofit educational and research institutes worldwide publish high-quality research for all pharma to use.

History & mergers

The discovery of drugs has been industrially organized for more than 150 years and any of the major drug companies can trace itself, or some part of itself, through consecutive mergers and acquisitions back to the mid-1800s. This industry is now in a phase of consolidation through a wave of mergers and acquisitions that mostly date back to the mid-1980s. Significant was the Roche acquisition of Syntex in 1994, and the Glaxo acquisition of Burroughs Wellcome laboratories (March 1995) and subsequently its merger with SmithKline Beecham (December 2000), itself the product of multiple mergers.[111] The resulting GlaxoSmithKline (GSK) was then one of the top five drug discovery and drug production and distribution companies.

The past years have seen other mega mergers creating several companies with over $100 billion market capitalization each (see Table 7.1). These companies spend between 11% and 22% of their income of $35-50 billion per year on research, employing worldwide over 100,000 graduates in research and development of drugs. Large industrial drug development—"Big Pharma"—is responsible for 90% of all drugs approved and presently used, with the rest discovered by biotech companies and academia. Drug development is a very slow process, with product development of 10-12 years from scientific result to approved drug first being used in clinical practice. This is only comparable to the time it takes to develop a new civilian airliner, an activity today confined to a few major entities such as Boeing, Airbus, Bombadier Aerospace, and Embraer worldwide.

Basic & translational research

The pharma industry, while maintaining its own large research (mostly translational in the past decades) and development base, heavily relies on the publication of scientific results from academic and government research institutes and laboratories. There is a strong link between government-sponsored basic research and industry-developed drugs. Without tax payer-supported research opening up drug targets and mechanisms of therapy, industry simply does not enter the area; indeed it may leave an area despite earlier successes, as it has for pain.

The governments of the Western World, China, Japan, Russia, and India maintain large government-sponsored research institutes

---

111　See also Chapter 04.

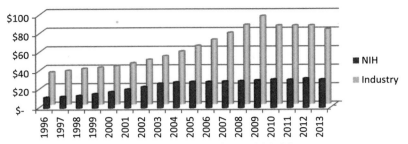

Figure 7.1: Industry's Global R&D Spending 1996-2011

The figures for industry spending are more speculative after 2009, partly because the industry appears to be less keen to reveal them. The 5% drop estimated for 2013 will probably take effect during 2012. The NIH research has become more translational research by nature (cf. 2009 NIH budget of $30.4 billion allocated mostly to preclinical basic research, but an additional $10.4 billion (not shown) was allocated to the NIH via the 2009 [Fiscal] Recovery Act). In 2011 the NIH requested budget increased from 2010's $31.1 billion to $32.1 billion. In 2012 the figure received an unexpected boost from the House of Representatives but should continue to be nearly stable at $32.0 billion instead of the requested $30.9 billion. This includes about $6 billion to cancer research across several institutes "to facilitate 30 new drug trials and double the number of therapies and vaccines in clinical trials by 2016."[1] The 2012 budget request also included a new program: NIH-The National Center for Advancing Translational Sciences (NCATS).[2] The 2013 request is $30.86 billion. Unlike many other budgets the NIH budget is often increased above the requested budget by Congress.

---

1 http://www.aacr.org/home/public--media/science-policy--government-affairs/aacr-cancer-policy-monitor/aacr-cancer-policy-monitor---february-2010/white-house-proposes-to-increase-nih-budget-by-$1-billion.aspx
2 http://officeofbudget.od.nih.gov/pdfs/FY12/Volume%201%20-%20Overview.pdf

[e.g., National Institutes of Health (NIH) in the United States, INSERM in France, Medical Research Council (MRC) in the UK, etc.] where they spend billions of dollars on research in life sciences (Figures 4.1 and 7.1). The same governments either directly sponsor universities (state universities) or, through a variety of tax breaks, encourage the existence and development of universities (private or independent universities). Today, all important universities unite research and education in life sciences. The reputation of the world's most important universities relies on their research achievements as measured in scientific prizes, research grants, and famous scientists in residence. The research grants used today by university researchers in the United States are predominantly from the government, with "extramural" programs that take ~83% of the NIH's annual budget ($31–32 billion per annum during 2010-2013). To this are added monies from private donations, industry sponsorship, and sponsorship by nongovernmental, nonprofit organizations often devoted to fighting one or a few diseases (Gates Foundation, Hereditary Disease Foundation, Alzheimer's Disease Foundation, etc.). The research grants from governments and nongovernmental organizations (NGOs) are supposed to cover the material cost of doing research and (contribute to) the salaries of researchers, postgraduates, graduates, and technicians. They may not cover them all very well, and it is common that the institutes to which the researchers belong receive a portion of the grants to cover institutional overheads.

Investors, through the stock market and in private companies, fund the pharma companies and the more risk-inclined investors invest also in biotech companies (see Tables 7.1 and 7.2).

Economic & social contribution

The pharmaceutical industry has become a very significant part of the economy and represents a *strategically important* industry. Its sales are far more stable and larger than those of the information technology industry or those of building airliners: activities with similar proportions of postgraduates employed.

The shortage of pharma products can directly threaten the stability of our society. When vaccines and antibiotics are not delivered, countries readily use an emergency designation that permits them to break intellectual property (IP)-patent protection to manufacture and distribute patent-protected drugs to head off epidemics and other medical emergencies.

The continuously reliable quality of drugs is as important as that of food, and in the United States the same agency, the Food and Drug Administration (FDA), controls both. In Europe, the European Medicines Agency (EMA)

Company	2013 market capitalization	2009 R&D budget	R&D % market cap
4. Johnson & Johnson (J&J)	$209B	$6.7B	3.5
2. Pfizer	$198B	$7.4B	4.1
1. Roche	$154B	$8.7B	5.8
3. Novartis	$138B	$7.1B	5.0
7. Merck	$125B	$5.6B	4.2
6. GlaxoSmithKline (GSK)	$112B	$6.0B	5.3
5. Sanofi-Aventis	$92B	$6.3B	5.9
XX. Bayer (Schering)	$79B	NK	NA
10. Eli Lilly	$62B	$4.1B	8.4
11. Bristol-Myers Squibb (BMS)	$61B	$3.5B	5.9
9. AstraZeneca	$59B	$4.2B	7.1
13. Abbott Laboratories	$54B	$2.6B	2.5
8. Takeda Pharmaceuticals	$30B	$4.6B	12.6
12. Boehringer Ingelheim	NA	$3.0B	NA
15. Astellas Pharma	$24B	$1.6B	7.2
14. Daiichi Sankyo	$12B	$1.9B	16.4
Totals	$1,250B	$76B	

Table 7.1: Largest pharma companies by market capitalization
The top 15 pharma companies and their market capitalization as of February 2013 (as quoted by CNBC) and R&D expenditures, after 17 years of mergers, ordered by market capitalization. Numerical ranking is by R&D expenditure. Large pharma are still trying to rein in R&D costs, especially the costs of failures.[1]

---

1   http://www.fiercebiotech.com/story/10-pharma-giants-form-nonprofit-gang-common-rd-foes/2012-09-19

	Company	2013 market capitalization	2009 R&D budget	R&D % market cap
2.	Novo	$103B	$1.65B	1.6
1.	Amgen	$65B	$2.72B	4.2
4.	Gilead Sciences	$60B	$849M	1.4
6.	Celgene	$42B	$745M	1.8
3.	Biogen Idec	$37B	$1.20B	3.3
5.	Genzyme (Sanofi)	NA	$805M	NA
10.	CSL[1]	$29B	$267M	0.9
9.	Life Technologies	$11B	$320M	2.9
8.	Vertex Pharmaceuticals	$9.7B	$454M	4.7
7.	Kyowa Hakko (Kirin)	$5.6B	$478M	8.5
11.	Amylin Pharmaceuticals (now BMS)	$5B*	$172M	3.4
13.	Cubist Pharmaceuticals	$2.8B	$119M	4.2
12.	Genmab	$900M	$123M	13.7
14.	Merial Animal Health (Sanofi)	NA	$115M	NA
15.	MannKind (NFP)	$611M	$109M	17.8
	Totals	$331B+	$10B	3.0%

Table 7.2: Largest biotechs by market capitalization
Ordered by market capitalization as quoted by Bloomberg.com on 31 January 2013 (except Amylin, which was from CNBC, August 2012). Numerical ranking is by 2009 R&D expenditure. Some market capitalization numbers are not available since the companies have been acquired. Revenues grew overall in 2011 and investment in R&D increased for 2012, but sometimes with generally fewer employees for smaller companies.[2]

1 Originally, Commonwealth Serum Laboratories, privatized in 1994.
2 http://www.fiercebiotech.com/story/bdo-biotech-rd-spending-hiring-rebounds-revenue-climbs-big-companies/2012-09-25 and http://www.fiercebiotech.com/press-releases/biotech-industry-rd-spending-jumps-five-percent-2011-bdo-study-finds

is a separate agency devoted to regulation of drug registration and the post-marketing follow-up of side effects and mortality from the use of drugs. These interventional arrangements by governments already clearly show that we place great importance on drug supply and drug quality in each country and internationally through organizations such as WHO. The cooperation between the regulatory agencies is increasing and it is clear that, for example, the EMA cannot ignore a 14-0 "No" vote by the FDA's expert panel for any drug, even if the EMA had earlier approved it.[112] It rapidly withdrew the European approval. The lessons also spread in both directions across the Atlantic, when the UK's NICE found that Roche's Avastin[113] is without effect in metastatic breast cancer patients; soon, the FDA came to a similar conclusion.

Governmental nonintervention & intervention

Where governments have not intervened, companies choose which diseases to treat and which drugs to develop. We argue that government intervention may now have become necessary.

Government intervention is clear and necessary in certain other cases, such as the steering of vaccine development and purchasing guarantees to meet expected epidemics. Examples include the purchase of millions of doses of the neuraminidase inhibitors Tamiflu (Roche) and Relenza (GSK) for swine and bird flu outbreaks, and the ordering of manufacturing and stockpiling of the antibiotic ciprofloxacin in response to the anthrax scare, thus demonstrating that governments can be more active although they own no drug companies in North America and Europe.

An intermediate position of intervention was taken by the U.S. government at the height of the HIV epidemics in the mid-1990s in Africa, when the government pressured the companies BMS, Merck, GSK, and Roche. They had developed HIV drugs for the wealthy, high-priced U.S.

---

112 See Chapter 11 for details, but rimonabant (Acomplia from Sanofi) was found to promote suicide ideation, which would, sooner or later, result in suicide in some patients and an unacceptable risk profile for an obesity drug. The FDA's expert panel's non-approval caused the EMA to reverse its prior approval.
113 See Chapters 10 and 11.

and European markets. The government intervened to "encourage" them to provide these drugs more cheaply to African patients through purchases by NGOs. The development of the HIV drugs had happened very fast compared to historical precedents. This was a result of pressure from patient advocacy groups and government-sponsored large-scale research in Europe and the United States. It has been a successful drug-development enterprise, with several effective drugs that slow disease progression, although none cure the disease. While we await an HIV vaccine, which will bring its own medical and ethical problems, such as whom to vaccinate, what risks to accept, and so forth, the deadly epidemics of HIV have been turned around. Adequate drug treatment, as long as it is available, can turn a deadly disease into a manageable chronic disease. It is a clear triumph of modern drug discovery, government-sponsored basic research, public advocacy and lobbying, and the industry's ability to capitalize on the knowledge generated by scientists. In this case, even though it is an infectious disease, governments did not directly suggest to industry that they work on HIV medicines; indeed, relatively few companies started, namely Roche, GSK, and BMS, and hungry biotechs, when grants specifically for HIV drug development were given. In July 2012, Truvada (a mixture of tenofovir and emtricitabine) from Gilead was approved in the United States for reducing the risk of HIV infection, that is, as a preventive medicine. Thus, we are clearly continuing to make progress vis-à-vis this viral disease caused by a rapidly mutating virus.

Crisis, what crisis? Tail wagging the dog?

The pharmaceutical industry has been an outstanding investment opportunity producing double-digit growth and double-digit profits for three decades. Revenue growth has been fairly resistant to economic cycles, because much of the sales often come from long-term or chronically ill patients' needs in more and more countries and markets. The issues the industry faces in this so-called "pharma crisis" have little to do with the great recession of 2008, other than that the cost of borrowing for acquisitions and mergers has skyrocketed.

The pharma crisis refers to the poor performance over the last 3-4 years of having new blockbuster drugs approved to replace blockbuster drug sales, when those drugs lose patent protection and when the generic pressure will cut the income of these significantly.[114] Only eight new blockbusters were probably approved between 2008 and 2012. For small molecule-type blockbusters the drop of earnings can be dramatic, as the pressure from generics can bring down the price by 60-70% and the sales may fall by 90%, because the generic producers will be so much cheaper as the competition between generic companies is growing. For biologicals, the biosimilars have not yet caused a similar drop; not all biological prices have fallen after the patent protection disappeared. Nevertheless, investors saw stock prices fall, albeit much less than in other industries in 2007-2008. Pharma managements, regulatory figures, and investors alike talk of a "crisis." This talk is forcing the managements to cut R&D expenditures by tens of thousands of jobs and billions of dollars. The industry is moving R&D spending from 18-22% to 14-15% of income. Analysts punish those companies who do not follow the industry lead in making cuts. The short-term needs of Wall Street and investors have adversely affected the future of drug development, as well as costing thousands of talented researchers their jobs.

One cannot deny that the cost per approved drug has increased steadily in the last 20 years; nor can one deny that not all problems of drug discovery are solved by throwing money at them. These are legitimate points of view of investors and analysts. What this does not take into account is that the bar for new blockbusters has been raised because of the prior success of pharma in controlling, for example, blood pressure, high blood glucose, high cholesterol, allergic reactions, and heartburn, that is, the large diseases. It also does not take into account that there are therapeutic areas of huge medical need left such as slowing Alzheimer's disease (AD) progression, or even preventing AD, treating COPD, alleviating neuropathic pain, and making safe and effective antipsychotics. Yet

---

114   As discussed in Chapter 06.

pharma leaves these needs unmet and reduces its efforts. It continues to fund drug development in oncology and diabetes, the former to build on its profits from the past 15 years, and the latter a growing epidemic at least partly because of obesity. Yet, neither is an unserved medical need compared to AD and neuropathic pain. The disagreement and argument we have with the present choices pharma makes is not what is pursued, but what is abandoned without attention to society's long-term needs. Pharma collectively has an effective monopoly on drug development. There are not any other credible actors for developing drugs for these large diseases when trials will cost $500 million to $1.5 billion. It would be more acceptable that pharma crowds the therapeutic areas where easier money is forecast, if it were investing in difficult areas as well.

The cuts in R&D reflect that the product development cycle is ~10-12 years, while the average pharma CEO, who no longer has a scientific or medical degree but now has a financial education, sits only 5-7 years as top manager. There is thus a serious disconnect between what it takes to make a new drug and the basis of their remuneration. This is a dangerous situation. As has been discussed for bankers in the years since 2008, society needs to come up with remuneration models that make pharmaceutical company managers the beneficiaries of a successful medicine that comes after their tenure has ended. They should be part of a future successful product to make them more responsible and responsive about the long-term future of the company that includes and is based upon R&D in its present model.

Academia-industry collaborations

Society via government funding has already taken over most of the basic research and acknowledged that the time lines no longer permit pharma to engage in nor pay for original basic research. Figure 4.1 shows how the spending by pharma on basic research (not on clinical and translational research) from about 1970 has been continuously falling, while the total spending by governments on basic research in life sciences and chemistry has grown nationally and globally, providing more raw data as the basis for drug development.

Pharma is re-adjusting its business development model in other ways. Pharma companies are establishing academic collaborations, but try to direct them toward clinical collaborations that have a faster effect on drug pipelines and approvals. These collaborations have mixed effects on both parties and the ideal forms have not been found and maybe never will, but it is clear that the collaborations initially appear attractive to both sides. In the past 20 years, collaborations have also been encouraged by the governments, which at first wondered whether it is right that government-sponsored basic research at universities should often also benefit foreign pharma companies. They now see that both the industry and research results are global, although research spending is national.[115] The industry and academic researchers often come from the same university, even from the same laboratory, yet their goals and even their language diverges rapidly, and understanding each other is a far from trivial problem. Some might convincingly argue that the presence of pharma's different goals perverts the academic research.

Academic researchers often cannot, or do not want to, adopt the pharma company's acronyms and hand-offs of the R&D project processes. By the time they learn the terminology and process flow in the collaborating company, this company disappears in a merger and will change all of these forms.

The industrial researcher's success is well quantified by the numbers of drug-development projects that have been leaving their laboratories to advance to the next stage. If they have been in the industry for 15-20 years they may have even been part of the development of a drug that is being used in the clinic. When industry researchers are looking for a new job, they refer to the number of patents they are listed on as inventors. The industry has a harder time appreciating the results that underlie academic promotions. The publication policies drive the university researchers to "publish or perish," while the patent policies

---

115   In Europe, some funding comes from the European Union and is restricted to member countries.

of the companies hold back the industrial researcher from publishing and thus prevent their work from becoming widely known.[116] In fact, almost all publications from Big Pharma are taken by competitors to mean that the project has been dropped. Only the phase 2 data disclosure does not necessarily mean this because companies, whether big or small, publish positive phase 2 data. Small companies want the clinicians who carried out the phase 2 trial to publish and speak about the results at congresses, and so forth, because they need to raise investor confidence and contributions so that they can continue with the project. Large companies have no choice but to allow important clinicians and their younger associates to publish the phase 2 data because they demand it; the younger associates need the publications and cannot wait. Companies do not usually want negative phase 2 data to be published for a variety of reasons, but mostly because it is already yesterday's news. Society would, however, benefit if negative data were also published, but the players—companies, authors, and publications—do not really like spending time and resources on it.

These different cultures of desire, need, and problems disseminating the results of collaboration, including the university having to prepare press releases on small and big breakthroughs, often result in tensions about publications. The academic partner wants and needs them and the industry partner delays and blocks them as much as possible within the contract. The idea of what represents a tangible result of value is also fundamentally different in academia and industry. A "publishable finding" is the result the academic researchers want, while the industry researcher needs a more tangible result. They need something that establishes, or dispels, the therapeutic value of a biological mechanism or target—so-called "proof of concept" or "proof of mechanism"—or establishes the use of a molecule, a putative drug, as a therapeutic tool. The time and money spent in industry between understanding a mechanism, or discovery of a drug target, and finding the proper molecule from millions screened

---

116 This is a significant problem if and when they seek to find a new position; they often cannot point to what it is they have done, and what can be clearly assigned to them even from a successful project that led to a drug.

and tens of thousands synthesized, covers a period of 10 years and up to several hundred million dollars. This is completely outside of the range of academic researchers' metrics, which measure time in grants' or PhD theses' durations, that is, 2-5 years. Their basic research funding is measured in stipends of $50,000 or basic project grants of $200,000–250,000 in the United States and of $100,000 in Japan and Europe, or sometimes multiples of these, while the industry knows that it will have spent $5-25 million to obtain phase 2 data.

Because of these differences, the open-ended collaborations, where the industry pays a few million dollars per year to a university to have first right of refusal to results produced, often end with mutual disappointments, and this form of cooperation is losing its popularity. The Scripps Research Institute, for example, had such agreements consecutively with J&J, Novartis, and, presently, with Pfizer. The success depends on whether the industry invests the time of good researchers into understanding and extrapolating early findings, described in early disclosures. The team-leading industry researchers are busy transferring their work into the clinic, and it falls upon their colleagues to follow the academic collaboration, and these colleagues may not have sufficient "pull" in their own organization. The industry people are too busy to dig deeply into the academic work, which is, somewhat perversely, often hard to recognize as a basis for therapeutics when it is truly original and new. The industry researchers know well what to watch for once they have heard of similar results in meetings or from journals, but by then it is not truly groundbreaking or original, although it still may be very useful. They often miss the really new pieces of knowledge that could have given their industry a year or more's competitive advantage.

There are no good mechanisms in place to acknowledge those in industry who take seriously the academic collaboration. Most people who are responsible for the interactions give the academic manuscripts just a cursory read and often miss the most promising, truly original, and often unexpected results. The academic researchers often contribute to this willfully. Some of them do not want the industry to engage fully and write patent applications based on their results because these take a lot of time and delay dissemination of results.[117] The academic researcher will indubitably be bombarded by industry people, who are not similarly trained and may not quickly appreciate the details, about what is needed for the patent. To the academic, it seems endless and they will almost never derive any money from it, as it may take 10-15 more years to develop the drug, and the portion of intellectual contribution of the academic lab is by then dwarfed by what the industry researchers have done. So the academic researcher, even if she or he had years of grants from the industry, wants the industry people to pass and permit rapid publication. A small group of academic researchers has an additional motive not to want much industry interest in their work; they want to start a biotech company, which, when the financial climate is good, is clearly going to make them richer in the event of success than the industry collaboration with their university. Thus, their descriptions of the results are often opaque, making the industry researchers search harder for patentable new data. In most university-industry contracts, the scientist is free to find outside funding from, for example, venture capitalists once the contracted large pharma industry has passed.

The academia-industry collaborations have a far better chance to be meaningful when a very concrete aspect of the drug candidate is being investigated in a "work for hire" manner by some very specialized academic laboratory. In these collaborations the expected results are clear and they, in a concrete manner, stop or forward the development of a drug or a class of molecules. Help by academic chemists to solve complicated synthetic problems once the medicinal chemist in the industry knows the structure they want synthesized is provided in the best-functioning collaborations. Industry-academic collaborations are, in summary, moderately helpful with the early, preclinical stages of drug development.

---

117   There is an inherent danger of being scooped academically if data are not disseminated without delay.

Now the industry is also trying to engage clinical research centers: the deals between Harvard Medical School and Merck in 2007 and University of California, San Francisco (UCSF)[118] and Pfizer in 2010 are good examples. The idea behind the UCSF–Pfizer agreement is that for new drugs we need observations made at the bedside. This is true; hence, the drive in the United States to educate MD PhD students in the past 30 years. These will be practicing doctors with a research background who may be better suited for recognizing and defining clinical findings that may be used to establish new therapies or therapeutic agents. How these will work out is too early to say. Certainly, the access to patient samples enhances the search by the industry for biomarkers that will be used in diagnosis and in the following of treatment using a new drug. The human pathological samples may permit *in vitro* testing of the drug candidate.[119]

Gaps in Big Pharma's research revisited
As discussed in earlier chapters, the industry in the past 3 years has decided to cut whole therapeutic areas and many diseases from its list of those to be addressed by drugs. In the remaining crowded areas, new strategies are used. As also discussed in Chapter 06, the major companies are evenly matched in terms of talent and technical and financial resources; thus, exclusivity of a new class of drugs in, for example, type 2 diabetes will not last longer than 6–12 months. The industry now focuses on producing best in class drugs and each major company has specific groups that follow in detail all public and nonpublic pieces of data from the clinical trials of the competitors to find or engineer into their drug candidate any property that may positively differentiate it from the drugs of the competitors in order to make their drug best in class. Almost no one speaks about aiming to make a first in class drug (the only thing of interest to the academic

---

118   See   http://www.ucsf.edu/news/2010/11/5826/ucsf-partners-pfizer-improve-drug-discovery-development
119   The industry is using more and more human cells derived from human stem cells to test its drugs so this dependence for human samples is becoming lighter on clinicians.

collaborator), which used to be the pride of companies like Merck, Roche, and so forth, 15-20 years ago.

As the EMA and FDA are not restricting the number of me-too drugs they might approve, marketing departments have to decide when is it no longer worth the effort to sell a drug that is number 5 or number 7 in its class if it has certain differentiating properties. Before reaching the marketers, the clinical trial organizers may discover that it is hard to recruit patients simply because there are too many trials ongoing for diseases popular with the industry: they are not popular with the patients. This is especially the case in large diseases such as RA, MS, type 2 diabetes, and so forth, and contract research organizations (CROs) are moving to the Ukraine, Russia, India, and so on.

Plugging the gaps in Big Pharma's research

How will the gaps be filled in the areas that Big Pharma has now dropped, such as neuropathic pain, stroke, and schizophrenia? And who will fill them?

The discussions are ongoing about several models.[120]

In an earlier period, 1985-2005, if there were biologicals that could be used to treat the disease then owing to their faster development, and to the higher ease of finding a biological molecule than an optimized small molecule, biotechs stepped into the void. They brought molecules forward for signs of efficacy in phase 2 trials. If the phase 3 trial design for the indication was not too large, they could take the candidates all the way to a NDA.[121] This is becoming less likely in the present situation as we have already plucked much of the low-hanging fruit. The likelihood of using biologicals in brain disorders, where the drug has to pass the blood-brain barrier, is low,[122] unless some new, safe, and fast way to introduce them into the brain is found. One must, however, add that some biologicals are active in diseases of the brain. For example,

---

120 See also later chapters, especially Chapter 12.
121 New Drug Application, as presented to the FDA in the United States.
122 It is not zero, as evinced by the antibody therapies in trials for AD.

therapeutic antibodies that bind Abeta amyloid peptide are now among the most promising drugs to slow disease progression in AD.[123] These antibodies reach the cerebrospinal fluid and there bind the peptide and "pull it" out of the brain. Postmortem studies of some patients who died while being treated with these antibodies exhibited antibodies in the brain tissue. Many of the indications that are underserved are large indications and thus the trials may be large and of long duration. The costs become prohibitive for biotechs. Pain and schizophrenia trials would cover billion dollar indications and are neither very large nor long; it is the very high failure rate that keeps big and small companies away from those trials.

We need to therefore address these questions of funding clinical trials for promising molecules even if Big Pharma presently finds these diseases not to be profitable markets. There are several government-sponsored clinical trial mechanisms in schizophrenia that are useful and promising, for example, TURNS.[124]

Regulation & politics

A politician in California told us that medical care already costs as much as it possibly can and "most of us live long enough and most of us have reasonable pain relief when needed." Thus, perhaps for political reasons, we should wait with any new drug that pharma does not bring forth until some major scientific paradigm shift reduces the risk of developing drugs such that pharma re-enters the area.

We do not quite believe that it is the nature of mankind not to use scientific knowledge immediately to cure diseases or treat their symptoms, or to develop new weapons, and we suspect that this politician will legislate for increased research should a disease strike close to him.

---

123   This is, of course, tempered by the August 2012 news that Lilly's solanezumab failed to show a significant improvement in both cognition and function (see Chapter 06).
124   http://www.turns.ucla.edu/

The roles played by the regulatory agencies are not discussed in detail herein. They do fulfill the most important role they were assigned: they are guarding patient safety, and they do it well. There are many problems in how all of this is organized and it is not sustainable in the long run that the people in the EMA and FDA, who are to regulate similarly educated colleagues in industry, earn one-fourth to one-tenth of what their colleagues earn in industry. It is also dangerous and wrong that pharma companies directly finance the FDA through their fees, rather than through taxes or other mechanisms with insulating layers between regulator and regulated. Many highly experienced FDA employees then end up in industry and earn in a few years what they had made in a "lifetime" of public service. They also improve adherence to regulatory requirements.

The "response letter" of the FDA to NDAs can affect small companies whose whole existence depends on the approval and subsequent success of this single drug, and which may not have the financial means to carry out the FDA-requested additional trials. The FDA response to NDAs can delay and even kill a new drug candidate. Yet, until now, developers have had complete discretion to release all or none of the FDA's concerns outlined in its "complete response letters." Currently, companies can put whatever spin they see fit on the FDA letter and this is not good for the public, investors, or competitors. The head of the agency's new drugs office, John Jenkins, said in 2011 that 7 out of 10 NDAs lack critical information. The regulators are now moving to disclose their complete findings about drug candidates; they do not want to leave it to the discretion of the drug developer. While Jenkins might agree that publishing the letters could go a long way to avoiding future pitfalls by developers, as a matter of law, the FDA is obliged to keep communications about unapproved drugs confidential. The FDA task force also called for the agency to report whenever a drug application is placed on hold, terminated, or withdrawn.[125]

---

125   At the end of this chapter we reference a contemporary report about the release of the FDA's complete response letters from *FierceBiotech*.

Clinical trials

The clinical trials are the most important, the most ethically sensitive, and the most expensive part of drug development, yet these receive relatively little attention, considering how central they are for establishing new drugs. To deal with the ebbs and flows of internal drug development projects, major pharma uses CROs to conduct trials. They can cover multiple sites in multiple countries, obtain ethical committee permissions, enroll doctors and patients, collect samples, analyze efficacy and side effects, and prepare documentation for NDAs. Large CROs such as Quintiles, Parexel, and so forth, have been hugely profitable as they have none of the drug development risk: they are paid whether the drug fails or not. They experienced, however, a reduction of projects from Big Pharma and thus decided to become sponsors of smaller companies to ensure a flow of clinical trials and to participate in the success of a drug. While the CROs have focused on the deal flow, the design of clinical studies in some areas is poor. In the past, there has been a wave of publications to detail the shortcomings of clinical trials and these could be easily fixed and often would not cost much more. It is a huge ethical and economic problem.

The large government-sponsored trials that promote "evidence-based medicine" are important examples of well-conducted, well-powered trials to answer important questions about new and old drugs and they influence the clinical trial industry positively.[126]

The discussions about the special place that the pharma industry and healthcare have in our society are escalating, as we need to put some brakes on spending for healthcare at the same time that our population in developed countries is aging; age is one of the most important risk factors for many diseases. The ethical aspects of the industry and its clinical trials are being clearly followed and improving as a result. A contentious area of discussion is when and how to publish the results of

---

126 At the end of this chapter we reference a contemporary Institute of Medicine (IOM) report about how such trials need to be improved and more efficiently implemented. See also Chapters 01, 03, and 11.

failed clinical trials. These trials have included human sacrifice and risk by taking healthy volunteers and subsequently patients. The majority of clinical trials fail and we hear all about how expensive this is, but the community outside the sponsoring company are not learning from the results. The corporate argument is that it would help the competition if the data on failed trials were disclosed; they do not let others see the data. While in an economic sense they are right, certainly for a short time period the data would help the development of new drugs and some mechanism must be found whereby these data are distributed. There are many reasons for this.

Firstly, other teams working on similar drugs may endanger human volunteers, without whose sacrifice no drug developments would be possible. If the first company already knows that it is dangerous to touch this particular mechanism or protein, it should make it public. The FDA and EMA can and do, of course, now warn the other companies as they approve and register all ongoing trials. The companies thus see when a subsequent trial design is going to repeat a dangerous exposure, already known from the first company's results, although broad publicity would be better.

Secondly, when the broader scientific community—not only the few experts called in by the company to save the drug—look at the data, there may be people no one thought to ask, who understand why the drug failed and could suggest ways to resurrect this drug or how to make better drugs to the same drug target.

Thirdly, the canceling of a trial without explanation may put off other companies working on the same drug target when in fact the target choice may not have been the reason for termination of the trial; instead, there was a problem with the given molecule selected by the first company, that is, the mechanism is fine but a better molecule is needed to utilize this mechanism. Most Big Pharma have a backup molecule as insurance, and would still aim to be first. Thus they are still not interested in disclosing their data so as not to assist competition. Meanwhile, the competing companies have combed the patents of the first company and have synthesized similar compounds to those that they believe have been put into the clinical trial. These competitor compounds are then run in the same animal experiments before possibly entering into a clinical trial.

Much of the industry opposed the clinical trials register,[127] which they now look up thousands of times a day and quote in every internal presentation. There is no better way to observe the competition and to learn about their trial designs: how long a treatment and how many patients they think they need to show efficacy. The answers are in the trial registry and to the experienced statistician and trial designer these numbers also tell how many responders and how large a response the company conducting the trial expects.

The changes in FDA and EMA stances on long-term benefit-risk ratio for obesity and type 2 diabetes drugs in particular, which is discussed more fully in Chapter 11, are contributing strongly to improve the quality of drugs and making pharma a more ethical industry, sometimes against its short-term will.

Although the products of the pharmaceutical industry are so essential to our society and they can be so dangerous, it is one of the industries that does not give a guarantee to its products. These thoughts are discussed in Chapter 09 in the section "The 'hair-dryer' & 'toaster' drugs."

IOM report on National Cancer Institute clinical studies[128]
The system used to conduct cancer clinical trials in the United States is "approaching a state of crisis," with waste and inefficiency creating difficulties for those wanting to undertake these studies, an IOM report has found.

The National Cancer Institute (NCI) supports a network of clinical studies. The largest component of this group is the Clinical Trials Cooperative Group Program. For 50 years, the program has played a

---

127   See clinicaltrials.gov in the United States, although there are several other national or regional sites.
128   Hollis LJ (2010) Report: U.S. cancer trials are in a state of crisis, *FierceBiotech*, April 16, http://www.fiercebiotech.com/story/report-u-s-cancer-trials-are-state-crisis/2010-04-16 Link to report: http://books.nap.edu/openbook.php?record_id=12879.

key role in testing promising therapies. And while it has made many important discoveries over the years, multiple layers of oversight have made the system "inefficient and cumbersome." According to the IOM's report, the average time it takes to design, approve, and activate a clinical trial is two years, and only half of the trials undertaken are completed.

Stagnant and declining funding, inefficient processes, extensive and complex government oversight, and a lack of resources, "have contributed to the program's difficulties in translating research into "timely clinical applications," according to the report. Recognizing that there is a problem, NCI Director John Niederhuber asked the IOM to come up with recommendations to improve the system.

IOM says the following goals should guide the improvements to the current system: enhancing the speed and efficiency of the design, launch, and conduct of clinical trials; making optimal use of scientific innovations; improving selection, prioritization, support, and completion of clinical trials; and fostering expanded participation of both patients and physicians.

FDA proposes release of complete response letters[129]

After a long-simmering controversy over regulatory transparency, an FDA task force has proposed releasing its complete response letters to drug developers as part of a wide-ranging plan to let the sun shine in on safety issues, plant inspections, and the agency's specific reasons for rejecting a new drug application.

BIO has yet to respond to the set of 21 proposals assembled by an FDA task force headed by FDA Principal Deputy Commissioner

---

129 Carroll J (2010) FDA proposes controversial release of complete response letters, *FierceBiotech*, May 20, http://www.fiercebiotech.com/story/fda-proposes-controversial-release-complete-response-letters/2010-05-20#ixzz20un9qyUK.

Joshua Sharfstein. Despite some deep-seated reluctance on the part of developers, the movement toward opening up has been gaining steam for years as controversies erupted over the dangers presented by marketed drugs such as Vioxx.

Currently, developers have complete discretion to release all or none of the FDA's concerns outlined in its complete response letters, documents that can delay and even kill a new therapeutic. And on more than one occasion developers have been harshly criticized for spinning the contents in their favor. The head of the agency's new drugs office, John Jenkins, said a few months ago that 7 out of 10 NDAs lack critical information. "Publishing the letters could go a long way to avoiding future pratfalls by developers," Jenkins said. The FDA task force also called for the agency to open up any time a drug application is placed on hold, terminated, or withdrawn.

"We should have done this a long time ago," Scott Gottlieb, a fellow at the American Enterprise Institute and FDA deputy commissioner for medical and scientific affairs during the Bush administration. "The public deserves to see the agency's explanations for its decisions."

"Investors are frustrated because very often you have companies that like to spin what is in those complete response letters, and there's no way to know what's really in them," Capitol Street analyst Ipsita Smolinski told Reuters. This way, "there's no question. Everybody has access to the same information."

Chapter 08: Diagnosing toward personalized medicine

"Without diagnostics there can be no treatment; without available treatment, we need not diagnose"[130]

Everyone knows how difficult it is to diagnose small children and adults who might be unable[131] to self-report their symptoms. Otherwise, humans are obviously a self-reporting species. They speak of their health and of its failings. They can direct medical attention to areas where pathological change, loss of function, pain, and so forth, is apparent to them. Sometimes the real site of the origin of the disease state is elsewhere, but the patient is clearly attempting to point the physician toward some direction; it is in their interest. However, some patients are frequently unable or unwilling to describe exactly or truthfully how they acquired an injury or a disease. Oftentimes they report to the physician some secondary and tertiary explanations for their real underlying symptoms. Objective diagnosis, based on one or several laboratory tests, imaging, or measurement of other standardized and quantitative parameter(s), is preferred but not yet always possible.

Thus, diagnosis is the basis of whether and how to treat. As such it has expanded in its significance dramatically in the past 30 years, parallel with the expansion of treatment options for many diseases, because of the large progress in developing diagnostic markers for diseases.

The expansion of diagnostic modalities—the increase in the number of different diagnostic tests that can inform about different aspects of the disease, its progression, or of the effects of the treatment—has been serving as an important basis for the increase in medical interventions by drug treatment, surgery, devices, or radiation, and

---

130 A maxim with which all may not agree.
131 Because of stroke, coma, dementia, and so forth, or simply by being too young.

The Future of Drug Discovery. http://dx.doi.org/10.1016/B978-0-12-407180-3.00008-8

so on. There is a lot of discussion about whether there are too many diagnostic tests that are ordered by physicians. Underpinning this is the physicians' fear that they will be criticized, sued, and/or punished for missing something because of not performing or asking for all feasible tests. In the United States, it is estimated that physicians carry out 30-50% more tests than what would be necessary to set a specific diagnosis and enable treatment selection. In other countries, such as the UK, Sweden, and Germany, an insufficient number of tests may be performed. Yet, there is no one who disagrees with the assertion that early, correct diagnosis saves huge amounts of human suffering. The costs of treatment and the treatment time may both be curtailed dramatically. Treatment outcome may be grossly improved by correct and early diagnosis; one only has to compare outcomes between early discovered cancer and later diagnosis. The steady introduction of new diagnostic tests, their pricing, and the ever-growing extent of their use is driven by recognition of this.

Growth of diagnostics

The diagnostics market sales grow at a healthy 5-6% per annum even during the present economical crisis. Part of this growth is that we now test new patient groups in Asia and Africa, but most of the increase is based on the introduction and use of novel tests.

The diagnostic market has grown almost twice as fast as the pharmaceutical market and it has also been much more consolidated. There are three large, dominant players and they collaborate with and acquire the hundreds of smaller players. The "big three" are Abbott, Roche, and Siemens (incorporating Bayer Diagnostics and Dade Behring, etc.). In imaging, the big players are Siemens, General Electric, and Philips, just like in medical instrumentation, and there are many Asian and Israeli competitors. Many larger diagnostic areas, such as digital microscopy, sequencing of the human genome in patients and their tumors, and protein fingerprinting of tumors, are being developed and pushed by several smaller companies awaiting acquisition by the big ones

	2009	**% of Sales**
Pharmaceuticals	8,896 mCHF[1]	22.8
Diagnostics	978 mCHF	9.7

Table 8.1: Roche divisional R&D expenditures
Roche is the largest diagnostics company. It spends on R&D in the faster expanding DX market only 9.7% of the sales, compared to 22.8% in pharmaceuticals. These amounts suffice to outspend its rivals according to the company.

---

1   In millions of Swiss Francs; at the time of writing, 1 CHF = US $1.022 or 0.833€.

(cf. Roche's $5.7 billion unsuccessful spring 2012 bid for the San Diego sequencing company Illumina[132]; see Table 8.1).

In vitro diagnostics (IVD) uses body fluids (blood, urine, or saliva) or tissue samples to determine the presence of a given ion, molecule/ metabolite, peptide hormone, protein, nucleic acid, viral particle, and so forth, and its concentration. Each patient sample is handled in a most industrial manner: automatically, rapidly, impartially, with a minimum of human intervention. Samples are rigorously marked and identified multiple times by the different test machines, because no diagnostic laboratory that mixes up patient samples can survive. Although we all take it for granted, the big issues are in the large hospital laboratories, with the introduction of ever more sensitive tests that will measure a few copies of a novel virus in a very small blood sample. The key to the success of a clinical diagnostic laboratory is reliability, speed, small test volume, and low price, in that order. There are plenty of commercial outfits such as LabCorp[133] (owned by Roche) that compete with the in-house hospital laboratories; they can be better on several or all of these parameters. It is only cases such as the acute following of a myocardial infarct patient, or a sepsis patient, where turnaround times from collecting the samples

---

132   It was reported in January 2013, that according to Roche the deal was off the table and Illumina shares fell. See http://www.bloomberg.com/news/2013-01-07/roche-comments-may-mean-no-illumina-deal-in-near-term.html
133   Laboratory Corporation of America Holdings.

to delivering results must be below an hour, where the hospital laboratory has a huge advantage compared to central large laboratories.

Point of care measurement of metrics such as blood glucose, blood pressure, and coagulation time measurements by the patients themselves, or at least at their bedside or kitchen table, will also remain and are expected to grow.

The biggest issues concern the identity and handling of the samples that are to be divided into dozens and dozens of smaller volumes for the different tests. The results of each test should end up on the same document that connects them to the patient. The time of collecting the sample should also be recorded, especially since for the same patient many samples may be under analysis in the same laboratory as the state of the patient may be rapidly and dramatically changing and new samples are drawn.

Why is the diagnostics industry becoming so important for the pharmaceutical industry?

Diagnosis is the entry to selection of drug treatment. If all drugs were very cheap and without side effects, and delays in treatment did not matter, then, and only then, would diagnostics be less important. We all know that we want the right treatment selected and administered as soon as possible, and we want the drug that will be efficacious, while causing the least number of side effects, and also that our insurers want the cheapest, fastest, and correct treatment, in that order.

Biomarkers

Biomarkers, that is, metabolites, hormones, proteins, or protein fragments, whose concentration in body fluids changes as a result of the disease and of treatment, are increasingly used in the development of the drugs and tested and validated during the clinical trials. The Food and Drug Administration (FDA) suggests that the use of biomarkers may cut drug development time by several years and reduce failure rate in drug development by up to 10%.

In the early phase of drug development, changes in biomarkers serve as the "proof of concept" measure for the effectiveness of a new drug and show that the drug has a therapeutic window that permits using doses that can cause meaningful therapeutic effects. When these biomarker changes are ascertained upon realistic dosing of the drug, the pharma company's confidence in the mechanism of action and in the particular drug molecule increases to the level that decisions about seriously costly clinical development and investments of $100 million to $1 billion will be made. Thus, the increasing importance of biomarkers for drug development is easy to understand.

In oncology, biomarkers are often mutated genes and their mutated protein products, which might be monitored using sequencing, polymerase chain reaction (PCR), and microarrays, and by *in situ* hybridization and immunohistochemistry using antibodies that distinguish the mutated and native proteins. Imaging of biopsies is also used to follow the success of the drug treatment and to confirm dosing and treatment duration.

Targeted cancer therapies

The past years have seen the introduction of focused or targeted therapies into oncology. These therapies were first exemplified by trastuzumab (Genentech's Herceptin), a therapeutic antibody used in the treatment of breast cancer in patients with mutation in the HER2+[134] gene. The mutation first has to be shown in the biopsies, using fluorescence *in situ* hybridization (FISH), before treatment can be recommended or agreed to, according to FDA guidelines, and reimbursed, according to insurer guidelines. Herceptin's response rate for those that can be treated is close to 60%.

Thus targeted therapies, as opposed to generic chemotherapies that kill all dividing cells, among them the cancer cells, but also all hair follicle cells, and so forth, became sought after. The recent 2011 approvals by the FDA include two targeted therapies, with their companion diagnostics:

---

134   *Human Epidermal* growth factor *Receptor* 2-positive.

one for treatment of melanoma with a *BRAF*[135] mutation; and one for treatment of non-small cell lung cancer (NSCLC), with an ALK[136] mutation. The pharma industry had to be able to develop inhibitors for the two enzymes B-Raf and ALK, which recognize the mutated forms of the enzymes and thus inhibit it in the tumor cells. The companion diagnostics help to stratify patients and thus the response rate for these two cancer drugs is the sensational 60% or higher, whereas earlier melanoma and NSCLC therapies had 5–10% response rates. Unfortunately this remains the response rate for those patients not carrying these particular mutations.

Other examples of new targeted therapies on the market include imatinib (Novartis' Gleevec) for chronic myelogenous leukemia (CML), cetuximab (Merck's Erbitux) for metastatic colorectal cancer and head and neck cancer; gefitinib (AstraZeneca-Teva's Iressa) for certain breast, lung, and other cancers;[137] and panitumumab[138] (Abgenix-Amgen's Vectibix) for metastatic cancer of the colon or rectum.

The main genetic changes giving rise to cell transformation, and thus cancer, are mutations in oncogenes, genes encoding tumor suppressors, DNA repair genes, and the recently discovered microRNAs (miRNAs). Mutations in oncogenes are the easiest to treat using antagonists. It is expected that the number of targeted therapies in oncology will increase. There are over 20 drug candidates in development that target mutated forms of proteins. Not all of these will have a robust effect and not all of them will be safe, yet an entry of several new targeted therapies is expected and this is an important advance in response rate and in outcome. Although they are small molecules, the pricing of these drugs is, however, often in line with the prices of therapeutic antibodies at $20,000–75,000 per year. The argument is that the therapeutic window of these drugs is

---

135 *BRAF* encodes the protein B-Raf, a serine/threonine-specific protein kinase that is involved in cell growth.
136 Anaplastic lymphoma kinase.
137 Although the FDA approval for NSCLC was withdrawn for new patients in 2005, after its initial approval in 2003, because it could not be shown to extend life. It is used for NSCLC in Europe for patients with epidermal growth factor receptor (EGFR) mutations.
138 Approved by the FDA in 2006 and the EMA in 2007.

as good as those of therapeutic antibodies, that is, they are very selective and relatively nontoxic. The somewhat ironic and macabre longer term view is that these drugs, when successful, save lives and that thereafter patients may develop other tumors that are resistant to the focused therapy. This is what is happening with Herceptin. This phenomenon in oncology is similar to the protracted use of antibiotics, where microbes develop new resistant forms to avoid our drugs. Treatment, in some way, enables or forces the tumor cells to develop a Herceptin resistance. Thus we create the continuing need for new drugs. Indeed Genentech-Roche is developing two drugs [pertuzumab and trastuzumab emtansine (trastuzumab-DM1, T-DM1, an antibody-drug conjugate)] to treat those who have become Herceptin resistant.

Companion diagnostics

When the use of a biomarker becomes essential for the drug treatment, from deciding on treatment initiation to decisions about its continuation, then we speak of a biomarker measurement that becomes a "companion diagnostic" (CDx). The definition of CDx is "diagnostics that are necessary to select successfully patients for therapy, distinguish likely responders from non-responders, identify patients at high risk for adverse events, or select an appropriate dose for safe and efficacious use of the therapy." As of the end of 2011 there were only four companion diagnostics in which the FDA and European Medicines Agency (EMA) mandate the diagnostics as a condition for the treatment. The number of companion diagnostics is increasing and 25 are expected to be mandated within the next 2 years. CDx is such an attractive initiative that one understands that diagnostics companies are drawn into the orbit of pharma companies—even when they do not have the same owner such as Roche and Abbott—to start developing CDx roughly at the same time as the company starts serious drug development. For the diagnostics companies, which are used to a much lower rate of risk than pharma companies, the CDx investment is a new ball game. If the drug does not materialize, which has a 90% chance, then the companion diagnostic is useless, unless the competitors' me-too drugs to the originally planned drug may use the same biomarker. Still, the diagnostics companies are used to development times to market of 1-2 years for PCR- and ELISA-based tests; now the time lines become more like drug-development time lines. This favors big diagnostics companies with staying power, as evinced by these press releases:

> Des Plaines, Ill., U.S.A., March 3, 2010—*Abbott announced today that it has entered into an agreement with GlaxoSmithKline (GSK) to develop a molecular diagnostic test intended for use as an aid in selecting patients who may benefit from a skin cancer treatment in development by GSK.*

or

> London, England & Glostrup, Denmark, January 18, 2010—*Astra-Zeneca and Dako Denmark announced today that they have entered into a collaboration agreement to develop companion diagnostic tests for multiple AstraZeneca oncology projects, including biologics and small molecules, in various stages of discovery and development.*

or

> Washington DC, U.S.A., August 17, 2011—*The U.S. Food and Drug Administration today approved Zelboraf (vemurafenib), a drug to treat patients with late-stage (metastatic) or unresectable (cannot be removed by surgery) melanoma, the most dangerous type of skin cancer. Zelboraf is specifically indicated for the treatment of patients with melanoma whose tumors express a gene mutation called BRAF V600E. Zelboraf is being approved with a first-of-a-kind test called the cobas 4800 BRAF V600 Mutation Test, a companion diagnostic that will help determine if a patient's melanoma cells have the BRAF V600E mutation. Zelboraf is marketed by South San Francisco based-Genentech, a member of the Roche Group. The cobas 4800 BRAF V600 Mutation Test is manufactured by Roche Molecular Systems in Pleasanton, Calif.*

Indeed, companion diagnostics have been approved by the EMA and the FDA and introduced foremost in the area of oncology. For example, in 2007 the EMA recommended the granting of authorization for Amgen's cancer drug, the humanized therapeutic antibody panitumumab (see above), whose antigen is the EGFR[139] in patients whose tumor contains a non-mutated *KRAS*[140] gene. The EGFR is overexpressed 3- to 10-fold in colorectal cancer and the therapeutic antibodies cetuximab (Erbitux) and panitumumab (Vectibix) block the activation of the EGFR dimer and cause apoptotic cell death.

Those with mutated *KRAS* were shown not to benefit from treatment with this expensive biological, making the companion diagnostic test for the *KRAS* mutation an excellent tool of personalized medicine, both for selecting patients for trial and, now, for treatment and following for how long this is an adequate treatment. As expected from really useful diagnostics, this test thus increases the response rate, helps the patient, and even permits charging a higher price for the drug and for this test. The company DX, which has brought the *KRAS* mutation test forward, has other customers because the *KRAS* mutations in NSCLC suggest other drugs to be used. Thus, the companion diagnostic becomes a companion to several drugs produced by different pharma companies. This is in accordance with the best interest of patients and the wishes of the regulators who do not wish that the same company should control the diagnostic test and the drug whose use it predicates.

Tougher regulation of diagnostics

The recognition of the importance of diagnostic tests in medical care leads not only to the expansion and use of the diagnostic tests but also to a harder regulation of these tests. Many tests were based on so-called "home brews" where, using antibody from an academic laboratory, one would

---

139   Also targeted by cetuximab (ImClone-BMS's Erbitux).
140   The protein product of the gene is the GTP-ase KRas or KRAS. Mutated KRAS is oncogenic and associated with the development of many cancers.

bring out an ELISA[141] to measure an antigen that is recently described. Now serious diagnostic tests from larger companies obtain FDA approval for clinical laboratory improvement amendments (CLIAs). These are achieved after rigorous clinical trials that, in the application for a CLIA waiver, demonstrate "insignificant risk of an erroneous result" with both "failure alerts and fail-safe mechanisms" and "accuracy," including selection of patients and quantitative data.[142] The collection of data samples and the requisite analysis might take 3 years and could involve hundreds of human samples. Thus, we are approaching the stringency of clinical trials aimed at the approval of drugs with the same ethical problems and same risks of failure; this, however, should not surprise anyone.

So, when one wants FDA-approved diagnostic tests, which have an added value close to that of the drugs and which are used to select and follow patients on the drug, the time and effort approaches that of drug development. The old maxim applies: "there are no free lunches." When a CLIA test is finally approved, it represents a huge competitive advantage that permits running trials and asking higher prices. For example, DiagnoCure Oncology Laboratories' U.S. CLIA certification of its parent company's Previstage GCC Colorectal Cancer Staging Test enables the company to promote it, perform it, and report the results worldwide.[143] The company Genomic Health makes a good example here of how this works in oncology, where "focused therapies" with expensive drugs are entering the therapeutic alternatives and where basic science is more advanced at the molecular and cellular level than in, for example, psychiatry. Genomic Health was founded in 2000 to develop differentiated

---

141   Enzyme-linked immunosorbent assay.
142   Recommendations: Clinical Laboratory Improvement Amendments of 1988 (CLIA) Waiver Applications for Manufacturers of *In Vitro* Diagnostic Devices, http://www.fda.gov/medicaldevices/deviceregulationandguidance/guidancedocuments/ucm079632.htm
143   See, for example, DiagnoCure wins US approval for colorectal cancer staging test, *InfoGrok*, 28 August 2008, http://www.infogrok.com/index.php/pharmaceutical/diagnocure_wins_us_approval_for_colorectal_cancer_staging_test.html and DiagnoCure press releases including http://www.diagnocure.com/docs/news/297.2010-08-03_DOL_receives_NY_State_Laboratory_Permit.pdf and http://www.diagnocure.com/docs/news/314.2011-01-20_-_Positive_Initial_Results_from_Colon_Cancer_GCC_Assay_Study_-Final.pdf

cancer tests based on examining which mutated proteins are present in a tumor biopsy from a patient whose sample is sent to their laboratory. They obtained, 7 years later, FDA approval for their test OncoDX that suggests to the physician who sent the patient sample to the company which treatment would be best for the patient. The FDA approved the test as being useful in predicting treatment choice because the outcome—progression-free survival of the cancer patient—was significantly better. The path to approval required Genomic Health spending about $50 million on sequencing, predicting treatment, awaiting results of the treatment, and comparing its outcome with the outcome of treatments given to patients whose tumor DNA was not sent to Genomic Health. The company has become highly profitable through reimbursement for the tests; similar to the way payments for the drugs they recommend are reimbursed. Today the company is worth about 15 times the investment. But, note that these sophisticated diagnostics undergo as long a trial with patient material and patient outcomes as drugs do and they may fail almost as often as drug trials fail. So diagnostics, when it becomes expensive, becomes also slower and more risky to develop. The main income of large diagnostics companies comes from the completely automated HIV, hepatitis, and other viral tests and from the blood tests that they carry out on billions of samples.

What makes a diagnostic test good?

In the development of drug treatments, the diagnostic tests and, ever since X-rays, imaging have always played an important role. With improved understanding of the pathophysiology of a disease we can suggest better diagnostic tests, better in the sense that they are:

1. more related to the core symptoms of the disease, or
2. more specific for the disease, or
3. provide earlier diagnosis, or
4. all of the above.

Consider fever as a diagnostic test for bacterial infection. Yes it is sensitive, but very nonspecific and does not suggest a specific therapy.

However, one can follow the therapeutic effect of broad spectrum antibiotics by measuring when the fever subsides, or conclude that the antibiotics did not have any effect as the fever persisted. We want more specific diagnostic tools yet wish for the sensitivity of the febrile response.

One of the greatest challenges, as discussed throughout this book, is the treatment and prevention of Alzheimer's disease (AD). It is, thus, understandable that there is much focus on new diagnostics, and in the summer of 2010 the National Institute on Aging (NIA) and the Alzheimer's Association cooperated to update the diagnostic criteria for AD for the first time in 25 years. We can recall that development of multiple sclerosis drugs took on greater speed when radiological diagnosis was agreed by the FDA; (ACR)-30 scale[144] has given new speed to the development of rheumatoid arthritis drugs: new agreed-upon diagnostics are very important.

The neuropsychological assessment of mild cognitive impairment is much improved and these positive results have initiated a series of biological sampling and imaging. See, for example, the report from the discussion at the Alzheimer's Association International Conference on Alzheimer's Disease 2010 (AAICAD 2010)[145] from which we quote here below:

- *Predictive genes in early onset Alzheimer's indicate that the initial events ultimately leading to both clinical symptoms and pathological brain changes begin with disordered beta amyloid metabolism.*
- *The e4 allele of the* APOE *gene is well accepted as a major genetic risk factor for late onset Alzheimer's disease, which is defined as onset at 65 or older.*
- *Biomarkers for Alzheimer's have been developed and are being validated. These fall into several categories:*

---

144   See Chapter 02.
145   New Guidelines to Catch Alzheimer's Drafted, *Dementia Weekly/Alzheimer's Weekly*, 7-14 August 2010, updated 16 October 2011, http://alzheimersweekly.com/content/new-guidelines-catch-alzheimers and see also http://www.alz.org/research/diagnostic_criteria/.

o *Biomarkers of beta amyloid pathology, including amyloid PET imaging and levels of beta amyloid in cerebrospinal fluid (CSF).*

o *Biomarkers of neuronal injury, including levels of CSF tau and phospho-tau.*

o *Biomarkers of neuronal dysfunction, including decreased uptake of FDG on PET scans.*

o *Biomarkers of neurodegeneration, including brain atrophy on structural MRI scans.*

This new list shows new modalities for assessing AD with molecular markers in CSF and measurement of general brain metabolic activity using imaging of fluorodeoxyglucose (FDG) changes[146] and of amyloid plaques with agents being presently developed, and not yet approved by the FDA. Yet Lilly, a company heavily involved in trying to develop AD drugs and therapeutic antibodies, acquired the company Avid, which makes the PET-imaging agent florbetapir,[147] which has been used in recent scientific publications on, for example, the effects of antibodies to beta amyloid (or Abeta or Aβ) peptide.

Lilly and other companies, such as J&J, Elan, and Pfizer-Wyeth, will use this or other imaging agents as companion diagnostics for their amyloid-lowering drugs.[148] Avid's Amyvid is a very good example of companion diagnostics as we will see them in the future. Namely, everyone understands that approval of a drug will not be based on whether it lowers amyloid load in the brain, but whether it slows or prevents loss of cognitive function, such as memory. However, for the companies that have made the bet that an increase in amyloid load is one of the causes of

---

146 Such changes may not be specific to AD and may result from, e.g., major depressive disorder (MDD).

147 Amyvid, aka (E)-4-(2-(6-(2-(2-(2-([^{18}F]-fluoroethoxy)ethoxy)ethoxy)pyridin-3-yl)vinyl)-N-methyl benzenamine, or ^{18}F AV-45, or florbetapir-fluorine-18, i.e., a compound containing the radiolabel fluorine-18 that binds to Abeta. It is the first beta amyloid imaging compound to enter multicenter, investigational new drug (IND) clinical studies in the United States.

148 Of course, Lilly has suffered two significant reversals in its quest to show an improvement in cognitive decline using its amyloid-lowering drugs, as evinced by both semagacestat and solanezumab (see Chapters 05 and 06). It is to be hoped that its entire program will not be dropped.

cognitive decline, it is mandatory to know that their drug indeed lowers amyloid load, as a companion diagnostic imaging agent can show them. If this happens, then they feel encouraged to conduct the long trial to see whether indeed lowering amyloid load will slow or stop cognitive decline and, thus, will provide an approved drug treatment for AD. Lilly is a leading CNS company that invested most heavily in AD drug development, and buying the maker of the companion diagnostics in December 2010 would seem reasonable to acquire a competitive advantage. However, the fate of this companion diagnostic is unclear. Although Amyvid has undergone serious clinical trials, it has not yet received FDA approval. The concern was the reliability of "readers"[149] and the "inter-reader" consistency, thus bringing into question the presented results, even though "efficacy was established" and, in addition, "there were no significant safety concerns raised." The FDA has also recommended how to amend the study to move Amyvid closer to approval. On top of this obstacle and delay for Amyvid, several pharma companies like Bayer, and diagnostics giants like GE and Siemens are developing competing companion diagnostics for measuring amyloid load. Will it be shown that a reduction in amyloid load can drive an improvement in cognitive decline? The FDA was keen that "a negative scan [using Amyvid] would be clinically useful in indicating that Alzheimer's pathology is unlikely to be the cause of a patient's cognitive decline," which is not the same thing.[150]

In general, the route to have the FDA approve companion diagnostics in major diseases is clearly through long, rigorous trials and the approval process will be more and more similar to that for drugs. But such diagnostics will be an inseparable part of personalized medicine, which represents the wish (and parallel unease) of big pharma to abandon "one size fits all."

---

149   That is, those that examine and quantify the data records.
150   As discussed in Chapter 06, these trials are on the way to failure.

Chapter 09: Personalized medicine

Personalized medicine has been for the past 15 years a sound bite in speeches by pharma executives, medical directors, and politicians to describe the *future* of medical care, yet there are only a handful of drugs approved that require genotyping of the patient before commencing the treatment. As mentioned in Chapter 08, the breast cancer drug trastuzumab (Herceptin), a therapeutic antibody against the HER2+[151] protein tyrosine kinase receptor, is the first drug to require genotyping. It shows very high efficacy compared to most oncology drugs and thus serves as the poster child of what personalized medicine will provide.

The promise is that by knowing as much as possible about the patient and the disease, even the DNA sequences, and the mutated proteins that may result, of each individual tumor in the case of the metastasized cancer, the proper selection of treatment may be made, leading to better outcomes (see Table 9.1).

What is new here? One may say: "nothing." Doctors going through the anamnesis[152] with their patients have always tried to establish symptoms and their current course, record all earlier diseases, earlier treatments and responses, and diseases in the family as pointers to genetic contribution. Then one orders specific laboratory tests and examines the laboratory results where electrolyte, glucose, metabolite, hormone levels, and red blood cell counts, and so forth, are listed and the deviations from normal range indicated.

Personalized medicine as a goal is not new. Every serious physician has always wanted to tailor the treatment to the specific patient at hand. It is the medical, technical, and scientific basis for being able to do so that is improving. The hindrances to progress are our knowledge

---

151 Also known as or Neu, ErbB2, CD340, or p185; see Table 9.2.
152 The information gained during the discussion between physician and patient of the patient's medical history.

The Future of Drug Discovery. http://dx.doi.org/10.1016/B978-0-12-407180-3.00009-X

Promises
Higher response rate
Higher efficacy
Lower side effect frequency
Better symptom control
Safer combination of drugs
Prerequisites
Laboratory data, blood chemistry, FISH of biopsies
Genetic information, SNPs, whole genome, somatic mutations
Imaging

Table 9.1: The promises & prerequisites of personalized medicine
The promises are many and appropriate for certain conditions for which some testing needs to be performed to obtain the prerequisite information. Somatic mutations, which are acquired after conception, are responsible for many cancers. It is understood or assumed that when these promises are achieved then a higher price can be charged.

about how to organize the huge amounts of data, the shrinking amount of time the physician has per patient, and our ability to pay ever-increasing costs.

Personalized medicine basics

In medical science, we have seen a strong development of imaging, and other diagnostic tools. Principal among them is DNA sequencing, which has been intensively developed over the past 15 years and which culminated in the original sequencing of the human genome in 2001, an achievement that cost hundreds of millions of dollars. By 2012 the price of determining the genome of an individual had rapidly plummeted to $500–1,000 dollars. This means that the hardware of our biology, our genetic makeup, can rapidly—in 1 or 2 days—be determined for each of us by DNA sequencing and with still decreasing costs. The sequencing capability and the information technology are at the point where one can put on a small silicon chip the entire DNA sequence of three billion bases that determine each individual.

The remaining problem is how to interpret these patient-specific DNA sequences and use them medically. We all carry a very large number of mutations, meaning that our sequence is different in one or other nucleotide base[153] from that of what would be the theoretical "standard" healthy human genome. It is estimated that we acquire ~200 mutations in the three billion bases in a generation, so the mutation rate increases very slowly. Thus, the number of genetic diseases also increases very slowly. However, as we live longer, many diseases where age is an important additional risk factor now have a higher incidence than before. Somatic or acquired mutations occur in individuals after conception and thus are not inherited. They accumulate with age since it is thought, possibly, that the repair mechanisms "cannot keep up."[154]

Most of these mutations are "silent mutations." They are without any effect on the performance of the protein that the gene encodes and, thus, have no effect on our health or on our diseases. There are, however, some single point mutations that cause serious diseases such as cystic fibrosis and Gaucher's disease. These genetic diseases are almost always diagnosed because of the severity of symptoms arising from the single mutation that is destroying or reducing the activity of the protein encoded by the gene. In these cases the sequencing just confirms the diagnosis based on the symptoms of the phenotype. So far the knowledge of the mutation has not helped us with therapy; instead we try to intervene at the level of the faulty protein, in most cases by supplying a functional protein replacement. The first drug to try to eke out some function from a mutated and dysfunctional protein is the January 2012 approved ivacaftor (Vertex's Kalydeco), for a special group of cystic fibrosis patients, that is, just 4% of the 30,000 U.S. patients with this orphan disease. This small molecule drug binds to the mutated chloride channel and makes it work to some extent. This is the first drug to combat a mutation causing loss

---

153 The nucleotide bases of DNA are adenine, cytosine, guanine, and thymine, each denoted by its initial "letter," i.e., ACGT.
154 There may also be sound reasons why it would not be good in an evolutionary sense if mutations were always repaired.

of function and, hopefully, it will be followed by others. It will, as of 2012, be priced at $294,000 per year. The Cystic Fibrosis Foundation was involved in its development; again, this is a welcome sign for collaboration between pharma and society. Engineering inhibition of the mutated, but not the "healthy," protein is becoming more common among cancer drugs.

There are many mutations that have been identified to be associated with a higher risk of a disease. But we have not been able to determine which combinations of mutations and which combinations of environmental, dietary, and so forth, factors play a role in the increased incidence of the disease. A very important example is the increased risk of Alzheimer's disease with ApoE4 (ε4). Homozygotes (ε4/ε4), 2% of the U.S. population, are most at risk (10- to 30-fold), but heterozygotes (ε3/ε4, ε2/ε4), 20–25% of the U.S. population, also have a 2.5- to 3.5-fold increased risk.[155] In Europe the percentage of ε4/ε4 homozygotes is reported at over 9%. These are very large numbers for a disease and in part contributes to the projection that 1 in 2 people above 85 will have the disease.

The situation regarding what to do with the knowledge about one's genetic risks has been simpler in Europe than in the United States. In Europe, we have been interested in determining mutations because in many cases one might propose preventive surgery for a genetic risk factor, for example, that makes it 90% likely that a person before the age of 45 develops familial adenomatous polyposis (FAP), a benign stage of an inherited disease with a very high potential to transform into the malignant disease of colorectal cancer (the third most deadly disease). Society would carry the cost of genetic screening, medical advice, and subsequent preventive treatment, if there is any, for all members of the society. In the United States until the last health reform bill,[156]

---

155   Roberts JS, Cupples LA, Relkin NR, Whitehouse PJ, Green C, REVEAL (Risk Evaluation and Education for Alzheimer's Disease) Study Group (2005) Genetic risk assessment for adult children of people with Alzheimer's disease: the Risk Evaluation and Education for Alzheimer's Disease (REVEAL) study. *J Geriatr Psychiatry Neurol.* Dec;18(4):250-255.

156   The Patient Protection and Affordable Care Act (PPACA), informally currently referred to as "Obamacare," which might have been reversed as of early 2012, and which might be emasculated by any future Republican administration.

one could be excluded from health insurance plans because of "pre-existing conditions," and none is more pre-existing than being born with a mutation. Thus, the advice to each person was not to look for mutations until you fall ill, not even if close family members are ill.

The only current case in the United States would be to know if you have an already diagnosed cancer. So, for breast cancer it is medically important whether you have the HER2+ mutation, because it will change the breast cancer treatment to the better trastuzumab. One should note that ~10% of the 230,000 breast cancer cases[157] discovered annually in the United States has the genetic basis identified. Trastuzumab treatment alone has a response rate of ~15%, but in combination with chemotherapy it rises to 67% (see Table 9.2 for current necessary supplemental tests).

However, for complex diseases science is a long way from being able to predict risk from our genome, what the best treatment might be, and the best lifestyle that may affect outcomes. For example, schizophrenia has an incidence of 1-2% and debuts around age 20. It has clearly some genetic basis since in first and second degree relatives the incidence is higher. Yet 50 years of genetic studies, 15 years of which have been using SNPs[158] and longer DNA sequences of patients and their families, has only come up with minor genetic factors, none of them accounting for more than 2% of the risk of having the disease. Scientifically, this is a great disappointment as we thought that the identified genetic defect would set us on course for a better therapy or even, some day, for disease prevention. But this example shows that for complex diseases to manifest there may be dozens of genes and environmental factors that must act in some determined sequence. We are very far from knowing what all these factors are. Thus, personalized medicine using adroitly our own genome sequences is far away. This is not because we do not have the sequence, but because we lack the in-depth understanding of it.

---

157   99.5% of cases are in women and 0.5% are in men.
158   Single-nucleotide polymorphisms, pronounced "snips."

Disease	Test	Treatment
breast cancer[1]	HER2+ (HER2/neu, Neu, ErbB2, CD340, or p185) overexpression	trastuzumab (Herceptin, Genentech-Roche) and lapatinib (Tykerb/Tyverb-GSK)
metastatic colorectal cancer (mCRC)[2]	epidermal growth factor receptor (EGFR aka HER1) expression, *KRAS* mutational analysis	cetuximab (Erbitux, BMS-Lilly; Merck, KGaA) and panitumumab (Vectibix, Amgen)
acute lymphoblastic leukemia (ALL)[3]	Philadelphia chromosome positivity (Ph+)	dasatinib (Sprycel, BMS)
persistent or recurrent cutaneous T-cell lymphoma (CTCL)[4]	CD25 positivity	denileukin diftitox (Ontak, Eisai)
non-small cell lung cancer (NSCLC)[5]	*ALK* mutation	crizotinib (Xalkori, Pfizer)
metastatic melanoma[6]	*BRAF* mutation	vemurafenib (Zelboraf, Plexxikon-Daiichi-Roche)
cystic fibrosis[7]-subtype of the disease mutation	G551D mutation	ivacaftor (Kalydeco, Vertex)

Table 9.2: Genotyping mandated by the FDA: diseases, tests, & therapies

---

1   Trastuzumab can only be used in breast cancer patients who overexpress the HER2 receptor (see text for details). Lapatinib is used in treatment of women with combined ER+/EGFR+/HER2+ overexpression and in HER2+ patients whose disease has progressed after other treatment including trastuzumab.

2   Studies and trials have indicated that cetuximab, in combination with chemotherapy if possible, is effective in treating metastatic colorectal cancer, but not earlier stages. *KRAS* encodes a protein on the EGFR pathway and, additionally, it has been found that cetuximab and panitumumab are only effective with a non-mutated *KRAS* gene. The FDA has requested information about *KRAS* mutations to be on the label, and this predictive biomarker test has been introduced before starting these expensive monoclonal antibody therapies. Cetuximab is also used against head and neck cancer without the need for assessing EGFR expression.

3   Dasatinib[8] is used in patients with Philadelphia chromosome-positive acute lymphoblastic leukemia (Ph+ ALL). It is also used in patients with chronic myelogenous leukemia (CML) and is being tested for other cancers including prostate.

4   Denileukin diftitox has been approved in a supplemental biologics license application (sBLA) for the treatment of patients with persistent or recurrent CTCL whose malignant cells express the CD25 component of the IL-2 receptor.

5   Crizotinib is an ALK (anaplastic lymphoma kinase) and ROS1 (c-*ros* oncogene 1) receptor tyrosine kinase inhibitor for NSCLC patients with an *EML4-ALK*[9] fusion gene.

6   Vemurafenib is a B-Raf enzyme inhibitor that the European Medicines Agency approved in February 2012 for patients with the very aggressive *BRAF* V600 mutation.

7   Ivacaftor is a different type of drug that tries to restore some function to the chloride channel known as the "cystic fibrosis transmembrane conductance regulator" when the mutation leads to replacement of a glycine (G) residue at position 551 of the protein with aspartic acid (D).

8   A tyrosine kinase inhibitor named after a chemist in the BSM development team, Dr. Jagabandhu Das.

9   The abnormal gene fusion of *EML4* (echinoderm microtubule-associated protein-like 4 gene) and *ALK* (anaplastic lymphoma kinase gene) leads to the production of an abnormal gene product (EML4-ALK), which promotes malignancy of cancer cells.

ENCODE

The part of the human genome that is known to encode proteins represents only about 1.5% of the whole genome. Another larger chunk was recognized as regulatory, that is, stretches of DNA that modulate the protein-coding genes. The "rest" was thought allegedly by many to be "junk"; maybe DNA that had fallen over evolutionary time into disuse, that is, not transcribed and with no discernible function. Not very surprisingly, the data published in September 2012 from the ENCODE (Encyclopedia of DNA Elements) consortium[159] shows that a lot of the non-protein-coding DNA has now been characterized and comprises a complex series of "switches" determining when specific genes are active. The hypothesis is that if there are errors in these sequences then this could result in disease states. Indeed, many of the single nucleotide variations found in disease states occur outside the protein-coding sequences. Speculation is that these gene-switching sequences represent potential drug targets.

But, that would be a very long way into the future. Unraveling the sequences that are important and showing that altering a switch would affect the disease state favorably without affecting many other switches working normally would be only one of the many problems. It is far from "emerging personalized medicine."

---

159   It was started in September 2003 by the U.S. National Human Genome Research Institute (NHGRI) as part of the National Institutes of Health (NIH). The new data came from the over 400 scientists from 32 institutes around the world. So-called genomic medicine research is also emerging from other major institutes such as the Wellcome Trust's Sanger Institute in Cambridge, UK, and the Broad Institute, in Cambridge, MA, backed by MIT and Harvard.

For now, we do not know how to fix a single mutated chloride channel in the single gene disease of cystic fibrosis.

Emerging personalized medicine

The dream to select patients for a clinical trial who have the highest chance to benefit from the treatment is shared by patients, physicians, and pharma companies. The earlier praxis was that when a large trial with large enrollment was finished, and the overall results were not sufficient to lead to approval, then we try to define—in diagnostic terms—the subgroup that benefited from the drug therapy. Good medicine and good economy suggested that one should let them continue to use the drug, especially if there were no other already approved drugs, as an open label, that is, not blind, extension of the trial. The next logical step was to find something common, diagnosable in the responder group, and then rerun the trial in a new group of patients selected for having this diagnosable property. This new group might include some of the earlier trial's population if they had been given a placebo, say. Today, genome analysis may provide the common attribute if we can find genetic markers that only the responders carry. HER2+ is such a marker. It is almost assured that the second trial in this select, genetically homogeneous (with respect to this genetic marker) population is more likely to be successful and lead to approval of the drug to treat this genetically determined population of patients. If this is a large portion of all patients, this is a dream situation for patients and pharma, because a large enough market can be charged a higher drug price as the efficacy is higher than average.

Side effects can be and are often genotype dependent and stratifying patients such that we exclude those who can suffer injury from the drug is one of the best ways to create safer drugs.

If this genetic marker only occurs in a small group of patients, then the pharma industry might be of a split mind about "what to do." The industry has grown strong and profitable on "one size fits all" type drugs, and it is impulsively averse to splitting a large indication with multimillion patients into a small indication.[160] The embarrassingly large number of failed expensive trials, however, pushes the industry to use as many genetic and other markers as possible to improve patient selection for the trial, and as many biomarkers as meaningful to follow treatment progression. The hope is that in a more homogeneous and enriched population the treatment signal is better revealed and thus the trial will produce results that lead to approval of the drug. Once the approval is granted, the industry would want to forget that the positive results were obtained in a select population of the patients and see that physicians prescribe the approved drug to all sufferers of the disease, a potentially dangerous impulse and suspect off-label promotion. This is a big problem for the Food and Drug Administration (FDA) and also somewhat of a problem for insurers. The FDA is against systematic off-label use because safety and efficacy were not established in the larger heterogeneous patient population. The insurers have to fight to maintain that they pay for these often very expensive drugs only when genotyping indicates that the patient will benefit, if the drug is only approved for this genotype. The insurers would prefer that the FDA makes it mandatory to carry out the genetic test before the expensive drug is prescribed.

Genotyping and drug prescription for a few drugs has already become intertwined and, thus, the concept of companion diagnostics has arisen (see Chapter 08). There is an emerging class of drugs that targets a mutated enzyme in tumors such as KRAS, B-Raf, ALK, and so forth, and for the use of these "designer drugs," or focused cancer therapies, genotyping will be mandatory. Hopefully they will show a similar efficacy gain as Herceptin has in HER2+ breast cancer (see Table 9.2).

However, the number of drugs that pharma has currently developed for a specific genotype, that is, for a small group of patients, is very small, even though there are drugs in trials. Pharma still makes most of its

---

160 Unless the indication becomes so small that it qualifies for orphan drug status and becomes profitable thanks to the special tax laws regarding those drugs.

income from conventional one size fits all type drugs that work in several genotypes and are safe enough to be dosed widely within a heterogeneous patient group. They are, of course, not optimal for almost anyone, but they are acceptable and good for almost everyone. When they were developed they were not a result of some cynicism about market size, but we simply could not have genotyped the patients. How new drugs will look with respect to genotype selectivity is unclear. There are still relatively few attempts to develop such drugs today and, thus, in the next 10 years there will not be many drugs that require genotyping. The estimate is that at the present rate of approval for drugs with companion diagnostics, this class of drugs will reach 20% of all oncology drugs by 2025, that is, possibly 1-2% of all drugs in use at that time. Pharma is not voluntarily splitting larger markets into smaller ones when the cost of developing the drug for the smaller market is only slightly lower than developing the drug for the larger one. If there were two drugs for a disease where one requires genotyping and the other not, unless there is a huge difference in efficacy, people will choose the one that does not require genetic testing. The cost of trials in a genotype-based selected population will be somewhat lower, despite the additional cost of genotyping, as a higher response rate is expected making the required enrollment smaller.

Adverse drug reactions may rank as high as the fifth leading cause of death

The undisputed great use today of pharmacogenomics is to help us to determine how quickly a patient will metabolize a drug. This thereby helps us to improve the safety of a drug therapy by use of simple genetic tests that show when a drug-metabolizing enzyme is mutated in this patient making the patient, for example, a slow metabolizer of this drug. A most common example of the power of pharmacogenomics is in the case of alcohol intoxication. Persons who have a mutation in their aldehyde dehydrogenase become much more intoxicated on the same volume of alcohol. Less mundane examples are mutations in catechol-O-methyl transferase, which lead to a smaller response when treated with drugs for Parkinson's disease such as levodopa. Warfarin is a commonly used anticoagulant, in particular after operations and also chronically after stroke to reduce the risk of the next clotting. However, there are patients who have a mutation in CYP2C9[161] that makes them slow metabolizers of this very commonly used drug. Today we do not have to wait until one of these patients suffers an internal bleed; a $25 test can determine whether it is safe to use warfarin in these patients and this is now mandated. In these cases the pharmacogenomics portion of personalized medicine brings increased safety. Since 2010, the MM-WES[162] test increased the safety of the use of warfarin.

When drugs can be personalized then they may be provided like most other goods and services we pay for, namely, they will come with some guarantee. The thoughts below relate to this potential expectation.

The "hair-dryer" & "toaster" drugs

Today the pharmaceutical industry is one of the very few industries that can sell a product that cannot be returned by the customer if the customer finds out it does not work. This has serious implications for the models of how pharma companies will have to test, promote, and sell their drugs. It can impact insurance companies, both private and national, that will look at the issue of drugs, which have a relatively low response rate, with, say, only 20-30% of those taking the drug responding positively. Low response rates are characteristic of many of our most expensive cancer drugs, whether they are small molecules, tyrosine kinase inhibitors, or therapeutic antibodies. When one considers that these drugs can cost between $50,000 and $100,000 per year per patient and that their use is associated with serious side effects in many cases, even in those patients who will not respond with beneficial therapeutic effects, then for the squeezed healthcare systems it becomes rapidly a question of should we pay for such drugs where the treatment for one patient—whether it works or not—will cost us as much as the vaccination of 10,000 children.

---

161 Cytochrome P450 2C9 is the enzyme that metabolizes over 100 therapeutic drugs, including warfarin.
162 The Meco-Mayo Warfarin Effectiveness Study.

The FDA's approval letter for such a large-selling drug like the therapeutic antibody bevacizumab (Genentech-Roche's Avastin) makes for sober reading. Bevacizumab inhibits angiogenesis—necessary for tumor growth—as it inhibits the vascular endothelial growth factor (VEGF-A). Approval in 2004 was based on patients with metastatic cancer of the colon or rectum.[163] The treated group was shown to have an increase in progression-free survival, of 4.2 months in study 1 and 3.8 months in study 2, compared with the placebo-treated group. Now this "extra few months," of course, is an average, and within this number there are some lucky patients who have lived 1-2 years longer because of this treatment. Overall response rate was increased only 10% and 23%, respectively, in the two studies, with kidney, heart, and hypertension side effects in the same range.[164] This presents, of course, the huge dilemma that in the absence of really good diagnostic procedures, which would help us, the industry, the insurance companies, and the doctors to select these people, society should have a hard time denying anybody this therapy as long as the healthcare system is financially solvent. But we are not that far from that point.

Therefore, it is very, very important to understand that we will have to come closer to the "hair-dryer drugs," that is, drugs that we can not only guarantee that you will not endure the pharmaceutical equivalent of an electric shock when you use them, that is, to say they are relatively safe, but also that they may be returned, or not paid for, in the case of no obvious therapeutic benefit. Another analogy, for which we are grateful to an adviser on this book from within the industry, likens the problems of variable responses in patients to that of a less than perfect toaster. We use his words:

> What do we do when we don't have a diagnostic or prognostic [market] and the drug is expensive? Imagine buying a toaster and finding out you can make perfect toast, your wife burns the bread,

---

163   See also Chapter 10.
164   Study 1 metastatic carcinoma of the colon and rectum, FDA, 2004, U.S. BLA Amendment: Bevacizumab-Genentech, Inc. 1 of 27: GNE_clean_PI_Feb_13.

your daughter fails to brown the bread at all, and your son finds out that it blows a fuse when he tries to use it. This would be unacceptable and selling goods as defective as this is prohibited and would lead to company collapse.

If you all had different somatic mutations [leading to] the same tumour and received the same therapy, this would translate to you benefitting with 2 extra years of life, your wife endures plenty of adverse events, but some extension of life, your daughter is resistant to the treatment but has few adverse effects, but your son dies of the disease and the last few weeks of his life are blighted by adverse events. This is just about acceptable as long as the average life extension, or progression free survival, is a few months, however, given the cost to society for "end of life" therapy it seems inconceivable that this can be sustained, especially during a prolonged and deep recession in the West.

How we will construct models in which we give this type of guarantee to patients and insurance companies is unclear. But that we will have to find such models is quite clear.

The future of personalized medicine

Personalized medicine as we discussed in Chapter 08 is our best hope for the type of precision medicine that will arrive at the point where we prescribe drugs to people whose likelihood of being responders is close to 100%, and for whom we will be able to prescribe the class and the particular drug—when more are available to choose from—to which they are more likely to respond and tolerate the side effects. Today we, even on blood pressure medicines, often have to go through three iterations before the right combination of several classes of antihypertensive drugs and the right doses of these classes of medicines are found. This is despite our having extensive experience with these particular drugs, since most of them have been around between 15 and 25 years and have been used by tens of millions of people.

The improved diagnostics will also be important for the drug companies in another way. Namely, the biggest problem of drug companies is that 90% of the projects become total failures: not a penny is recovered from the expenditures of several hundred million dollars when the drug has reached phase 3 and failed there. In 2009, large drug companies with extensive experience in developing drugs such as Roche, Lilly, and Pfizer, experienced failures of much-touted phase 3 drugs where they were hopeful of producing new effective medicines that would generate several billion dollars a year from each of them.

There are many reasons for these failures, but the biggest is that we are not very good at selecting patients for trials. We have already described that we are not very good at selecting the patients for the available approved drugs. Unfortunately for the drug companies, they are also not very good at selecting the best patients for a drug trial. It is not uncommon that there are relatively small and successful phase 2 trials with 200–300 enrolled patients. The cost of such a trial is at the very limit of the finances of a biotech company. But the phase 3 trial in which 4,000–10,000 people will be enrolled may fail because the larger group has a more heterogeneous response. The best defense, of course, is to find drugs that have very large robust responses, such that the variability does not erase the signal. This is, however, too often not the case as we tend to underdose drugs for fear of side effects and then we reduce the therapeutic signal. If unlucky, the positive therapeutic signal drowns in the interindividual variability of a larger trial. Thus, the response rate and efficacy of personalized medicine is very attractive, but how to fulfill its promise is not yet clear in most indications.

Knowledge management

Knowledge management is an emerging field of personalized medicine. It is important for the best personalized medicine to recognize that during our lifetimes so much medically relevant information is accumulated about us: blood group; vaccinations; diseases we have overcome and forgotten; the response or lack of response to drugs then prescribed for us; the allergies we had acquired and the ones we have now under control but can be rekindled; the viral diseases we brought into a dormant state, but viruses like herpes are still with us; the bacteria that are encapsulated but not dead as after many tuberculosis infections, and which can be brought to activity by, for example, TNF-antagonist therapies for rheumatoid arthritis, and so forth. The list goes on. Neither we nor our personal physician—if such still exists where medical care is delivered—is up to date on this potentially important information. Much of the information in a mobile society might be anywhere. The electronic medical records (EMRs) are supposed to assist doctors with patients who do not remember all their ailments from earlier days, although do not suffer from any memory disturbance but just follow human nature and forget unpleasant things and periods. Also, none of us carry all our X-rays, CT scans, and MRIs, or remember the date when we broke a bone or what the last bone density measurement was, what our last estrogen level was, or when the last tetanus vaccination took place. These data can now be stored in one place instead of being distributed among all the hospitals we have ever visited.

EMRs have been a reality in many European healthcare systems for years and are now being introduced in the United States not only in hospitals but also in the office of every general practitioner. The expectation is that not only will billing information be better but there will also be a real improvement in the quality of medical care.

Others want to go one step further and have patients carry all of their data at all times. The idea is that modern information technology now enables all medical and genetic data of a patient to be stored on small devices that could even be implanted. This device could then carry data on all of the patient's vaccinations, hospitalizations, and drug allergies, even the ones the patient already forgot, and all images made of this patient: chest X-rays, MRIs, and so forth. These data may be stored safely in various hospital archives, but are too often not at the fingertips of the physicians. The physician would add to these data from the current examination, and expert systems may then be used by the physician if she or he wants to use them to bring up similar case studies from the medical literature without running to the library.

The programming of these systems is difficult but not impossible for IBM, Microsoft, Google, GE, Siemens, Philips, or many others that are present in hospitals with electronic record keeping, invoicing systems, archiving of laboratory data, and so on. The key issue in knowledge management is the physician's desire to retain decision making, and the credibility and responsibility associated with the medical decisions. The genetic variations add so much new and yet not fully digested data to the basis of decisions that they now risk being overlooked except when it comes to pharmacogenomics and drug prescription where the safety benefits are clear.

What does this mean for drug treatments?

The maxim that no doctor remembers more than three drugs within the same class of medicines is more or less true and any marketer will attest that hard-pressed, stressed doctors in their 15 minutes with the patient rely on prescribing not the latest drug in a class but the one with which they have the longest and best experience. Almost no heart specialist, and definitely no general practitioner, can list five or six beta blockers, five or six ACE inhibitors, and five or six diuretics, but they know which are the top combinations of two drugs from these classes of antihypertensives in terms of efficacy, lowering blood pressure, and each drug's interaction with the other. When the patient is on other drugs, in particular on rarely used drugs, it becomes more complicated and makes the doctors even more conservative in their prescription choice of the antihypertensive. It is also clear that only a fraction of the drug-labeling information, which lists and explains interactions already known—drug interactions, dosing strategies—is an active part of doctors' prescribing choices.

The electronic record, if it is annotated to warn the physician about allergies, over-reactions, and earlier idiosyncratic responses, will do much to personalize medicine. There are many versions that are in development that may affect drug prescription routines. In most versions the FDA labels of the prescribed drugs that the patient is taking are matched to the drugs the doctor is prescribing and checked for known drug interactions. The doses the doctors choose are checked with respect to the other drugs the patient takes, and the doctors are warned when they deviate from the recommended dosing so that it is not done by accident but by their decision. So far this is not personalized medicine, just better use of public data and patients' personal medical drug regimens. When the individual pharmacogenomics data are added to this, they will show that this patient is a slow metabolizer of, for example, warfarin, because another key drug is metabolized by the same mixed function oxygenase cytochrome P450 2C9 (CYP2C9); then we will make an additional step in personalizing drug use, that is, improving the safety and efficacy of drug use—a goal of all doctors in all times.

Finally, it is envisaged that the system will not only check the doctor's choices but will make recommendations based on the treatment algorithms that, for example, the National Health Service, or the American College of Physicians, and other professional bodies, have compiled from specialist advice. The implementation of recommendations is today usually at the sole discretion of the doctor and many insurance and malpractice cases hang on what is the present best praxis, and whether it has been followed.

Knowledge mining & learning algorithms

An additional development is also taking place in which increasingly sophisticated disease models are built using more and more patients' data. The information would comprise all possible data from, for example, stroke patients including the images, functional consequences, and treatments prior to and directly after the stroke, and so forth. When such data from thousands of patients, treated in many hospitals, are "mined," then one may come to treatment models of very complex disease states that will affect the treatment of an individual patient, including the use of the drugs prescribed. These models, often based on learning algorithms, are experimental tools and the most well-documented parameters, besides age, height, weight, and available images of the patient, are the drugs they are given and their dosing. The major idea is that no single specialist, no single hospital, nor any hospital system has seen all of the millions of patients with the same disease worldwide, but that—providing patient integrity can be maintained—information technology today enables collecting and learning from all patients' data for the benefit of all future patients.

The real clinical use of these models will require large and long randomized trials showing that the use of such models positively and significantly improves the treatment outcomes and reduces suffering and cost. That is, these models will be subject to a long, expensive approval process similar to those for the new CLIA-type[165] diagnostics and the very drugs whose use they will ultimately modify.

---

165   Clinical laboratory improvement amendments (see Chapter 08).

Chapter 10: How much can drugs cost?

The discovery, development, and sale of medicines is a highly profitable business enterprise and, despite complaints from the pharmaceutical industry, the market has been growing for the past 45 years in a spectacular manner. The industry, using the breakthroughs in life sciences, has produced highly useful drugs that have reduced mortality and suffering in numerous diseases. The successes of the industry are evident from the number of cases that are treated because the physician, the patient, and the insurance provider all agree the drug has beneficial effects.

The cost of medical care in the developed countries that today account for over 80% of the world market (with the $2.6 trillion in the United States alone accounting for 41% in 2010) is, however, growing in an almost uncontrolled fashion; now it is over 10% of the developed world's GDP. This leads to political discussions and decisions about whether the system should be mostly government sponsored, like the National Health Service (NHS) in the UK and the national healthcare systems in Scandinavia, France, and so forth, or whether it is better with mixed private and governmental insurers, as in the United States, the Netherlands, and Germany.

The absolute sums per capita per year spent on healthcare are much higher in the United States at over $7,000, than in the other OECD[166] countries with an average of just over $3,000 (see Figure 10.1 comprising largely 2010 data). Yet the sums spent on drugs are not that different, at ~$950 in the United States and ~$700 in the other OECD countries. The major contributors to the inflated medical bills in the United States are unnecessary tests, expensive

---

166 Organization for Economic Cooperation and Development; it is not clear if the voting public understands that the U.S. costs are so much higher than in other very capable medical systems where reimbursement depends on government intervention. It is not evident to Europeans, or even Canadians, why U.S. politicians cannot seem to come to terms with the economic benefit of a healthy population backed by comprehensive and government-controlled healthcare policies. However, most of the expenditure and growth in the United States is in the private sector. See Health Care Marketplace Project's "Health Care Spending in the United States and Selected OECD Countries April 2011" http://www.kff.org/insurance/snapshot/oecd042111.cfm

The Future of Drug Discovery. http://dx.doi.org/10.1016/B978-0-12-407180-3.00010-6

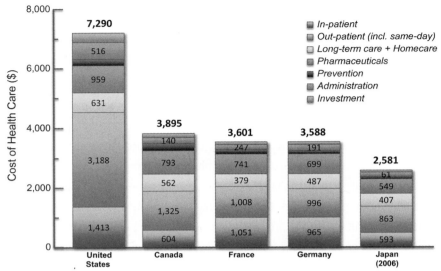

Figure 10.1: Distribution of Healthcare Costs in Selected OECD Countries
The average amount spent on healthcare per capita per year is much higher in the United States, at $7,290, than in the other OECD countries with an average of $3,415. But the sums spent on drugs are not that different, at $959 in the United States and ~$700 in the other OECD countries. Given that as many as 10% of the population, that is, ~31 million[1] in the United States, are uninsured, but will likely become insured, there will probably be a much wider range of money spent at the individual level.

---

1   Some estimates are as high as 49 million (16%).

procedures, medical devices, the high average salary of doctors, and the high insurance cost against malpractice litigation compared with OECD countries.

Thus, the pharmaceutical industry manages to carve out of the widely different total expenditures in the United States versus other countries the same sum, because its products are globally approved and sold, and because the market flows would not easily permit very large price differences between markets for the same product; the market, in this example, works. The overall cost of the medicines is remarkably similar when we consider the different medical philosophies and traditions of the countries in the OECD. For example, the use of antidepressants, pain killers, and drugs to prevent pregnancy is dramatically different in the different countries. Yet these are not the expensive drugs and the differences in their use do not disrupt the general uniformity of the medical profession's diagnostic procedures within "normal" values of international health standards.

The U.S. dominance as the largest market for medicines, in terms of earnings not number of patients, will eventually be eroded and China, India, and Brazil will dominate the market for all drugs, including the most recent proprietary drugs. Differences in philosophy of drug prescription may become visible, with different portions of the healthcare expenditure being used for medicines in such countries. However, we do not expect this to happen in the next decade.

The question that is much discussed is whether the sum spent on medical care can and will grow and whether the sum spent on new medicines can and will grow.

Will the sums spent on medical care and new medicines grow?

Until now, pharmaceutical companies operated under the assumption that it is possible to increase the total cost of drugs. There was no notion of having to sacrifice income on some drugs to be able to sell others. In addition, despite the waves of mergers and acquisitions, the industry still consists of many players with none controlling 20% of the market, the sign in other industries of consolidation. These players see that they can take market share from other companies if they make better drugs and market them better than the competitors.

Society has not yet put a serious effort into pushing the companies to produce more cost-efficient and better drugs by, say, insisting at the level of the regulatory agencies that any new approval represents a more efficacious drug than the already approved ones. The European Medicines Agency (EMA) and the Food and Drug Administration (FDA) insist on patient safety and on some signs of efficacy, but do not require that the new drug is superior or better than others used to treat the same disease.[167] This is left to the market, physicians, and marketers to insist that a company tries to have a

---

167 However, in Germany an attempt is being made that is being watched closely by other countries. Two years after approval, the new drug is to be compared with older ones for the same indication. In order for the manufacturer to maintain a higher price, superiority must be shown. Otherwise the price must be lowered to match that of the older drug. See later in this chapter.

more efficacious and/or safer drug. The regulators are becoming increasingly involved in judging whether the benefit to risk ratio is appropriate, which is an important and logical step toward asking for better drugs.

The answer to the first question of whether medical costs will grow is that, with the same levels of governmental income and taxation as today, medical care costs cannot grow unabated. Healthcare has already taken from education and other essential services. The efforts to rein in medical care costs are active and seriously pursued, although the political differences are making agreements difficult in each country. But, there is a great understanding that this has to happen. If so, then can the share taken by medicine grow within this fixed sum? Or will it have to remain the same, or does it have to shrink?

The 1960s to 2000 saw the successes of effectively treating cardiovascular diseases by addressing hypertension and hypercholesterolemia. This led to a major drop in myocardial infarction- and stroke-caused mortality.

According to the National Heart, Lung and Blood Institute (NHLBI), if death rates were the same as those of 30 years ago, 815,000 more Americans would die of heart disease annually and 250,000 more would die of stroke.[168]

In view of this, society did not ask too much about the price of these medicines despite cholesterol-lowering statins being expensive. Statins were the first truly preventive medicines, yet we did not hesitate to buy these drugs for close to $10 billion per year as it was clear that they had a large effect on cardiovascular disease-caused mortality. The use of statins has increased in the past 20 years despite the tremendous cost (see Figure 10.2).

The "number to treat"

The use of statins underscores a very important concept for all healthcare systems: the number to treat. This concept was not discussed at all until the mid-1980s and seriously only since the mid-1990s.

---

168 As reported verbatim in many bulletins. See, for example, http://www.phrma.org/research/heart-disease-stroke

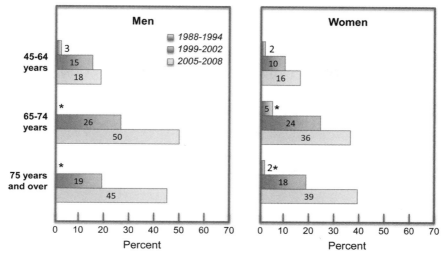

Figure 10.2: **Statin Drug use within "the past 30 days" in the United States**
Estimates are considered unreliable. Data preceded by an asterisk have a relative standard error (RSE) of 20-30%. Data not shown have an RSE of greater than 30%.[1] The percentage of adults 45 years of age and over using statin drugs increased from 2% in 1988-1994 to 25% in 2005-2008.

---

1   From CDC/NCHS, Health, United, see http://www.cdc.gov/nchs/data/hus/hus10_InBrief.pdf for figure under "prevention," and see http://www.cdc.gov/nchs/data/hus/2010/fig17.pdf for the U.S. data from the 2010 National Health & Nutrition Examination Survey. Respondents reporting use of a prescription drug containing any of the following ingredients: atorvastatin, cerivastatin, fluvastatin, lovastatin, pravastatin, rosuvastatin, or simvastatin were classified as taking a statin drug.

When we treat a diagnosed HIV patient or a diagnosed cancer patient the *number to treat* equals *one*; there is only this diagnosed person for whom we have to find an efficacious and tolerated treatment to have a positive effect on quality of life and mortality. When we treat with statins everyone with high cholesterol then, statistically, the *number to treat* to avoid *one* myocardial infarction is close to *100*. In other words, we would expect only 1 in 100 of the people taking the statins to have a myocardial infarction if they were not taking it, but we do not know which one it would be. This would be fine if the preventive drug is cheap and we are very rich. The statin prices have already fallen as a result of the first major statin—the one that was used to reduce cardiovascular mortality—simvastatin (Merck's Zocor) becoming generic in 2006. It has now been followed by the largest selling statin atorvastatin (Pfizer's Lipitor), which lost its patent protection in late 2011. Thus, statin use will continue but society will pay less for it.

The discussion of the number to treat has not yet started in earnest. To obtain the relevant numbers one needs large studies and meta-analysis of many studies over a long period. The methodology of these is not beyond criticism, and it is clear that only governmental studies will have the numbers and the credibility to produce the numbers that politicians and healthcare economists can start to work on. When these numbers are eventually produced by, for example, NICE in the UK, serious ethical debates will have to take place. Choices will have to be made as to what is more important to treat. But, we must remember, the disease is always someone's disease and its treatment should always be a priority. Even in the most ethnically (genetically) homogeneous countries we see large regional and other differences in disease prevalence. The United States is probably the most heterogeneous country, ethnically and economically. This OECD country shows tremendous differences in disease prevalence, as detailed for all chronic diseases by the Milken institute report "Unhealthy America."[169] Any decisions based upon economic expediency to use the number to treat concept openly to decide which diseases to treat with which drugs would inevitably lead to political and ethical discussions. Today's treatment guidelines, that both governmental and private insurers publish, deal with the medical decisions about the first-line therapies with which to start. These just deal with what we know from the clinical practice about efficacy and safety and how long these treatments last before new drugs need to be used. The number to treat choices between diseases and drugs are not discussed in these instructions; it is the choice, rather, between different drugs to treat the same diagnosed disease that is discussed, and where recommendations are made these often are rather soft.

---

[169] See http://www.milkeninstitute.org/publications/publications.taf?function=detail&ID=38801018&cat=resrep and http://www.milkeninstitute.org/publications/publications.taf?function=detail&ID=38801020&cat=ResRep

The price of the most expensive drugs

The recommendation to use the generic version of a drug is an easy one to make. But we have not saved on medicine costs despite the use of generic drugs increasing as many of our first waves of successful medicines of the 1980s and 1990s have become available from several generic manufacturers. The reason is that the drugs that became generic were relatively cheap to start with as these were synthetic small molecule drugs such as beta blockers, antihistamines, proton-pump inhibitors, serotonin reuptake-blocking antidepressants, and so forth. They cost $1,000-3,000 per patient-year before the generic entries into the market. The drugs that bring our medical bill up are the *biologicals*.[170] Few of these have come off patent protection.

The hope of politicians was that the high cost of biologicals will be stemmed by the "generics" called *biosimilars*.[171] However, the biosimilars suffer badly as they gear up for approval and beyond for serious competition on the market. Initially, the manufacturing instructions and documentation that the regulators have required for the approval of the proprietary biological that typically costs the consumer $25,000-75,000 per year—with orphan drugs up to $600,000 per year—were not very precise. Thus, the biosimilars may not be fully identical to the original biological. For example, the glycosylation patterns[172] and the molecular foldings of the proteins depend on from which organism, yeast strain, bacterium strain, or cell line the biological was produced, and vary with the density at which the cells were grown. Amgen even had problems in producing

---

170 See Chapters 02 and 03.
171 See also Chapters 04 and 06.
172 "Many bioactive natural products are glycosylated compounds in which the sugars are important or essential for biological activity. The isolation of several sugar biosynthesis gene clusters and glycosyltransferases from different antibiotic-producing organisms, and the increasing knowledge about these biosynthetic pathways opens up the possibility of generating novel bioactive compounds through combinatorial biosynthesis in the near future. Recent advances in this area indicate that antibiotic glycosyltransferases show some substrate flexibility that might allow us to alter the types of sugar transferred to the different aglycons or, less frequently, to change the position of its attachment." Méndez C and Salas JA (2001) Altering the glycosylation pattern of bioactive compounds. *Trends Biotechnol.* Nov; 19(11):449-456. See also Chapter 06.

and reproducing EPO in the United States as well as Germany in its own factories using its own experts.[173] Thus, no physician is sure that when a biosimilar like GSK's competitor[174] to rituximab (IDeC's Rituxan) comes into the clinic it is going to be effectively identical to the rituximab they have used for 15 years and about which there are 7,812 indexed publications in 2011 detailing efficacy and side effects. These data help physicians to confront potential difficulties in their patients and the eagerness to switch to the slightly cheaper biosimilar is low. After the FDA guidelines were published in 2011, the estimates of how much cheaper biosimilars will be were around 10-15%. That is not a convincing and commanding price gap when even recruitment for the studies showing equivalence between biologicals and biosimilars is very difficult. Yet the developed world's medicine costs are markedly affected by our use of very expensive biologicals.

Some insurers such as the NHS of the UK are choosing to retest the efficacy of expensive biologicals as their approval is often based on small studies where the results are not robust. For example, as mentioned in Chapter 09, bevacizumab (Genentech-Roche's multibillion dollar Avastin), the cancer drug that blocks angiogenesis,[175] may cost up to $100,000 per year.[176] Avastin was approved by the FDA[177] using data

---

173   Amgen also endured other problems with EPO as documented by *FundingUniverse* here: http://www.fundinguniverse.com/company-histories/Amgen-Inc-company-History.html
174   Ofatumumab (Arzerra) targets another part of the CD20 protein, i.e., a different epitope to rituximab, so patients and physicians are unsure about equivalence of efficacy.
175   Blood vessel formation; thus, Avastin restricts blood supply to tumors.
176   The huge price tag has also attracted unscrupulous criminal activity. In February 2012 vials of the injectable drug were found not to contain bevacizumab. The labeling was different, having the Roche logo instead of Genentech's, and the labeling was in French and Arabic, which curiously, the FDA announcement (http://www.fda.gov/Drugs/DrugSafety/ucm291960.htm) did not mention, although it was shown by Genentech (http://www.gene.com/gene/news/press-releases/press_statements/ps_021412.html) and reported at the time by the U.S. National Public Radio (NPR). Allegedly, shortages of the medicine were thought to be behind the fact that respected hospitals were found to have secured "Avastin" from more unusual suppliers.
177   See also Chapter 09; the initial approval of Avastin in 2004 is hardly a congratulatory note but rather a highly conditional letter that rigorously sets forth further marketing hurdles (see http://www.fda.gov/ohrms/dockets/dailys/04/sep04/090304/04e-0402-app0001-05-Attachment-D-Avastin-Approval-Letter-vol1.pdf).

from at least three different trials.[178] The first phase 3 trial with a "large" population of patients with metastatic colorectal cancer showed a longevity improvement of 4.7 months (20.3 months vs. 15.6 months overall survival) by adding Avastin to the chemotherapy regimen. The second approval was based on a trial with 829 patients with advanced or metastatic colorectal cancer who had received previous treatment. Recipients of Avastin had a "25% reduction in the risk of death," which translates to a "33 percent improvement in overall survival" or "median survival for patients receiving Avastin was 13.0 months, compared to 10.8 months." The third approval came from a study of 878 patients with unresectable, locally advanced recurrent or metastatic non small-cell lung carcinoma (NSCLC) who achieved a median survival of 12.3 months with Avastin and chemotherapy as compared to 10.3 months on chemotherapy alone. Improved longevity of a few months may indeed be the important benchmark, but what are missing from these data are issues about the quality of life during the whole treatment regimen.[179] Avastin, besides the statistically significant increase in median survival, caused, in the first trial, increases in "nosebleeds, hypertension (high blood pressure), proteinuria (too much protein in the urine, a possible sign of kidney malfunction), ... weakness, pain, diarrhea, and leukopenia (a reduced white blood cell count)." In the second trial there was a small percentage of serious side effects including somewhat rarely fatal

178 See Genentech's website http://www.gene.com/gene/products/information/oncology/avastin/ under Status and http://www.gene.com/gene/products/information/oncology/avastin/avastin-crc-facts.html under Clinical Trial Data. It is disappointingly hard to find summaries on the FDA website; one needs to look for the pdfs of the approval letters themselves.
179 FDA "approval" for Avastin's use in the treatment of breast cancer was subsequently withdrawn in 2011, despite the fact that physicians and patients were convinced it had saved, that is, extended lives, because statistically there was no improvement in longevity even if there was an improvement in suppressing tumor growth. The FDA had withdrawn an "accelerated approval" rather than canceled an actual approval. While the FDA was not prohibiting Avastin's use in breast cancer patients, its modified ruling makes it less likely that insurance companies in the United States will reimburse treatment costs. The FDA encouraged Genentech to uncover why some patients could do better and if these patients might be identified prior to treatment (see, for example, http://www.cancer.org/AboutUs/DrLensBlog/post/2011/11/18/FDA-Withdraws-Approval-For-Avastin-In-Metastatic-Breast-Cancer.aspx).

"gastrointestinal (GI) perforation and slow or incomplete wound healing." The third trial for new approval revealed "a higher risk of stroke or heart problems (blood clots) compared with people taking chemotherapy alone" and some additional side effects of "severe hypertension, kidney malfunction, nervous system and vision disturbances, and neutropenia (a reduced white blood cell count that may increase the chance of developing an infection)."

Approval, thus, does not always mean unbridled celebration by pharma, physicians, or patients. Nevertheless, ~60% of the profit of Roche is from oncology medicines and ~15% from sales of Avastin. Also one needs to be fair when reading the average increased survival times of 4 months. It may mean that certain patients had gained 2 years while several others gained no time and just experienced the serious side effects. If we were better able to predict who will benefit from the drug, the price tag would be a lot more acceptable.

When studies like these are repeated in larger patient groups, the statistical differences seen in the smaller study can easily disappear when the effect is not very robust. One might say that the company and those responding patients whose survival is prolonged were lucky. Since the average survival is quoted, there will be patients with much longer survival time. All of this makes these decisions ethically difficult or impossible, yet the decision to retest the expensive drug in a larger study can never be attacked, in particular when response rates are low and side effects are serious and highly frequent. If one or one's insurer is to pay the $100,000 per year or over $8,000 per month for, say, 20 months to achieve a life prolongation of "only" 5 months, while almost guaranteeing serious side effects and with only a relatively small chance of benefits, it almost invites insurers to try to block the use, and, in the UK and elsewhere, actually to block approval of use of the drug in a given country. But, we are employing better drugs with higher response rates and better efficacy and better safety. Therefore, the resistance to the high costs will be reduced, although it can never disappear as our resources are limited.

Cancer drugs, which are using up a very large portion of our medical expenditures, have to become better.

Another very expensive cancer drug—costing perhaps $30,000 per 8 weeks of treatment—cetuximab (ImClone-BMS-Lilly's Erbitux) was approved during 2008. The primary data in the approved FDA submission were from a two-arm phase 2 trial with a total of 329 patients.[180,181] Patients were "randomized to receive either Erbitux plus [the chemotherapeutic agent] irinotecan (218 patients) or Erbitux monotherapy (111 patients)." The results of the 111-patient Erbitux alone group were "a 10.8 percent objective response rate, a median duration of response of 4.2 months and a median time to disease progression of 1.5 months." The 218-patient group with combined therapy "had an objective response rate of 22.9 percent, a median duration of response of 5.7 months and a median time to disease progression of 4.1 months." In other words, the new drug did not really show a good response rate and did not work very well for very long or delay the disease progression much. This may be considered an important first step which "validates the concept that non-chemotherapeutic molecular drugs are active in the treatment of colorectal cancer."[182] A first step maybe, but again there is tremendous room for improvement.[183]

Eroding the high-priced drugs

These two very expensive cancer drugs are not only under scrutiny by insurers and regulators but they are also under competitive pressure by small molecule drugs such as tyrosine kinase inhibitors. These

180   See http://investor.bms.com/phoenix.zhtml?c=106664&p=irol-newsArticle_print&ID=494936&highlight=

181   See http://www.druglib.com/druginfo/erbitux/description_pharmacology/

182   As attributed by BMS (see footnote 15, Chapter 01) to Howard Hochster, MD, Professor of Medicine, New York University School of Medicine, who continued: "It adds a new dimension in the treatment of this disease and allows oncologists new options for treating patients that have this disease when irinotecan-based chemotherapy is no longer effective or tolerated."

183   Some scientists said in reference to Erbitux possibly being prescribed for lung cancer patients that it was not worth it (see, for example, http://www.bloomberg.com/apps/news?pid=newsarchive&sid=a477Nm93JYxM). Lilly withdrew its FDA application to extend the drug's use to lung cancer. If the drug was used in the treatment of all 550,000 cancer patients who die yearly in the United States the scientists estimated it would cost $440 billion or "100 times the annual budget of the National Cancer Institute."

biologicals are monoclonal antibodies that bind to the outside of the cell. Bevacizumab (Avastin) binds to the soluble vascular endothelial growth factor (VEGF) required for vascularization, and cetuximab (Erbitux) binds to the receptor for epidermal growth factor (EGF). They block signaling through the VEGF receptor and through the EGF receptor, respectively. The intracellular portion of both of these receptors have enzyme—protein tyrosine kinase—activity that we are now more and more successfully inhibiting with cheaper, orally available drugs for VEGF receptor protein kinase, currently pazopanib (GSK's Votrient), and for the EGF receptor protein kinase there is erlotinib (OSI Pharmaceutical-Genentech-Roche's Tarceva). There are, of course, differences between efficacies, dosing schedules, and so forth, of the antibody and the kinase inhibitors, but they address the same biological pathway and thus may bring, when properly adjusted, the same benefit. This type of erosion of the high-priced drugs is the most desirable one; when science and drug development produces cheaper yet better competitors, the choices are "no brainers."

Some drug prices are set freely by the companies; they need to recoup their investment while they can and lower them when the competition emerges. But, the present trend is that when there are competing drugs to treat the same condition, regulators, for example, those in Germany, which has possibly the highest drug prices in Europe, require that the producer of the drug, after a year or two of its clinical use, demonstrate value. This ensures follow-up after a sufficient number of patients have been treated to enable comparison with existing therapies. This analysis should show an added benefit of the drug that might justify the higher price. This proving of better efficacy and/or safety is, of course, on the wish list of all marketers in the companies. But that the demand to prove it comes from regulators is new and important in setting limits to prices of new, me-too type drugs. For novel drugs that treat a disease for which no treatment is otherwise available, the formation or determination of the price remains much in the domain of the company.

Quality adjusted life year costs: the QALY

When governments try to set a limit on how much societal insurance will pay for medicines, it is bound to be a complicated ethical and political issue. It will involve the concept of "quality adjusted life year" costs as described in the UK by the NHS,[184] but similar descriptions and calculations are now presented by all countries wherein one attempts to evaluate the cost efficiency of treatments. This not only applies to drugs but to medical procedures as well. Once formulae arrive, the rules can be applied. In the United States, the litigation-prone atmosphere conjures up many more diagnostic procedures than in Europe. Several surgical procedures vary dramatically between countries based on medical philosophy and tradition, which affects total medical cost. For example, in Germany, urologists and oncologists are reluctant to address prostate cancer in men above 70 by surgery; the conclusion they have reached is that the intervention causes more problems than it solves and that at this age the prostate cancer is often slow growing and their patients will die of other causes. The U.S. approach is much more aggressive with treatment by all means, including radiation, surgery, and, recently, therapeutic vaccines. This is, however, undergoing some revision. Prostate cancer screening (the PSA[185] test) is no longer recommended by the U.S. Preventive Services Task Force (USPSTF, 2012), which concluded that "the potential benefit does not outweigh the expected harms."

With the rapid advances in modern medicine, most people accept that no publicly funded healthcare system, including the NHS, can possibly pay for every new medical treatment that becomes available. The enormous costs involved mean that choices have to be made.

It makes sense to focus on treatments that improve the quality and/or length of someone's life and, at the same time, are effective uses of NHS resources.

---

184   See, e.g., http://www.nice.org.uk/newsroom/features/measuringeffectivenessandcost effectivenesstheqaly.jsp
185   Prostate-specific antigen (PSA) or kallikrein-3 (KLK3).

NICE takes all these factors into account when it carries out its technology appraisals (TAs) on new drugs. Its expert review groups (comprising both health professionals and patients) examine independently verified evidence on how well a drug works and whether it provides good value for money.

To ensure their judgments are fair, they use a standard and internationally recognized method to compare different drugs and measure their clinical effectiveness: the quality adjusted life years measurement (the "QALY").

How is the QALY calculated in the UK?

The QALY is in use in the UK to evaluate the worth of treatment. It is a rational, though harshly objective, evaluation of the effects of treatment with respect to quality of life, life extension, and cost. How much longer you might live is weighed against the possible reduction in quality of life through side effects, one of which can, of course, be death. Something that helps you live longer, but with increased pain and sickness, might be considered worse than something that may shorten your life, or at least may not extend it, but make one less disabled and more pain free. The rating of quality of life can score from the best possible health at 1.0 to the worst at zero or even less than zero. Table 10.1 shows how this is worked in practice in the UK.

What about cost effectiveness?

Having estimated the "QALY effect" between two types of treatment, the drug treatments are evaluated in terms of cost per QALY, that is, "the cost of using the drugs to provide a year of the best quality of life available."[186] One QALY is unusual for a single patient and is more usefully thought of as, say, 10 people each improving by 0.1 QALY over 1 year. While each patient case is matched to each drug for evaluation, if it costs, in the UK, over £20,000[187] per QALY, "it would not be considered cost effective."

---

186   See http://www.nice.org.uk/newsroom/features/measuringeffectivenessandcost effectivenesstheqaly.jsp
187   Currently about $30,000 and €25,000

Patient x has a serious, life-threatening condition
• If he continues receiving standard treatment he will live for 1 year and his quality of life will be 0.4 (0 or below = worst possible health, 1= best possible health).   • If he receives the new drug he will live for 1 year 3 months (1.25 years), with a quality of life of 0.6.
The new treatment is compared with standard care in terms of the QALYs gained:
• Standard treatment: 1 (year's extra life) × 0.4 = 0.4 QALY   • New treatment: 1.25 (1 year, 3 months extra life) × 0.6 = 0.75 QALY
Therefore, the new treatment leads to 0.35 additional QALYs (that is: 0.75 – 0.4 QALY = 0.35 QALYs).
• The cost of the new drug is assumed to be £10,000; standard treatment costs £3,000.
The difference in treatment costs (£7,000) is divided by the QALYs gained (0.35) to calculate the cost per QALY. So the new treatment would cost £20,000 per QALY.

Table 10.1: How a QALY is calculated
This is the information taken from the NHS: NICE[1] website. It is a matter of judgment as to how patients and physicians can put a number on quality of life. Since it is a predictive measure it must inherently rely on independent data obtained from reported clinical trials and eventually knowledge bases since upon it is decided whether someone will receive a treatment, particularly a new treatment; it is not a postmortem analysis.

---

1   National Health Service (NHS): National Institute for Health and Clinical Excellence (NICE), both of the UK.

We would not like to speculate on how this would be seamlessly integrated into the American system of healthcare followed by malpractice suits. In the United States, refusing to give and pay for treatment is only practically possible if such a treatment has not been FDA approved, and not because it is too expensive. Of course, this "treatment at all costs" only applies to the insured and legally self-sufficient. The poor and uninsured would not have any QALY yardsticks if it were to be integrated into the U.S. health system.

Chapter 11: Modeling drug discovery until 2025

In 2009, the top 12 pharmaceutical companies were employing over 1 million people worldwide (see Table 1.2). Since then they have cut payroll by over 40,000 positions, which may not seem very much had it not mostly come from R&D. R&D represented about 15% of the workforce; thus R&D has been reduced by ~25%. This is a very significant number. It means that employees with a long university education with postdoctoral specialization in areas such as metabolism, neurodegeneration, or heart disease have been let go. Perversely, this highly qualified and experienced workforce is cut when the companies have plenty of cash on hand: Pfizer, Merck, and GSK announced multibillion dollar stock buy back plans in 2011 in order to boost the stagnating value of their stocks.[188]

What is behind these industry-wide cutting decisions? They were started first and most forcefully by the Sanofi-Aventis CEO in 2009 and copied by other executives in the industry—those, who were fast enough to do so, at least. Those that delayed or hesitated to cut R&D expenditures resolutely were liable to lose their authority with their board of directors. For example, Pfizer's CEO Jeff Kindler was "let go" in December 2010, because he failed to reverse the trend of falling stock prices. He only lasted 5 years in an industry where the product development time is 10-12 years. Indeed, one has to ask how can management not focus on stock price and short-term financial gains, when they will not be around when a putative product, a new innovative drug, the R&D for which starts today under their stewardship, will become a new drug. Any approval of the new drug, following a New Drug Application (NDA), would be expected long after they left, if everything went well. The chances are that a project that starts with novel science will yield a new drug is about 1 in 100 at the prevailing 2012 rate of efficiency of drug discovery. Thus, when they cut

---

188   See Chapters 01 and 04.

The Future of Drug Discovery. http://dx.doi.org/10.1016/B978-0-12-407180-3.00011-8

R&D they do not seem to feel any sense of "loss," only an improvement of the bottom line that is immediate.

Worse is that they make clear to their remaining employees, with eloquent and fully credible threats, that they will continue to cut R&D by billions of dollars, with no clear discussion as to what extent. Will they cut it by 25% or 50% or 75% or 100%? For example, Pfizer's R&D cuts were $1.5 billion in 2010, coming after ~$4 billion worth of cuts in 2009 from the joint R&D budget of Pfizer and its acquired Wyeth. It was explained as, or excused by, removal of duplications in the joint R&D platforms and projects in the combined organization. Merck has used a similar explanation involving its recent "merger" with Schering-Plough. The acquisition of Wyeth itself followed Pfizer's continuous strategy of growth by acquisition rather than by attempting the more difficult organic growth. Since Wall Street investors have a shorter term view than almost any species on the planet, acquisition is much preferred to succeeding on one's own R&D merits. One should note that many drug targets were pursued at both of the merging companies—Pfizer/Wyeth and Merck & Schering-Plough—and in many therapeutic areas there is a shortage of drug targets.

A secondary problem is that companies and investors have a much different view about important parameters in measuring a company's worth. If a company really focuses on itself and consolidates and cuts a non oprofitable arm of its business, it will be frowned upon by U.S. analysts. They want to see growth in top-line revenues, not only in bottom-line profits. If revenues grow and profits fall, then one only has to fire management to improve profits. European companies are measured much more on the bottom line and a budget, which embraces cutting non profitable programs. European companies can tolerate revenues decreasing but profits increasing; such management is much more acceptable.

Consolidation does seem to be a partially sound motivation. But beware corporations' business-speak pronouncements of being "better focused"; it often just means that:

We have let go some of the brightest minds in our organisation and are primarily going to work on non-innovative projects in disease areas in which we have already been successful, rather than cater for society's needs. If another company is successful with innovation, we would have saved enough in order to acquire it. Innovation is all well and good, but we are trying to make it risk free.

But, in trying to answer the question of how far might the cuts go, we can imagine the answer is "all of R&D." Expenditure on R&D amounts, at the time of writing, to 14.5-22% of the income of the companies.

This process of cuts and threats of further cuts does not create conditions for highly creative work. Society still needs novel medicines to treat diseases with which it still has to deal.

So what is happening and what will happen about the new medicines that we badly need?

Early twenty-first century realities

It is clear from the decisions made and publicized, and from other decisions made and not publicized, by Big Pharma management that the time of double-digit growth and double-digit returns is over for a number of reasons. One has to accept that this is an industry, like many others, with single-digit growth and single-digit returns. K. Frasier, chairman and CEO of Merck, one of the U.S. blue-chip pharma companies, finally admitted this in 2011.[189] The big companies have relied on blockbuster drugs with sales over a billion dollars per year, and for some companies, such as Lilly, many if not most of such products have lost patent protection in the past 3 years. The constant race to replace blockbusters with novel blockbusters has been on ever since the day the patent was awarded. This race is now, however, failing across the whole industry, in every company.[190] Not all companies have the same reliance on patent-protected

---

189 See also Chapters 01 and 06.
190 See also Chapters 06 and 07.

blockbusters.[191] Such companies may be less vulnerable; however, this safety of income flow is paid by lower profit margins. When one sells generic or over-the-counter drugs price competition is immensely harder than when selling patent-protected prescription drugs.

All executives, stock analysts, banks, and stockholders speak of pharma being in crisis. Even the outgoing chief of the European Medicines Agency (EMA) in 2011 accused the industry of having wasted over $60 billion of its $80–85 billion annual R&D investment in the prior year.[192]

Long-term safety (gets) in the face of short-term pharma

As all pharma executives, and in particular those responsible for R&D, will immediately allege the number one culprit in this "crisis," which justifies the cuts of workforce and projects in rich companies, are the overly cautious regulators, the Food and Drug Administration (FDA) and the EMA. The accusation is that:

> With their increased safety mindedness and with their new focus on safety–benefit ratio, the FDA and the EMA made it so hard to develop new large-selling, blockbuster drugs for millions of patients in obesity, for example ... it is impossible or close to impossible to bring new obesity drugs to the market with their insistence on SAFETY ... what is worse, these regulators have started to insist on long-term safety ... and they have the temerity to take into account that a patient's life is longer or should be longer than the period she or he was on the weight loss drugs ... and then the novel require-ment that these new, to be approved, and already approved drugs, should have an overall benefit not only for the looks, curves and body weight, but also should reduce the risk of diabetes and heart disease.

191   For example, J&J and GSK have less than 30 % of their income from patent-protected proprietary drugs (see Chapter 06 for more details).
192   http://www.burrillreport.com/article-outgoing_emea_chief_criticizes_pharma%E2%80%99s_rd.html   and   http://www.fiercebiotech.com/story/ema-chief-blasts-60b-wasted-rd-spending-each-year/2010-12-16

It is true that the FDA was inaugurated to ensure food and, later, drug safety and for a long time they did not require proof of efficacy, relying on physicians not prescribing and insurers not paying for drugs that lack efficacy. However, in the past decade the FDA and the EMA want proof of efficacy, although they still do not insist on proof of superior efficacy to existing treatments, again relying on physicians and insurers taking care of that choice. In addition to expert panels proving efficacy, they judge the safety-to-benefit ratio and recently made it a major part of the decision to approve a drug. This is well illustrated by the fate of the cannabinoid receptor (CB1) antagonists for treatment of obesity, on which all large pharma companies had trials (Sanofi, Merck, Pfizer, etc.). The Sanofi drug [rimonabant (Acomplia), synthesized in 1994] that was first up for approval was turned down by an expert panel, in a broadcast discussion watched by thousands of stock market analysts and, of course, by all the competitor companies. The scientists and clinical experts of the panel found that the risk of suicidal ideation, which the drug caused in a significant number of patients participating in the trials, outweighed the benefits of the weight loss; in 1994 no one thought of testing this serious safety issue. Within a few months Pfizer and Merck stopped the clinical development of their cannabinoid receptor antagonists, as they found no reliable way to ensure and demonstrate that their compound, addressing the same target protein with the same molecular mechanism of action, would not cause suicidal thoughts and, eventually, suicides. This can only be tested in humans. The resulting "badmouthing" of the FDA for being overly cautious was unprecedented, and only understandable in view of the projected sales of these drugs being $3 billion or more per year. Yet it was the expert panel, not FDA employees, which unanimously (14:0) voted down rimonabant. The EMA, which had earlier approved the drug, withdrew its approval in January 2009.

This is against the background that most experts on the expert panel are university professors who have at one time or another advised pharmaceutical companies, and they tend to approve rather than turn down efficacious new drugs unless the risk is too high. In addition, and here comes the clincher, the regulators, wise from earlier failures, "now maintain that any drug on the market, whether old or to be approved, should not shorten life expectancy or bring serious cardiovascular and other risks."

The executives point out that these kinds of thoughts on long-term safety were not around between 1980 and 1999 when many of today's blockbusters were approved and certainly were not made into binding requirements by almighty regulatory agencies. They tell us that the FDA and EMA "moved the goalposts" and thereby made it impossible in many areas to estimate the risk one takes when embarking on drug development in this area. Thus, they have "no choice" but to cut research programs whether or not there is medical need, good scientific rationale, and, possibly, a large market. The FDA and EMA requirements "make it unlikely to succeed in bringing the drug to the market and their long-term safety requirements make the approval so far away in time that it is almost irrelevant for the immediate and 3-year financial health of our companies."

The path away from innovation

This new and incredibly strong risk aversion of all major pharmaceutical companies, which now forces them into very crowded niches of oncology, inflammation, diabetes, and so forth, is thus being fully explained by the regulatory environment. No one admits that every merger and acquisition (M&A) and every cut of R&D leads to selecting and firing the people who want to develop some novel drug using yet unproven, thus risky, mechanisms of action. By the removal of these people one creates a research environment in which being the best clerk, following the "process" and not an intellectual impulse, is the only way to survive and advance. Most large pharmaceuticals have cleansed their R&D from the uncomfortable presence of innovative people who disturb the process, and then seem to be surprised that no new beta blockers and no new statins are invented. Indeed, those who have achieved these drug discovery breakthroughs had a hard time even after their discovery product made billions of dollars. The man who synthesized the largest selling drug, the statin Lipitor—~$11 billion per year over the last few years—was let go.

It is true that the number of approvals per amount of research expenditure has been falling over the past 10 years and spending more money has not helped as the number of approvals is still 25-31 drugs per year, although the amount spent on R&D has increased dramatically (see Figure 7.1). The bar is significantly raised, and we acquire better medicines.

Evidence-based medicine

It is also true that the FDA and EMA have become more safety conscious. In particular, meaningful long-term safety considerations have been enabled by evidence-based medicine (EBM) as pioneered by large national clinical trial programs to test long-term efficacy and safety in large numbers of patients in the UK, the United States, and large European countries. They have executed very large and long—3-5 years—comparative efficacy and safety-focused trials that private companies did not do, or could not do, or certainly would not want to do. As discussed earlier,[193] the prime example of a government-conducted EBM trial is the case of the U.S.-sponsored trial of the estrogen replacement therapy (HRT) and breast cancer and cardiovascular risk from the Women's Health Initiative (WHI) study. The study, with its relatively huge numbers of post-menopausal women (~16,000), had a planned duration of 10 years. The study code was broken early because the data clearly warned of increased breast cancer and cardiovascular risk. As soon as the results of the study were announced, gynecologists, who had in large numbers prescribed estrogen replacements, called in their post-menopausal patients before the patients had a chance to besiege their offices, to discuss the risk-benefit ratio of these natural hormones taken as medicines. Wyeth, the company whose economy most depended on this therapy, eventually came under such pressure that when other research projects also failed, it was bought by the ever acquisitive

---

193   This is worth emphasizing again in this context (see also Chapters 01, 03, and 07).

Pfizer. It was not that Wyeth was in any immediate financial danger, as it was still earning money and had highly successful drug, vaccine, and hematology businesses, but investors and management lost confidence in research in the wake of the damage to the earning engine of HRT. The final straw may have been the difficulties with the antidepressant and potential anti-menopausal desvenlafaxine (Pristiq or Ellefore), which had been developed to replace the blockbuster venlafaxine (Effexor).

Today, the industry is making several attempts to dismantle by qualification, rather than discredit, the results provided by the WHI study. Refining the analyses using smaller well-defined patient groups is aimed to reveal more benefit and less risk. This is how it should be. If we could determine the risk-benefit ratio for each patient, then we would do so. We would make decisions about treatment using this individual value. This is, after all, the goal of personalized medicine: to determine and improve the risk-benefit ratio for each patient.[194] Thus, there is nothing sinister in the industry doing meta-analysis of the big trials to find small groups that could benefit from using the drugs.

There is also nothing sinister, rather it is desirable, that many large, long-term studies are being conducted by national agencies to elucidate efficacy and safety of drugs. After all, these are drugs that are used by millions of patients over long periods, and which often represent serious expenditures for public health plans. The individual patients and the public have the right to expect that there is efficacy and safety and that the drug does not create new, dangerous medical situations.

Thus, the requirements on the safety front increase and make drug development longer and costlier, while the drugs that are approved are better than earlier drugs. However, industry and investors are not yet adjusted to the economic consequences of their earlier successful, safe, and efficacious drugs being generic today, nor to the new scientific findings that require longer testing, measuring many more parameters, before new drugs are approved. These new requirements make development of certain drugs much longer and much more expensive, and industry simply

---

194   See also Chapters 08 and 09.

abandons these projects. These decisions are solely based on financial considerations and do not take into account the need of society for drugs in the abandoned areas. Companies have tended to abandon the same areas for effectively identical reasons.[195]

Risk of failure leads to risk aversion

But, where does this leave us when we ask who will develop new drugs?

Pharma companies have decided to be open about it in some cases. They want to focus on a few diseases that they deem will be profitable to treat and leave the rest of the diseases that are only promising. The abandoned projects are either promising to too small a market or require too long or too hard-to-do clinical trials. They have even lower odds of success than the average in an industry that as a whole has indeed low odds of success. Engineering companies have in general a higher probability of success. Thus, they too are less keen to invest in high-risk medical-clinical projects. One such huge medical imaging company has, in our personal experience, declined to accept our recommendation to invest in an imaging agent whose FDA approval had only a 10-15% chance. An executive explained that for them a reasonable engineering project has a risk of being 20-30% too expensive or take 20-30% more time to develop and generate sales, but almost never both. It certainly will not have a risk of 85% that they would lose the entire investment, as might be the case of the imaging agent with its need for FDA approval and long trial time, which we also see with the β-amyloid imaging agent.

Thus, the largest and most scientifically, technically, medically, and clinically capable companies with the largest financial means leave therapeutic areas to others, or to no one.[196] These include diseases such as neuropathic pain, which is experienced by one in five above 50 years old;

---

195   See Chapter 12 for possible incentives to encourage research in abandoned areas.

196   One might also hope that the researchers equally abandoned might form their own biotech companies to take their insights and develop their dreams without the backing of their particular Big Pharma, but it is terribly difficult especially in those areas where risk is indeed usually higher. Venture capital companies (VCs) that have the funds and are not dependent on a successful and lucrative project handover to Big Pharma within 2 years, are increasingly rare.

respiratory diseases, including asthma, being on the rise, particularly in children, and the present mostly steroid-based treatments being far from ideal; and chronic obstructive pulmonary disease (COPD), a disease on the rise with huge prevalence (16.9%) in over 50 year olds. They also leave diseases such as epilepsy and Parkinson's disease (PD), which are too small to provide a market for a blockbuster drug yet ironically too big (>200,000 sufferers) to be classified as orphan diseases. They are also too large to be classified as a rare disease by the EMA (no more than 5 in 10,000 people in the EU, currently <250,000 people).[197]

It is the prerogative of private, for-profit companies to seek and seize their best, legal profit-making opportunities. They are followed and often hounded by an army of stock market analysts because they are economically important, making up approximately 1–2% of the GDP of several countries.

Filling the strategic vacuum

The products of this industry are so essential and so strategically important that the countries with even the friendliest and closest ties to each other may stop delivery of ordered and paid for drugs and vaccines to the other country when their own population is not fully covered. For example, in 2008 the UK stopped the export of influenza vaccine to the United States. Governments do become involved not only in the approval and payment of drugs and post-market surveillance but also in export and import of drugs in the same way they try to control the movement of weapons and nuclear material. To put this into just a few words: *we cannot pretend that this is an industry like all others; this is a strategically important industry.*

So, who will fill the strategically important vacuum when the principal part of the private sector abandons it?

---

197 About 30 million people in the EU suffer from a rare disease. Most often these are diseases affecting less than 1 person in 100,000; http://www.ema.europa.eu/ema/index.jsp?curl=pages/special_topics/general/general_content_000034.jsp&mid=WC0b01ac058002d4eb

One may hope that biotech companies with VC funding pick up on the lack of Big Pharma competition in developing drugs for the neurological diseases of neuropathic pain, Alzheimer's disease (AD), PD, epilepsy, stroke, schizophrenia, and so forth; the respiratory illnesses like asthma and COPD; or in antibiotics development. However, this presumption may prove to be too optimistic a scenario for a number of reasons.

VCs: less capital leads to less venture

The supply of venture capital is severely down compared to the golden times of biotech from 1980 to 2005. Secondly, most VCs want to operate on the premise that phase 2b trials probably, and phase 3 trials definitely, will be carried out by a large pharma. They would commit to financing only the preclinical work, a phase 1 (~$1-3 million), and possibly a small dose-finding phase 2a trial (~$3-8 million). The customary total funding sum spent jointly by approximately five different VCs financing a company would be at most $25-50 million. Then, armed with good animal data plus some initial signs of clinical efficacy from phase 1 and phase 2a, thus having proven the mechanism, shown tolerance, and signs of efficacy of the drug candidate, a Big Pharma will step in and either buy the company or at least partner the project.

But, we now hear that Big Pharma, in these abandoned diseases and these therapeutic areas, still does not trust its own much bigger, and often better designed phase 2 studies to predict success in a phase 3 trial. By the time large pharma cuts its collective R&D budget, they have already closed down many projects with successful phase 2 data; an examination of the pipelines, public statements, and the appearance of few out-licensing candidates show this clearly. They have abandoned them once already, remember. So, it is less likely now that they will come to the biotech in these disease areas of high medical need but often failing trials. VCs are critically dependent on being able to show some return in their funds within 5-6 years and, thus, they do not have the funds, nor the patience, nor do their funds usually have the rules to permit them to go for a phase 3 costing at the very least $50 million, but more likely hundreds of millions of dollars. Surely there are indeed biotechs presently working in these indications. But one has to worry about their continued financing, especially in light of Big Pharma leaving these diseases either openly or just silently by not pushing its own trials and by not in-licensing anything from biotech or smaller pharma. This is an alarm for VCs that tells them not to invest in areas recently abandoned by Big Pharma.

The small- to medium-sized biotech companies with a capacity for preclinical and some clinical research comprising up to 300 full-time employees and spending $70-100 million a year have a hard time finding funding, as evinced by the very low number of IPOs and the lack of interest of VCs. When it becomes clear that Big Pharma is not looking to buy them or partner in these disease areas, their value will further fall.

Society-funded safety net

The basic requirements of Big Pharma when they were partnering were that biotech:

- should be working in an area in which society needs new treatment,
- has achieved something of interest and a proof of mechanism,
- has at least passed phase 1 or phase 2a,
- has a strong scientific rationale, and
- has convincing animal models.

Therefore, if the typically underfunded biotech fulfills these criteria, then we, surely, must not permit that their drug candidate be lost without giving it a government-sponsored and conducted clinical trial. *It is the least society should demand, isn't it?* THIS IS IMPORTANT!

Were the drug to be successful, then surely these companies and society will be better off having a new drug than a lost and forgotten drug candidate that no one has taken to test for real in clinical trials of appropriate design, size, and duration because of lack of funds. Their intellectual and financial investment up to the trials and their intellectual property would not be wasted.[198]

---

198   A mutually equitable reward system could be easily negotiated. It may involve having more keenly priced therapies for the home market and would, if approved overseas, earn export revenues.

Of course, should this scheme be realized, the biotech companies that will want to have their drug candidate clinically tested within such a program will probably quickly exhaust the resources available and selection will be a problem. It is also clear that there will be biotech entrepreneurs who will have a die-hard attitude and will sooner wait for the next wave of private funding rather than doing something with the government. Such ideologically founded motives will be hard to overcome, but one has to hope that common sense will prevail.

Our major thesis is to:

> save successful phase 2 projects from biotechs in areas of medical need with a government-supported clinical trials entity

This would not apply to me-too drugs. It is necessary so that we do not lose identified potential new treatments because of Big Pharma's reluctance. It is possible that phase 2 projects stopped at Big Pharma will need the same support.

Pharma cannot be expected to take the risks they cannot afford.

The history of the future

The Lilly CEO, John Lechleiter,[199] understood this. During a speech in London in February 2011 he proposed that Lilly, one of the most pressed Big Pharma companies, together with VCs, will start several VC-like funds of $50 million each clearly so as "not to have to use our own funds all the way." The problem is that this model has been tried without great success earlier. All Big Pharma, even the big CROs,[200] already have VC-like funds and they do co-invest with VCs, and sit on the boards of biotech companies, with first access to the news of success or failure, of new mechanisms, new molecules, and so forth. As the biotech company in which Lilly or a Lilly-controlled VC will own 51%, it is clearly geared to

---

199 He also took up a favorite topic of his during this speech highlighting the problems that bedevil the R&D field: "Our industry is taking too long, we're spending too much, and we're producing far too little ... Ironically, the crisis in our innovation model comes at a time when we have vastly more scientific knowledge and data than ever before ... But unless we change the way we do research, we won't translate this knowledge into advance."

200 Contract research organizations.

be acquired by Lilly in case of success. This may discourage some other VCs; it is inevitable. The worst any VC can hear is that someone limits the upside earning potential of their investments. Since the proposed Lilly funds direct the successful projects to Lilly, VCs think: "why not just buy Lilly stock?" It is not so cynical to ask this as Lilly will dominate these proposed funds' selection and financing decisions because of the power of its financial strength and its know-how in the field; such expertise will be better or more forceful than the *ad hoc* experts pulled together by the VC on a project basis. Nevertheless, there will be some VCs investing with Lilly as a part of their portfolio, but it is in no way replacing the R&D investments caused by Big Pharma cuts including those by Lilly.

How will we then make new drugs in these areas of medical need abandoned by pharma?

Since the pharmaceutical industry is not just any industry, but it is an industry of central significance to how our society functions, the governments have to step in. We all accept that governments and international bodies like the World Health Organization (WHO) are involved in regulation of drug approval, and when it comes to vaccines, we have accepted that government, by guaranteeing the purchase of millions of doses, acts as an engine of demand and financing. They do the same for the defense and aircraft industries, after all.

The argument is that epidemics threaten the stability of society physically, economically, and socially. On that basis one can make the same argument that every second person above 85 years of age having AD constitutes a similar threat to our society. These patients will present a demand for care that is estimated to bind 15-25% of all available labor.[201] Thus, if we do not succeed in preventing, postponing, or slowing disease progression, our society cannot continue in the same form. Thus, studies for prevention and postponement of AD need to receive governmental support because they are essential. As we have said in several places in

---

201   See also Chapter 05.

this book, the very long studies that are required are deemed too risky for the private sector and more and more companies have abandoned their research programs.

What would be the best way to dispense governmental support?

What would be the profile of a pharma company that will continue to work on AD drugs until it succeeds?

The preclinical research for small molecule drugs, which most drugs acting in the brain often are, has been developed into a scientifically and technically very complex and highly successful paradigm of iterative cycles of biology and chemistry research. It is a workflow that so far very, very few smaller biotech companies have mastered. The successful ones in small molecule drug discovery such as Gilead Sciences (California), Vertex Pharmaceuticals (Massachusetts), and Arena Pharmaceuticals (California) have all had to reach an R&D expenditure of above $200 million per year or they would not be able to employ, for example, the necessary 60-120 medicinal chemists that these programs involve even in these times of outsourcing. For these reasons it would be best for our society to find a system of incentives that enables and encourages Big Pharma to work on AD because of its existing highly specialized and very extensive and expensive R&D machine. While for biologicals such as antibodies biotechs have been rather more successful than Big Pharma, Big Pharma has absorbed them wherever it could through acquisition. Big Pharma now dictates what these absorbed biotechs work on, although, for example, AstraZeneca claims that its biologics business unit, Medimmune (incorporating Cambridge Antibody Technologies) is "operationally independent."[202]

Continued basic research support by governments is essential. It has to be finally said that in academia translational research has a less than glorious name, as it wins few scientific prizes. Many influential academic scientists believe that the intellectual effort and quality they exert is superior to

---

202 See http://pressroom.medimmune.com/press-releases/2007/10/29/astrazeneca-bolsters-its-worldwide-biologics-division-through-integration-of-cambridge-antibody-technology-into-medimmune/

those achievements in the pharmaceutical industry. One of the authors (TB) has served as the Senior VP in a major pharmaceutical company and as a professor and head of department in top academic institutes in both Europe and the United States, and he forcefully rejects the idea behind this academic snobbism. The academic scientist routinely writes in the grant application about the translational possibilities of the proposed work, but assumes that this imagined lesser work will be done by someone less talented in the industry once the great insights are produced by the academic applicant. Conducting a rigorous clinical trial and developing safe drugs to be prescribed to real people is as challenging as any research project but requires many more competences, and thus many more scientists working together, than any founding agency-forced collaborative project so far has been able to maintain in any collaboration in academia.

The main issue is that there must be a government-backed financial guarantee that these clinical trials will be conducted such that we do our best to prevent, postpone, and modify AD and other diseases. This is of great significance for our society even if Big Pharma presently does not want to spend money on trying to develop a drug.

Are we crazy? No. Some in pharma have been listening.

As we mentioned in Chapter 05, where we explained the importance of studying familial forms of a disease—no matter how rare—in order to elucidate mechanisms, and thus find drug targets, we also emphasized the importance of finding a preventive drug. Now is a good time to detail the ray of sunshine on AD.

A clinical trial has begun on a Colombian extended family that has the genetic predisposition to familial AD and wherein family members are likely to develop AD at age 45. It involves all the ingredients we have recommended throughout the book: government, nongovernmental organization (NGO), and industry backing; carefully selected participants[203]; and a viable candidate drug. In this case, announced

---

[203] U.S. citizens who also qualify may be recruited for the trial. The new entity organizers, the Alzheimer's Prevention Initiative (API), will work with the Dominantly Inherited Alzheimer's Network (DIAN) to identify potential U.S. participants.

in May 2012, the government is represented by the National Institutes of Health (NIH), with 5-year $16 million funding; NGOs are represented by the Banner Alzheimer's Institute (BAI) in Phoenix, Arizona, with a promise of a philanthropic $15 million; and the remainder of the $100 million trial is guaranteed with money from Genentech-Roche. The trial will use crenezumab, originally discovered by the Swiss company AC Immune SA, but licensed to Genentech since 2006. About one-third of the 5,000 member family has the presenilin-1 gene mutation that is known to cause early onset AD.[204] The trial will be conducted on those family members.[205] Of course, the trial may fail. It is unclear if anti-amyloid treatment will delay or, amazingly, prevent onset of the disease. Another company may already have a better anti-amyloid candidate and, eventually, a better target. But even moderate success will open the doors to new candidates. Will it lead to a new treatment or generally available preventive medicine to "well but worried" candidates for AD onset?

Of course, the trial will depend on Genentech's established expertise in designing and conducting the trial.

In an additional twist, Genentech's owner, Roche, will put its own antibody (gantenerumab made by Morphosis) against the same amyloid peptide into an expanded trial (from 360 to 770 participants) for the same Colombian patient group. Now convinced that one can learn from familial forms of the disease, Roche has "two horses in the race."

Use of existing R&D machines is essential. Left alone, Big Pharma are becoming chiefly marketing companies. How do we discourage or stop them abandoning the often more than a century of drug discovery experience that they have accumulated? Society still needs the very specialized highly educated workforce, and the very complex, highly technical organization that has evolved in the past 25 years of modern "target-based drug discovery." Society just needs it to focus on problems

---

204   See Chapter 05.
205   See, for example, http://www.multivu.com/mnr/56128-banner-alzheimer-s-institute-genentech-nih-prevention-trial-genetics

that society recognizes as important. We must find a way to achieve this through:

1. public–private partnerships,
2. tax advantage,
3. guarantees to purchase drugs,
4. payment for the work and setup required,
5. other incentives, or a combination of some or all of these.

One can be fairly sure that the Manhattan Project or the Apollo missions would not have been the successes they were technically and scientifically had the government taken a hypocritical stance describing these as essential for the country, but not willing to be completely engaged and involved financially, lest some private interests come under too much competition. This ideological hypocrisy needs to be broken when it comes to finding drugs for the severest of our healthcare problems. The country that has matched or preceded the technical physical science-based programs of nuclear weapons and rocket technology of the United States, that is the Soviet Union, marshaled all resources as part of its now abandoned planned economy, but it was not interested in the life sciences to the same degree. It did not embark on drug development, since drugs are for individuals not the collective, while it had great success in vaccine development and vaccination programs.[206]

Successful generic firms such as Teva Pharmaceutical Industries (Israel) and Dr. Reddy's Laboratories (India), which spend between $300 million and $1,000 million per year on research, are doing everything to become Big Pharma and to diversify from the generic income. Teva has soon-to-expire patents on two proprietary drugs: glatiramer acetate (Copaxone) against multiple sclerosis (MS) and rasagiline (Azilect) for PD. Dr. Reddy's is currently more successful in launching new formulations of generics. Both act as VCs and invest in their own research, often into small molecule drug development. Their problems are, thus, becoming the same as those of Big Pharma and it is unlikely that they will now

---

206 Most pharmaceuticals for the Eastern Block were produced in Hungary.

crowd the areas left by Big Pharma because these behemoths found them too risky.

Middle-sized biotechs such as Europe's largest biotech, Actelion, have their own drug discovery potential. Actelion has $1.9 billion in annual sales from bosentan (Tracleer), an endothelin receptor (ET-A and ET-B) antagonist. It is a highly successful product for the treatment of pulmonary hypertension (judged too small an indication by Roche). Actelion's founders worked at Roche, from which the molecule Tracleer is licensed. However, Actelion has so far failed with all of the last six of its own development projects that it started in order to diversify. Now the company is under pressure from its owners, hedge funds, to be acquired. The appetite of such a large biotech to take on far more risk than Big Pharma is unlikely to be big.

Industry spin-out companies will appear in the areas Big Pharma abandons and, with some very few exceptions, these will have a very hard time unless there is some government support. Private capital has supported such spin-outs in the past because it was shown that when these were successful the parent company often exercised buy back rights and, thus, a large pharma partner was more or less guaranteed. In other cases, there were or might be competing Big Pharma in the same area. The pharma from which the spin-out came would not want to strengthen a competitor, and the leaders of the spun-out company would not wish to combine forces with the competitor, either because they wanted to work in a smaller company, where their success would not have to be shared so widely, or just to ensure the safety of their own positions, which might come under threat from the competitor's own researchers in the area. Often a combination of these factors, together with some eager VC backing where the financiers described the project as a victim of political changes but where science and technology was in the best order, led to the formation of spin-outs. A good example is the antibiotics company Basilea Pharmaceutica, which was formed after Roche-Syntex, the largest supplier then of hospital antibiotics with the cephalosporin antibiotic ceftriaxone (Rocephin), had endured 12 years of failures to bring a new product to the clinic. Roche thus spun-out its large, scientifically highly respected group of scientists and chemists working on antibiotics. Since then Basilea has had to forge deals with other large pharma like J&J. Now, J&J is just the largest example of Big Pharma backing out of the area and thereby giving back to Basilea the rights to their joint antibiotics development projects. In short, Basilea will be in a hard position to find financiers when several large companies with competence in the area have turned away from it. This is even though trials for an antibiotic are much shorter than for an AD drug and far more focused. The presence of the disease, the bacterial load, and its decline and the return to health of the study group can be precisely measured; the treatments are of a duration of weeks and not years. Yet we see no promising, truly novel antibiotics approved in the past 10 years and the pathogenic bacteria have not stopped mutating and becoming resistant to the present drugs. Again, if we want novel antibiotics, we will have to take the long view and support them as one does with other societal needs.

The sad picture emerging is that those parts of the drug discovery, drug development, manufacturing, marketing, and post-marketing surveillance process that are easy to industrialize fully, such as manufacturing, may be extremely effectively done by many actors, as the success of generic drug companies worldwide shows. It is easy to find bidders for these parts. Clinical trial design, organization, and registration of drugs are done efficiently by large CROs who work for Big Pharma and for biotech and the governmental CROs[207] have mastered this to the same or higher extent, and also work globally to find the right patients for a trial. Thus, we can be sure that were we to have a serious clinical candidate for disease modification in AD, and someone to finance the trial, that this will be done competently.

Which diseases are international, urgent priorities?
The WHO is charged with and carries out the task of following international healthcare development and emergencies and epidemics. It is very

---

207   Such as WHI used to be and NICE is now.

focused on the countries with low levels of medical care delivered, such as in Africa and Asia. The problems of these countries are not at the level of drug development but at the level of political stability, the lack of transparency of institutions, and policies that endanger even the delivery and distribution of drugs donated and developed for them. The other huge problem is the extremely low number of trained medical personnel. While the industry develops diagnostic tests that can be successfully administered many times by analphabets in countries with 1 doctor per 50,000, a different set of problems is being mostly discussed in this book. It is an ongoing task to address the major diseases in these countries such as malaria, sleeping sickness, leishmaniasis, tuberculosis, and HIV/AIDS, to mention a few, in the focus of international efforts by NGOs,[208] governments, and WHO.

In the developed world, which can now be argued to encompass the majority of mankind, healthcare standards are improving and most of these countries not only use but also produce drugs, even if these drugs are in many cases generic drugs. Nevertheless, the majority of antibiotics and antivirals used are now produced in India, Brazil, and China, and these large countries aim to develop proprietary drugs too.[209]

The healthcare problems such as the emerging epidemics of AD and type 2 diabetes with obesity will hit all countries. The urgency to develop drugs for these indications is to meet a global risk and to address a global market opportunity. Benefits from the results of change from the completely profit motive-guided selection of which diseases to treat and which drugs to develop will take many years, and most likely decades. This leaves us with selection of the diseases to which we want to attach such importance that we make their treatment a national or international priority. This is a medical-social-political problem, where the economic cost of the disease burden, the human suffering it causes, and the changes

---

208   Such as those already listed earlier in Chapters 04 and 05, as well as Medicines for Malaria Venture, Drugs for Neglected Diseases initiative (DNDi), Foundation for Innovative New Diagnostics (FiND), and so forth.
209   See Chapter 12.

it causes in our society can only be tackled by politicians using medical, scientific, and economic expertise. Surely AD and type 2 diabetes, both looming epidemics, and drugs to treat stroke, schizophrenia, and neuropathic pain, as well as the need for novel antibiotics and vaccines, will make the list? Of these, pharma has picked only type 2 diabetes, with exceptionally high research and clinical trial activity in the area; the others will need strong, determined, and sustained political will and governmental support.

One must also remember that part of the problem in areas of medical need has been that science has not delivered enough drug targets for pharma to work on, nor sufficiently sophisticated and more translatable animal models to judge early the likelihood of clinical trial success.[210]

Step 1: intensify research

Step 1, which does not necessarily require too much intervention, but needs the will of scientists, would be to intensify the basic research in these areas of intense concern. This means more programmatic research and less free, investigator-initiated research as the total research budgets are shrinking in real terms again.[211] This is, ideologically speaking, a sad development because the world has benefited in an incredible manner from the research based on the scientific curiosity of individual, talented researchers working in areas and on questions that were thought by others with concrete goals in mind to be "off the chart." Yet, for example, the work on the nematode worm *C. elegans*[212] taught us about the rules of programmed cell death, work in yeast richly contributed to cancer research, and so forth. Society should recognize and accept this: new medical treatments cannot develop without basic research—often carried out on unpretentious, often bizarre and largely unknown animals, even if many millions of these live in your garden.

---

210   See also Chapter 06.
211   See Figure 7.1.
212   *Caenorhabditis elegans* to give it its immediately forgettable first name, which may mean "mud worm." It is arguably the elegant one of its genus, apparently.

Today we can treat, for example, most leukemias and lymphomas, a significant portion of breast cancer patients, and so forth. The success of cancer therapies draws on the huge governmental investments in basic research. Similarly, turning HIV from a deadly disease into a chronic disease is based on a huge and ongoing basic research enterprise. Thus, for a while, we have to make bitter prioritizations and spend a lot more on the basic research in areas like AD or, more generally, neurodegenerative disease.[213] This will have to come at the cost of narrowing—not killing completely—support for other areas. It turns out that when talented researchers looking for grant support come into an area they have not earlier worked in, they bring game-changing ideas. They may not like the mechanism by which they were led there, but their achievements have been often dramatic.

Step 2: new results, new targets, new biotechs

The increase in basic research intensity will lead small biotech companies in this area to form around new results that reveal new drug targets. But, as discussed above, this will only happen if there is some serious prospect of being able to take into clinical trials the fruits of these research and drug development projects.

Since time is of the essence when we think of AD epidemics, one must admit that small start-up biotechs learning the tricks of drug discovery for the first (or maybe the second) time are not the most efficient way to go about it, and this is why it would be useful to make a governmentally or partly governmentally supported spin-out of 500 or more R&D staff that has a large critical mass of experience in drug development and the disease in question, be it AD or another chosen disease.

The new biotechs would need some old heads. There are many examples of currently approved drugs being discovered in academia, but they have

---

213 This is important: being too narrow sometimes precludes finding the solution. Molecular and cellular mechanisms are often common between different diseases. Studying neurodegeneration can lead to greater understanding and greater benefit than studying AD alone.

all been clinically developed and marketed from well-funded biotechs, if not from within Big Pharma.

The cost and the effort from the large companies that goes into forming and hiring a working R&D group in the highly complex process that is drug discovery is often ignored. When such groups are cut from the company's future, there are large but calculable, often tax deductable, restructuring costs for the company. But the loss for society is enormous. Costs may only at best be enumerated in the form of unemployment benefits, which are in some societies very short lived. There is no estimate of the cost of lost opportunity to society or of how much society might have already benefited from a drug in a critical disease discovered by this group. There is too much emphasis on how much drugs cost rather than how much society benefits.

Step 3: government-backed initiatives

The NIH started directly to support drug discovery in 2005. There are high-throughput screening centers and toxicological and other services run by the NIH, yet it has not discovered a single drug. One may argue that 7 years is too short, but we see no live phase 2 candidates. Many outside observers classify this program as a "failure"; hopefully this is too rushed a judgment. As well as not having had any successes, it does not have the experience of hundreds of failed projects. In addition, the budget for this translational research is $750 million, and even this amount has run into large opposition from basic scientists. Yet even if the budget continues to be approved it is a drop in the ocean. A major trial costs up to $1 billion over 3-5 years. Thus, at most, the NIH could run 3-5 trials. This would mean that, with the present attrition rate of drug development projects in the best, most experienced 100-year-old pharma companies, the NIH might have an approved drug every 6-10 years and not without some considerable luck.

The NIH and NIH-supported academia and its government-backed counterparts in Europe, China, and Japan do so well at basic research in biology, discovering new pathways, and novel targets—prerequisites for drug discovery, earlier diagnosis, and patient selection—better than anyone. It is hard to understand why the NIH wants to build an embryonic translational research division. Perhaps the protagonists did not understand the scale of the problem or were too focused on political fruits: how nice it would be if the government could be said to have developed this new drug. But for the patients, only efficacy and safety count; who made the drug is irrelevant.

The medicinal chemistry part of such an enterprise is, for example, so very important. Although NIH supports chemists through its National Institute of General Medical Sciences (NIGMS) programs, its efforts are dwarfed by those of Big Pharma. The chemical library that NIH screening centers access is much smaller and seemingly of lesser likelihood to contain drug-like molecules than the libraries of 4–10 million compounds of any of the top 15 pharma companies.[214] If the NIH seriously worked on drug discovery, it would have to improve dramatically the ratio of chemists to biologists within research, which is today approximately 1:30 while in drug companies it is approximately 1:2. Better and possibly best would be if the NIH became the custodian of a large pharma spin-out wherein one could preserve some institutional memory from Big Pharma's successes, failures, and learning, and fuse this with the basic science and the clinical trial prowess of the NIH. While we most often speak of the United States and the NIH, there are similar setups, with a similar scientific quality and similar, but abandoned, industrial backgrounds in countries such as the UK, France, Switzerland, and Germany for drug development. Successive M&As have reduced those still employed in Big Pharma and left many well-trained drug developers available for work. There are riches of talent for scientific discovery among the unemployed.

Smaller diseases such as Fragile X and Huntington's disease are today being pushed at the research and early, pilot phase 1–2a trial level by NGOs, and we must not leave these NGOs completely without support

214   See Bartfai, T & Lees, GV (2006) *Drug Discovery: from Bedside to Wall Street*, for more information on this aspect of drug discovery.

because phase 2b-3 trials in several of these diseases may be far beyond their organizational and financial capacities.

Government has intervened before in passing the legislation required to provide incentives for orphan drug discovery. Progress in our context will depend upon more lobbying than we can provide through this book.

Outsourcing & what parts of the drug discovery process are scalable?

The cuts in the R&D budgets by billions of dollars are accompanied by the cuts in the number of diseases the industry pursues and limited by thinking about which parts of the drug discovery project are scalable and which are not. In addition, which steps can be safely outsourced while retaining high quality, yet rather more economically, that is, cheaply? The industry's history of outsourcing is summarized in Table 11.1.

The results of the past 10 years in life science and chemistry laboratories in academia that are most similar to the early phase of drug discovery in the industry are:

- drug target identification and validation,
- the understanding of the biology of the disease in cellular and molecular terms, and
- defining the site and mechanism by which to intervene.

Before 1950	In-house research and using the literature
1950s	In-house research and university consultants
1960s	In-house research and contract research at universities
1980s	In-house research and biotech companies, CROs for excess clinical work
1995	In-house research, biotech companies, and outsourcing, off-shoring to India and China starts
2005	In-house research, biotech incubators, outsourcing, and option funds
2011	Joint VC financing; VCs, and Big Pharma to identify projects

Table 11.1: Forms of outsourcing in pharma
In clinical development CROs became important in the 1980s and today account for ~ 60% of clinical trial activity: 35-60% for Big Pharma and 95-100% for biotech.

The experience seems not to lend itself to any large-scale enterprise. Project groups of 6-20 people have been most successful in these endeavors, and increasing this number did not provide the industry any proportional shortening of times required or better results. Thus, this portion of the industry's budgets is being relentlessly cut and, whenever possible, renewed by new, young, and thus cheaper talent from academia. The screening assays via the chemical library with its extensions and replenishments seem to lend themselves better to outsourcing; the chemists of many Big Pharma become designers but not synthesizers of the compounds that make up the library of Big Pharma. This is made possible as Russian, Indian, and Chinese companies now offer chemistry services (synthesis and analytics) at 25-50% of the cost in the United States or Europe. Equally important is that the quality control of the synthesized compounds is unequivocal. Using agreed analytical methods, with the same instruments as the designer and user of the compounds, purity and structure are ascertained, and, thus, there is not much temptation to misjudge and cheat each other in these outsourcing deals. Of course, we do not know the effort and costs that go into delivery of agreed compounds, but we know what the delivered product is and how pure it is.

The biological work up of the molecules, however, is a battleground where protagonists of keeping the important toxicology and efficacy assays in house point to many mismanaged outsourcing deals. Examples are cited where the prices for *in vivo* animal toxicology have been pushed down and the quality and reproducibility of the data suffered, ultimately causing embarrassment and delays. The size of toxicology and histology laboratories is important: no one wants to use a lab that does not have a great deal of experience, and large volume, and is not kept up to date. But this is only worthwhile for a laboratory if it has sufficient numbers of compounds going through. There are no advantages to having one's own toxicology and histology laboratories in terms of the price of testing and it is not strictly scalable. The keeping of modern methods and quality sets a minimum size. This is certainly possible for academic and biotech drug discovery when it has been achieved for the hospitals. Clinical laboratory work in individual hospitals is being outsourced, for example, to LabCorp (Roche) because of cost advantages and up-to-date tests, except for tests needed for urgent treatment decisions in emergency medicine.[215]

Efficacy testing in complex models, for example, of behavior, is one of the most expensive and also the most dangerous to outsource despite the advent of powerful video recordings, and so forth. The very start of the outsourcing exemplified a cost-cutting exercise where finance departments wanted to believe that this is possible without loss of quality and credibility. Of course, this is not the case here, as it is not the case almost anywhere else. The fact is that in providing efficacy testing of advanced drugs the companies in France, the United States, and the UK are keeping up very well against the cheaper competition from China and India because, so far, the quality and scientific standard has been better and more stable. The gap may be shrinking, but it is clear that timely reliable data are worth paying for when 1 month of a drug on the market may mean $100 million income; thus, delay from faulty testing is a foolish consequence of falsely "saving."

The outsourcing of clinical trials saw its peak in early 2000 when all Big Pharma companies relied on some CRO to handle some of their trials while their own clinical research departments were fully occupied. The major cuts of research and the M&As have left a reduced need for CRO involvement with Big Pharma, and most CROs focus on biotech-produced clinical candidates. In these cases, CROs, with their significantly better and deeper experience than biotech, play a bigger role in the design of the trials and not only in their execution. The latest trends are that CROs in search of "virgin" populations that have not already all been treated with all the generic drugs frequently used in the West, moved eastward. First came the multiple sclerosis (MS) trials in Eastern Europe and then the rheumatoid arthritis (RA) trials. The advantage of finding patients who, for example, are not on methotrexate although diagnosed with RA is clear. The population of unmedicated sufferers is shrinking because a

---

215   See Chapter 08.

U.S. or European trial in RA will have to be conducted as an add on to methotrexate, which is the standard of care in these countries. There are sometimes clear genetic bases for certain necessary outsourcing of clinical trials: Japanese approval of a drug requires that it has been tested on ethnic Japanese, and soon similar requirements for the bigger population of Han Chinese will be the reality.

It is clear that CROs today are sensing the drop in earlier parts of drug discovery activities and they are in competition to acquire the contract for fewer and fewer clinical trials. One strategy is that a CRO-owned VC is investing in many biotechs in case they produce a successful clinical candidate. This is so that in the event of success of a new drug, for which the CRO has conducted the trials, the CRO will be a co-owner rather than a "work-for-hire" participant.

Real really beats virtual

Could one achieve the development of these much needed drugs using competing virtual companies? It seems that cost cutting in Big Pharma together with the appearance of cheap, reliable, and high-quality platform companies in Russia, India, and China, which synthesize chemical libraries of hundreds of thousands of compounds, led to the assumption that in drug development everything can be outsourced and that the end result will be the same but achieved more cheaply, and perhaps more expediently. Indeed, there are CROs that do toxicology testing, efficacy testing, and so forth, and thus one could imagine that with a sack of money one can in a quasi-virtual pharma company produce a drug to be tested by a CRO. The case of Boeing's Dreamliner may, however, serve to make us pause. While the product development cycle for airliners and drugs is similar at 10–12 years, making an airplane is more predictable, according to the engineers, than predicting or even measuring the interactions of the drug molecule with 10 million different patient bodies having different genetic and environmental vulnerabilities. Yet Boeing embarked on extensive outsourcing and is lagging behind its delivery plans by 3 years, and is worried about safety; work had to be repeated in house. The residual issues with outsourced battery development grounded the entire fleet. In drug development, we worry no less about safety and we do not work on simpler systems than humans in all of their manifestations. Pharma's best people are its most important capital investment, and they are being cut. The underappreciated—at least by the economically motivated and educated new bosses of pharma and self-styled gurus of Wall Street—aspect is that the R&D staff provide the only robust and experienced institutional memory of the risks and failures throughout the full flow diagram and context of the drug-development process, which has over 1,000 steps. It is less likely that these so-far hypothetical virtual pharma companies will be more successful than the former reality-based and vastly experienced large pharma companies in discovering drugs in these hard indications.

Our proposal is that it would be better to create a second tier of society-sponsored higher risk projects that would be executed in the same well-working framework of Big Pharma alongside the drug discovery pharma is undertaking for the areas in which they have decided to remain. The entities would have independence and separate accounting as spin-offs but would have the resources and intelligence of Big Pharma. While this may sound complicated, we have all seen recently some serious financial engineering, even if some of the engineering did not enjoy a good outcome; it is perfectly feasible.

The bottom line is that such a future, in which pharma companies exist only as a virtual administrative, management, and finance company, and outsource all their core activities, is not going to be successful, in our opinion, in producing novel drugs. Government-backed supportive intervention in the process would be.

Manufacturing in the near future

Manufacturing of drugs is a complicated process wherein quality control even by famous old companies often fails, and where the regulatory agencies play a key role in maintaining the safety of patients. Yet the generic manufacturers showed that it is fully possible to produce cheaply and reliably drugs that someone else has invented and someone else has tested in clinical trials. Thus, discovery and development, on one hand, and manufacturing and marketing, on the other, could be separated for these "priority drugs" to find the best scientific and technical possibilities that are still leaving some of the financial incentives in place.

Clinical trials in the near future

For the clinical trials in the key abandoned diseases at the core of the argument, *existing* governmental programs have the best track record and the best chance of success. Admittedly the whole industry of private CROs exists, and suffers now that Big Pharma has cut its drug-development programs. Therefore, the government can outsource this expensive, financially risky, long-trial-filled activity to these private companies. Or it can use the already government-financed NIH- or NICE-run networks that have conducted large, long clinical trials at the highest standards and with major results for our understanding of the risk-benefit ratios of approved drugs, such as the HRTs discussed earlier. Other government-sponsored trials, which were larger than private companies tend or want to do, include GSK's PPARG[216] activators used to treat diabetes, which cause long-term cardiovascular problems, or comparing older, generic and new expensive antipsychotics for efficacy. These important trials have had a major impact on how we use certain medicines, and also had a major impact[217] on the companies (GSK, Wyeth, and Lilly) that had these drugs as their major earners.

Positive outcome of the near future

What this really means is that, while Big Pharma cuts therapeutic areas but still retains a sufficient number of projects to maintain its experience, there will be no change in the quality of the in-house work under this schematic. Many have concluded that the lack of R&D efficiency gains in

---

216 Peroxisome proliferator-activated receptor gamma (PPAR-γ or PPARG).
217 The impact has often been thought of as entirely negative, but even if the trials caused physicians to exercise more caution in prescribing the drugs in question, the trials caused no litigation even if risks were revealed, and none of the drugs in question have been withdrawn. The outcome is far from entirely negative for society and pharma alike.

the past decades may be caused by the increasing size of the research organizations, and that the optimal size would be 400-500 researchers of all the needed specialties as one unit; even if one were to keep many more scientists on the payroll they should be in no larger groups than units of this size, as GSK discovered. The retained projects can support the up-to-date high-tech platforms such as chemistry, drug design, toxicology, and efficacy testing. The Big Pharma model, which focuses on production and marketing of proprietary drugs and increasingly generic drugs, ensures that one will keep a sufficiently large number of R&D projects to distribute risk over the still-selected therapeutic areas. We might be speaking of maybe 4-5 areas and not the 20 of recent history.

The biotechs compete well in the early preclinical research, in particular when the putative drug is a biological. Here, scale plays no important role. In the subsequent steps of drug development they too have to deal with CROs. Unfortunately, as smaller customers, they experience often worse service, even though poor service is more lethal to them than to Big Pharma. Many biotechs now use more expensive and more responsive CROs in recognition of this situation. When Big Pharma outsources clinical development, it has a solid internal organization to follow enrollment and execution, while small biotech, with just one or two medically trained experienced chief medical officers (CMOs), are much at the mercy of the CRO. Individual biotechs may be a customer in every tenth year for just one project; they cannot compete for the attention of CROs with Big Pharma.

Negative outcome of the near future

What happens if no governmental intervention occurs to produce drugs for strategically important diseases? There will be a significantly increased demand for enhanced drug candidate quality and a slow-down in progress.

As the finance and political processes in Europe and North America are again moving away from public projects it is entirely possible that, while the U.S. president is able to declare AD as a national emergency, it will not translate into any engagement in developing drugs to prevent or slow the disease. In this case scientists will continue laboring on, increasing understanding of the disease pathology in cellular and molecular terms. New "incremental" discoveries will be made with the limited resources for basic research. It will lead to ideas about clinical translation of these new ideas, but now the scarcity of VC financing and the lack of Big Pharma, which might have previously wanted to take over the projects, will make the drug discovery process slow, although it will not stop.

Any successful progress will be limited by pervasive visions in the field. Many scientists and clinicians believe that by using relevant animal models, they might find a much more robust drug that will have such a large therapeutic effect that it is expected that this can be demonstrated in a 6-month trial on 300 patients. This could certainly lead to some VC financing of such a trial and finding out whether the scientists were right or rather too optimistic. Given such a large therapeutic signal, with a large response rate and large therapeutic window with a good safety profile, one might indeed activate the attention of a Big Pharma. It will eventually, using its superior resources, make a me-too drug to this breakthrough Alzheimer drug. It will try to make a best in class drug that supersedes the drug from the biotech. Big Pharma might partner in developing the new Alzheimer drug, or do both drugs as it often chooses to do: it has a large purse.

It needs to be pointed out that the demand for significantly better, that is, less developmentally risky, drug candidates is going to lead to not only longer but also much more expensive preclinical research as we try to improve the qualities compared to what used to be an acceptable clinical candidate. Thus, VCs must be prepared that partnering will take a longer time and the sustaining of a biotech company will cost much more.

One may ask what is wrong with this scenario. And the most prevalent answer may be "nothing." Except for, that is, the inordinately long time it would take to find drugs for approaching epidemics. The fall-back, the most comfortable position is: "the market will solve it." *This is wishful thinking.*

As unjust as it may be from the point of view of a single individual suffering from a small disease, there is little doubt that we must mobilize societal resources for treating the looming large epidemics.

Perfect is not perfect

Demanding that drug candidates become better is always possible and is nothing new. Today many of the drugs approved in the 1960s would not be approved, although they continue to be used. Indeed, we spend ten to a hundred times more than we spent in the 1960s to prepare a drug candidate before testing in humans. Thus, we generate better drugs. But, when the situation is somewhat desperate, turning to really desperate as with AD, then society would accept less than perfect drugs to affect disease progression. The present drugs have both low efficacy and many side effects.

We must not accept that the programs stop until the perfect or close to perfect drug is found.

In other cases, it is likely that the new found austerity of Big Pharma, while it somewhat slows down drug discovery, will lead to even better drugs. It is like telling the strikers in a soccer team that they are not permitted to shoot unless they are about 10 m from the goal. This happens seldom, but it is also true that shots from that near a distance more often lead to goals than from almost any other distance.

Can we afford this strategy? If we must, sure we can, but do we not have to? There is no mutual exclusivity between simultaneously pushing stepwise the demands on the drug candidates, and thereby reducing the risk of failure, and continuing the process as is.

Pharma has discovered that there is a disconnect between its research spending and the drug approvals resulting from it, so it reduces its research spending; it wants to improve the quality of the drug candidates, and decided that it is easier in some areas than in others. Unfortunately for society, this does not serve our needs; we also need drugs in the hard areas.

Room, & time, for optimism?

Despite the large cuts in Big Pharma R&D, one may be optimistic and point to the recent past when biotech companies stepped in successfully to an area neglected by Big Pharma.

In 1980, oncology—now a darling of many pharma because of several very highly priced therapeutic antibodies ($30,000-$75,000/treatment cycle)—was not regarded as an essential therapeutic area by the Big Pharma companies; only 6 of the then top 20 companies had any presence in this therapeutic area. This has dramatically changed and examining the reasons for this may help to rekindle interest in some recently abandoned therapeutic areas.

The Big Pharma view on oncology as a therapeutic area of interest for drug development has changed for two major reasons:

1. The massive, decades long, government investment in cancer research revealed interesting drugable targets for the drug companies to work on, thus saving them the long and costly basic research.

2. The large basic science effort coincided with the birth and growth of the biotech industry based on the relatively easy availability of venture capital; several academic researchers could found the biotech company, whose first drug was often to be a therapeutic antibody for treatment of a cancer.

More details are given in Table 11.2.

This was a coincidence of many good elements: scientific breakthroughs in genetics and cell biology, and technology breakthroughs in imaging, recombinant technology, and sequencing. It cannot be expected to occur again, at least not in the same shape. But it gives rise to optimism that the often seemingly realistic pessimism of Big Pharma to the imagined intractable problems of solving the most difficult problems can be overcome. The problems need to be surmounted.

In the 1960s and 1970s, cancer certainly looked at least as insurmountable as AD has looked over recent years.

Factors that have made oncology a favorite therapeutic area for biotech & pharma
1. Government-sponsored large-scale research over decades revealed many drug targets; it is an area rich in drug targets and in knowledge of biochemical pathways.
2. Recognition that, although individual cancers present a fragmented therapeutic area, some large-selling drugs can be developed to treat many cancer forms because they address general underlying problems.
3. The ability for almost anyone to make recombinant proteins was opened in the late 1980s and continued to become a more streamlined and cheaper process with each passing year.
4. The antibodies are biologicals that had a very good safety record and required much shorter development time (5-8 years) than small molecule drugs.
5. The clinical trials in different cancers were the most favorable from the small companies' point of view: they are small and not of long duration.
6. The success of eventually mastering the design of non-toxic protein kinase inhibitors has given us a set of drugs that are effective in several cancers.
7. Diagnostics, imaging, and sequencing developments help to define cancers earlier.
8. Imaging assists in following the results of therapy of solid tumors; no area benefits more from imaging than oncology.

Table 11.2: Why oncology is a favorite therapeutic area for biotech & pharma

1. Most of the research was in basic cell biology—scientists had to know how cells worked before they could work out what was wrong with the continuously dividing cancer cells. 2. Similarly, radiation therapy can treat many cancers, and, for example, chemotherapy blockade of neo-vascularization helps to stop the growth of many solid tumors. 3. Technology made the making of therapeutic antibodies to treat cancers—an area where Big Pharma interest and competence was low—become an obvious choice for scientists, who, with government-funded research, have identified many potential drug targets that were tumor-specific antigens addressable by antibodies. 4. Compared with biologicals, small molecule drug development requires 20 times the number of researchers, chemists, and toxicologists; takes on average 10-12 years; and thus mostly remained in the domain of Big Pharma. 5. Less complex clinical trials enabled many biotechs to finance—in the better economic climate of the mid to late 1990s—full cancer drug development through phase 3; in addition, a narrower therapeutic index, that is, higher side effect-efficacy profile is accepted because of the high mortality caused by cancer. 6. Progress in developing these kinases as drugs was made possible because of the government-sponsored academic research on the pathway knowledge in many tumors. 7. Selecting patients most likely to respond to and benefit from the drug became possible with genotyping. 8. There is a greater willingness for drug development to continue when the tumor's shrinking or disappearing is visible to the eye, and for the insurers to pay the high prices.

Faster, longer regulatory practices

We did not discuss the changes in regulatory practices in clinical trial design and in drug approval times that are expected to make positive changes of 5–10%. Improving the cost of discovery of drugs will not assist with the abandoned areas of medical need, but it may improve profit in the areas chosen by the industry. Faster approvals would bring drugs to market and generate revenue streams earlier in patent life.

However, the regulatory agencies' main focus is not to change from patient safety. Indeed, while promising faster decisions, the request for longer safety data collection will work in the opposite direction. Administrative times being shortened cannot compensate for asking for a 5-year cardiovascular safety data collection. Faster approvals would then be in the realm of science fiction.

The more extensive use of biomarkers in clinical trials will increase investor confidence, but it is not expected to change in emphasis from real end points remaining the same. No matter how well a biomarker for tumor growth indicates that it has stopped, if there is not a progression-free survival benefit for the patient, the proposed cancer drug will not be approved. Even if it were to be surprisingly approved it should not be used. Showing lowered amyloid load in cerebral spinal fluid or with imaging in the brain will never replace the real end point of slower or no loss of cognitive ability in AD.

Chapter 12: Drug development models between 2010 & 2025

When this book is being written, in 2011-2013, it is the time to start most drug development projects that will lead to approved drugs in 2025. This is a long time and an uncommon characteristic shared by the pharmaceutical and airline industries. Both industries require large capital reserves and a high-tech background in their respective countries.

The parallels used to end here, since the number of customers for military aircraft was the number of governments while we used to think that pharmaceutical products are being purchased by millions of patients. But in reality, the different insurance schemes of the different countries in the end leave the governments as the major customers of drugs like they are of aircraft.

The number of military and civil aircraft-building countries is very limited and although large customers insist on technology sharing and being involved in delivery of parts, the technology has not spread much when it comes to the design of new models. In pharma the picture is not dissimilar.

The first part of this chapter deals with the complex set of requirements: scientific, clinical, legal, and financial—backed by an appropriate investment culture—that is needed for successful development of novel drugs. The national regulatory institutes, capital, and investment habits, and other characteristics were so favorable in tiny Switzerland, but were so hard to create in short order in some of the emerging new economic powers.

Why the pharma industry is where it is

The traditional Central European, French, British, and U.S. pharma industries as producers of novel drugs has been completed with a strong Japanese pharma industry, which still often chooses alliance with western firms over alliance with Japanese or Asian firms. The balance between

The Future of Drug Discovery. http://dx.doi.org/10.1016/B978-0-12-407180-3.00012-X

European and American firms is constantly moving since WW II with a migration toward the United States. Until WW II, Germany used to be the "pharmacy of the world." The rise of American pharmaceutical firms is somewhat owing to German immigrants like the Pfizers, Merck, and so forth and because of a second wave of immigrants in the 1930s. The U.S. industry is strong but not dominant, however. The advent of recombinant protein-based biologicals, which are an increasing proportion of new drugs since the 1990s, has moved the weight-point toward the United States. The United States pioneered the discovery and development of biologicals even if this involved European ideas and funds. In the period from 1960 to 1985, the scientific and technical prominence of the United States in molecular biology compared with Europe made the site of development of biologicals clearly U.S. based. For example, KABI, a large Swedish government-owned— at the time—plasma fractionation firm defined and financed several of the early projects of Genentech in San Francisco such as recombinant growth hormone (GH) and tissue plasminogen activator (tPA). There have been, at the time of writing, less than three approved biologicals originating from Germany, even though Europe caught up scientifically with the United States in molecular biology, genomics, and protein expression technology. The Swiss multinationals Roche, Novartis, and Serono are well represented in biologicals, but mostly from their U.S. sites or acquisitions. So why did European biotech-based biologicals not catch up, and what does that teach us about the future of the development of pharmaceutical products?

The major European and U.S. pharmaceutical firms, none of which yet controls 20% of the pharmaceutical market, are undergoing strong consolidation that started with the 1995 acquisition by Roche of Syntex, then crowned as one of the most innovative U.S. companies. Mergers and acquisitions (M&As) is a process, picking up fully after Glaxo-Wellcome, and the subsequent GlaxoWellcome-SmithKlineBeecham merger, which has generated companies of market capitalization of $100 billion or more. The capital intensity of the industry is one reason it did not spread geographically so easily, but, today, there are many companies in many countries that could buy a company like Schering-Plough, bought in 2009 for $40 billion by Merck, or Wyeth, bought in 2009 for $47 billion by Pfizer.

There is more to establishing a strong and innovative pharmaceutical industry than ownership of the company.

The top 10 drug companies by revenue and per employee earnings in 2009 were listed in Table 1.2. It is worth noting that all of the companies relied on a few multibillion dollar per year blockbuster drugs, which have or will lose patent protection in the coming years. In the case of Lilly more than half of its income originated from drugs that lost patent protection by the end of 2011.

It is worth noting that no Japanese, Chinese, or Indian companies are among the top 10 companies so listed.

Emerging economies & pharma

Table 12.1 lists the major factors that are identifiable in the development of the European, U.S., and Japanese pharmaceutical industries.

	Major factors in the development of the European, U.S., & Japanese pharmaceutical industries
1	Strong capital market and long-term financing available
2	Strong scientific background in chemistry and biology (home grown and/or imported)
3	Investment attitude that accepts that 90% of the projects end in total loss of the invested capital and human work—and that this often becomes first known after 8-10 years of investment—this in exchange for high earnings over a long period
4	Strong intellectual property (IP) protection
5	Strong regulatory framework in the home country and reliability and credibility of clinical trials
6	Mercantile attitude that produces drugs for the entire world—almost no home market is sufficient to recoup the costs of development
7	Prime production capacity
8	Internationally credible control authorities

Table 12.1: Factors key to pharmaceutical industry development
When discussing the different emerging economies such as Brazil, China, India, and Russia, major gaps in one or several of these factors are apparent and these are not easily filled in a short time. The hardest to foresee a major change in are factors 3 and 8.

The emerging large economies have impressed the world and their home public by their rapid growth wherein they have utilized natural resources and/or cheap labor, and the long-awaited and present availability of capital, which now they have in abundance. These economies have invested in major ways in education and in importing or re-importing a well-trained highly skilled workforce from the United States and Western Europe, such that there is an abundance of these. This is not the problem when considering a pharmaceutical industry.

However, it is noteworthy that the projects these economies invested in produce returns within a few years, not in 10-12 years, and the risks of these largely manufacturing and engineering projects are much reduced and easier to predict. They produce returns only 20-30% later than projected and cost only 20-30% more than calculated. But these projects will not match the risk inherent in the development of original medicines that are "first in class," lead to failure in 90% of the cases, and where failure means losing 100% of invested capital. And all of this is known only after 10-12 years and when $300-800 million has been spent in a failed phase 3. The most successful companies like Roche-Genentech, Pfizer, Novartis, and GSK have, in 2009 and 2010, experienced failures of phase 3 trials in no less than eight cases and these trials were each based, naturally, on successful phase 2 data. One cannot state that experience was missing. Simply the risk in phase 3 clinical trials is very large for novel medicines when the number of patients treated is expanded 10- to 50-fold compared to the phase 2 trial.

It is often emphasized that all major pharmaceutical companies have established research centers and cooperations with Chinese and Indian firms and that they thus employ tens of thousands of people in research. This is certainly a testimony to the quality of researchers who have been trained in these countries or who have returned from abroad. What is, however, not discussed is that these scientists work on projects that were designed and decided upon outside of the country in which they are carried out, and that taking the risk that 90% of these projects may fail after a long time and a large expenditure will be born outside of these countries.

With ever-increasing capital reserves, there will be capitalists and scientists in these countries who might be able to take the risks drug development involves, but we are far from this point if we aim for the drugs to be approved in 2025. Work on 2025 drug approvals needs to be started now.

Intellectual property & quality

The issues of intellectual property protection are rapidly advancing and will soon, it is hoped, be solved. The quality of clinical trials and the credibility of the data produced by the emerging markets' enterprise will take longer to establish. An increasing number of trials by large contract research organizations (CROs) are carried out in these countries. These lead to better education of trial-physicians and also to an improved level of general medical care. But the regulatory agencies remain somewhat weak, and impressionable. These and other factors suggest that in the short term, and in the pharmaceutical industry this is 10 years, the major source of novel drugs will remain in the countries that presently dominate discovery of new drugs. The large centralized nature of the emerging markets, chiefly in China, may change the economic fundamentals of the industry. In addition, they may also undermine the ability of the emerging markets' firms to carry out original research, or force them into novel forms of cooperation with western firms wanting to sell in China as a requirement for registration and market entry. These are fully in the hands of local authorities and subject to political decisions and policies that can be changed relatively fast. The attitude of investors and researchers, who will take responsibility for the failure rate of modern drug discovery, will be an issue that will take a longer time to address.

Switzerland's opportunity

The example of Switzerland, a tiny neutral country without raw material resources, which is the home of several large successful pharma and biotech companies, is worth discussing when thinking about what it takes for a country to develop or permit the development of a successful pharmaceutical industry.

Switzerland behaved as a huge importer of talent, second only to the United States, and then knew how to use and exploit it. Switzerland is a very small country and, to be successful, it needs to realize this and act accordingly. It needs to import what cannot be homegrown in sufficient quantity. Because talent is evenly distributed among mankind and Swiss education is good but not outstanding, there is an insufficient cadre to supply the requirements of the large number of both academic and industrial institutions that are the country's strength. Switzerland stumbles when it forgets this simple fact. In addition, there is the issue of capital resources. Switzerland has undergone great changes from a poor country, with no industrial capital excess as it was before WW II, to a rich country whose major banks and industry must spend their funds abroad or else import talented workers at every level as well as materials, which for pharma is luckily not a big issue.

One must therefore state somewhere that pharma, while not dependent on raw materials, needs highly educated chemists, biologists, clinical developers (physicians), and patients. It also needs capital, long-term stability in its political and regulatory environment. Regarding regulation, it is worth remembering that strict or lax is not the only issue; how it compares with other countries is what matters. French chemists moved over to the Swiss border town of Basel—the site of the headquarters of giants Hoffmann-La Roche and Novartis[218]—because patent laws in the 1830s were more favorable in Switzerland than France. Switzerland was fairly unique in this regard from 1950[219] to 1970, but after that others caught up and the uniqueness gives way to hard competition with everyone else. Switzerland is doing well in this competition but is becoming one of many.

---

218 The merged Ciba-Geigy and Sandoz.
219 After its neighbor to the northeast, Germany, was no longer equipped to be the "pharmacy to the world."

In the context of drug discovery and drug sales one must emphasize that Switzerland:

a. has an insufficient internal market to sustain drug development;

b. has, despite many outstanding individuals, a shortage of scientific researchers and economic leaders and has to import these continuously;

c. had political, religious, and financial stability, and low taxes, which made it a dreamland for many talented people from less fortunate countries; a dreamland located in the middle of Europe and not in the distant United States, and so for many well-educated people from Central Europe and the Balkans it was the preferred choice;

d. had an intellectual climate that was permissive for technical and scientific innovation but was insular in political and social science issues;[220]

e. had a remarkable language advantage, which in particular made Basel attractive to Germans and French; moreover, English was and is much better taught and spoken in Switzerland than, for example, in Germany or France, lowering the barrier for the influx of English-speaking individuals;

f. had a remarkable merit-driven employment and advancement policy that was attractive to many foreigners who had really bad experiences in their native countries;

g. provided a favorable temperamental fit: drug development[221] requires a long product-development time, a large capital base, and a resilience in the face of failure,[222] all of which were met by the Swiss owners' temperaments; and

h. benefited from the luck of neutrality.

---

220 Switzerland became a member of the United Nations (U.N.) in 2002 as the 190th country.
221 In our previous book we said that drug development was the most regulated human activity, but, on reflection, religion is more regulated, even though, if one does not like the rules, one can start a new one; pharma rules cannot be avoided.
222 For these reasons, we doubt that pharmaceutical development will be easy in China, where the authorities want fast returns. Pharma is full of failures and only 2 of 100 started projects make it to the market. The Chinese also have a reputation for punishing people who fail.

Its pharmaceutical industry really started to expand between 1950 and 1970, and then again between 1990 and 2000 following the molecular biology revolution.

In the first of these periods Switzerland was an intact oasis in a ruined Europe, so those who did not go to the United States but were willing to leave home for good working conditions in a research-based industry, could come from Germany, France, and Central Europe.

The United States had a large and generic flow of immigrants including some highly talented and highly skilled ones. Some of these found employment in the expanding pharma industry, which was in part owned by Swiss companies. In contrast, Switzerland had to shop around in a specific manner to fill specific, well-defined positions in its pharma enterprise with foreign talent. As a foreigner high up in a large Swiss pharma company's research organization, Bartfai saw daily the dilemma of the Swiss owner family: to buy talent abroad and bring it to Basel, or to set up research organizations abroad. This dilemma has been largely settled with the large investments in research facilities in the United States rather than Switzerland by the major Swiss companies in the past 10 years: Roche focusing on the Bay Area around San Francisco, CA, through its purchase of Genentech, and Novartis moving more and more of its research from Basel to Cambridge, MA, respectively. Since the 1950s, both companies have also kept large facilities in New Jersey: the home of many U.S. companies.

The experience of WW II and the deals made with the U.S. certainly played a key role in determining how the owners of Roche acted after the war. They opted for a dualism. They benefited from the more rapid biological innovation in the United States and invested by founding and funding The Roche Molecular Biology Institute in Nutley, NJ. While it became a motor in molecular biology in the United States and for the world, they also financed the Basel Institute of Immunology, which was a "cradle of creativity" for several decades resulting in Nobel Prizes for foreigners working there: Niels Kaj Jerne and Georges J. F. Köhler (1984) and Susumu Tonegawa (1987). Dualism is fine as long as the leadership of the company feels affluent and is not squeezed for rapid returns. Both research institutes have been closed for more than a decade as a result of those pressures and the corporate realization that they did not directly contribute to the commercial success of Hoffmann-La Roche. These events were indicative that the Swiss pharma industry started to measure success in increasingly Anglo-Saxon, that is, predominantly U.S., economic terms and moved to use Anglo-Saxon consulting firms that put a large emphasis on intellectual property over material property and on the time interval a project takes to bring returns independent of its importance.

Now, the ownership and leadership of pharma companies are largely not Swiss but international for the most part, even if the controlling block of shares may be held by a Swiss family as in the case of Roche. Even when they are Swiss, the pharma companies do not behave like traditional Swiss companies anymore. They are fully emulating the Anglo-Saxon companies, which force them into a fully mercantile behavior and may not permit them to retain within Switzerland the balance of research and development; this is what we are witnessing. Eventually the markets transform the producer and this is no different for Swiss pharma at the end of an epoch; companies remain very successful but become, by necessity, global, and are no longer Swiss.

Drug development is moving, but not completely

The scientific, clinical, and technological basis of drug discovery is expanding. The second part of this chapter tries to describe what is already a clear trend, and which requires observation and some limited anticipation. It will also seek to describe some models of drug discovery, which are being discussed today, but which are not yet fully, or not at all, implemented. We believe they will be needed and will thus be invoked, developed, and used in the next 15 years.

Of course, pharma can be innovative and change direction at the prompting of successes of biotech, such as in the case of cancer discussed earlier. Orphan and rare disease status may continue to be worth exploring. This can easily be seen on examination of the 2009-2011 lists of approvals in Tables 3.5-3.7, where other "creativity" is revealed.

Pharma can try "slicing" a bigger indication into smaller diagnostically or otherwise separable groups, or even into imaginary groups thereby "creating new diseases." This "creative" activity is a much practiced procedure by which innovative pharma and biotech executives try to split larger indications into smaller ones that would qualify for orphan drug status. The regulatory agencies do not actively fight this trend but also do not encourage it. Their dilemma is different from that of the insurance companies that simply refuse to pay when an expensive drug is not approved for a condition even if it may be useful in treating it. The regulatory agencies' problem, which they have often encountered in the face of pharma's "sleight of hand," is as follows: they have been asked to approve a drug for a small well-characterized group of patients suffering a disease in which trials can be short with few patients enrolled.[223] It is hard to judge efficacy and safety in a broader section of the population based on the small, short trial even when this produces significant changes in the agreed end point(s).

There are also major changes becoming discernible in the origin of scientific discoveries as the United States and European Union (EU) science funding is declining and Chinese research funding is accelerating as a portion of global R&D. This trend starts to be reflected in scientific publications. Nevertheless as drug development requires many activities besides basic life science and clinical research, the majority of novel drugs will still be developed in the period between 2010 and 2025 in the United States, Japan, and Europe, although with an increasing share of new drugs from China, India, and Russia, which

---

223   This is in fact a notable ingenious technique that has been used, for example, in the original approval of Botox for cervical dystonia, and subsequent variations.

may be reaching 10-15% of globally approved and used new drugs by 2025-2030.

But where does this leave us when we ask who will develop new drugs?

Pharma companies have decided to be open about it, or stock market analysts spoke for many of them. They want to focus on a few diseases that they deem will be profitable to treat and leave the rest of the diseases that have too few sufferers, yet too many for orphan disease status, or that require clinical trials that are too long and too hard with even lower odds of success than the industry average.

Medical need motivates

As this book claims, the medical need, the need of society to act as a healer and controller of epidemics, and the interest of capitalists in any potentially profitable enterprise, will ensure that we will continue to discover and introduce new drugs—even in the next 15 years—despite loud statements about the crisis of the pharmaceutical industry. The models of drug discovery are, however, changing and will continue to change.

The 15-year period may be very long compared to most society planning cycles, but is not too long compared to product development cycles in pharmaceuticals. While some projects reach from preclinical inception to New Drug Application (NDA) stage in a shorter time, the 15 years would be a time line in which a company might have one set of products approved and would start the next set of projects as earlier projects exit through attrition—abandonment and failure—(90-95%) or to approval (5-10%). It may also reveal whether they have continued confidence in the drug development model of the previous 10-15 years. The scientific and technological platforms are developing rapidly. They are being continuously changed as part of the investments within the still large R&D budgets. A budget of 14-20% of sales is enormous compared to those of any other industries.

Past & future trends

Mergers & acquisitions

The period from 1995 to 2010 saw a tremendous consolidation in the industry through M&As too numerous to mention in detail.[224] Yet, none of the large companies so formed controls even 20% of the prescription pharmaceutical market; the 20% mark is usually taken as a sign of a consolidated industry. All of these conglomerates buy continuously smaller companies and projects or products in the range of $20 million to $20 billion. For example, Sanofi bought Genzyme for $20.1 billion in 2011. There is no reason to believe that this trend of consolidation will stop. In fact, a prerequisite for venture capitalist (VC)-based biotech company formation and progression is the belief in the continued purchase of smaller biotech companies by Big Pharma, which has become the major exit strategy for biotechs since IPOs have dwindled dramatically in the past 5 years.

With no exception, the R&D in the combined companies is often smaller than the sum of their parts. At each contraction they lose experienced personnel and diminish the expertise at the heart of drug discovery. But Wall Street does not mind, except that studies have shown that between 2000 and 2010 about $1 trillion was wiped off of the value of the industry, as measured by market capitalization of the industry and the cost of acquisitions. This is from *PharmaNews*:[225]

---

224 For example, Roche-Genentech, AstraZeneca (ICI), and GSK forming from Glaxo-Wellcome merging with Smith-Kline-Beecham seems simple enough. But, Sanofi emerging from Sanofi-Synthelabo-Aventis-(Rhone-Poulenc-Hoechst-Marion-Roussel-Uclaf-(Marion-Merrill-Dow)) resists simplification as does Pfizer incorporating, at least, Pharmacia-Upjohn-Warner-Lambert-Parke-Davis, and so forth. Merck-Schering-Plough is complicated because of co-existing Merck KGaA-Serono and Bayer-Schering. The two Mercks are a result of World War I and the two Scherings are a result of WW II. Hoffmann-La Roche is a minor anomaly in the corporate name game. Fritz Hoffmann with Max Carl Traub founded Hoffmann, Traub & Co. in Basel in 1894. Traub left in 1896 and, meanwhile, Fritz Hoffmann had married Adèle La Roche in 1895, so he renamed himself and the company Hoffmann-La Roche. It may be the only case of a corporate divorce leading to a double-barreled name.
225 Grogan K. (2011) M&A strategy has failed miserably-Burrill Online PharmaTimes, April 13, 2011, http://www.pharmatimes.com/Article/11-04-13/M_A_strategy_has_failed_miser ably_-_Burrill.aspx

Big Pharma has pursued an aggressive strategy of mergers and acquisitions in an effort to grow their businesses, but this approach has failed and resulted in the loss of $1 trillion in value over the last 10 years.

That is one of the key findings in the latest report from Burrill & Co on the biotechnology industry titled *Biotech 2011-Life Sciences: Looking Back to See Ahead* ... on December 31, 2000, the combined market capitalisation of 17 of the industry's most active acquirers was $1.57 trillion, excluding Johnson & Johnson. By the end of last year, that figure had shrunk to $1.04 trillion, a loss of more than $500 billion in market value.

When the combined value of the acquisitions these companies completed during this time, $425 billion, is added, close to $1 trillion in value has been lost during the last decade, even without taking into account transactions of less than $10 million ... Big Pharma continues to produce roughly the same number of new drugs each year despite a steady increase in R&D investment, smaller companies have come up with a growing share of new treatments *"and done so more cost effectively"* ... while the major players are pursuing acquisitions of innovative biotech products and companies, they are now taking steps *"to leave in place the culture of these companies to protect the innovation they covet."* In other instances, big pharma is seeking to emulate biotechs through *"new R&D models that create small, focused, independent research units"* ... the loss of revenue drugmakers are looking at *"over the next several years does not just reflect the impact of competition from generic drugs, but also the failure of big pharma's R&D to generate innovative products to replace those going off-patent"* ... *"if the industry is to return to the type of growth it once enjoyed, it must innovate its way out of its current predicament."*

Big Pharma

We see the trend that Big Pharma will continue to grow, but one must observe that there are two fundamentally different strategies at play in the 10 largest companies and a hybrid of these models is also discernible in the intermediate period.

Model A. Stable large companies like J&J and GSK are working to reduce their dependence on blockbusters and indeed on proprietary drugs altogether. The share of these in their income is shrinking and is below 25-30%. Continued expansion of generic drug production, OTC products, and medical devices in the portfolio of products is aimed to make them even less dependent on the success of their R&D efforts. The explanations for the popularity of this model are many: this model is more like that of other less research-intensive industries; the present executives are often from industries like food, or consumer products with very low R&D and the markets for OTC and generic drugs are more easily understood in terms of raw competition by managers and analysts alike. Also, as many of their own blockbusters are losing patent protection, the question arises to them:

Should we stop making and selling these and take a loss of, say, $3 billion income and hope for another blockbuster that might be slow and erratic in its coming, or should we use our 15 years of knowledge of how to make and sell this drug and capture, say, $0.5 billion worth of the generic market?

Companies increasingly find that, in the absence of great R&D successes, the $0.5 billion sales per year does look attractive with their own, now generic drug.

Model B. In the recent months BMS, Pfizer, and Merck have made statements—usually following a successful NDA approval such as BMS' therapeutic antibody for treatment of melanoma in 2011—that they will increase their R&D efforts to develop high-value proprietary drugs. This is, of course, much in line with how all big companies functioned in the 1995-2010 period. Novartis and Roche also seem to approach the future with these sentiments.

Sanofi is not against R&D, it just does not believe much in its own research, and its trendsetting CEO, Chris Viehbacher, has made huge cuts in Sanofi's R&D, thus joining the ranks of Model A-ers, which is not surprising since he came from GSK. He seems to believe that one can buy or in-license new products and thus embarked on a buying spree often using funds earlier earmarked for R&D. He presented his and Sanofi's thoughts at an event at MIT in April 2010, which was reported in many places, including as follows in *FierceBiotech*:[226]

Sanofi chief outlines R&D, biotech investment strategy—Sanofi-Aventis CEO Chris Viehbacher took the podium at an MIT event to lay out the pharma company's R&D strategy, once again voicing his displeasure with big internal research operations and laying out a new approach to investing in small biotech companies. "My goal as CEO is never to inaugurate a new research and development center," Viehbacher told the group, according to a report in the Boston Business Journal.

The month before, under a possibly misleading title,[227] it was reported:

Sanofi-Aventis—The world's biggest R&D spenders—Under CEO Chris Viehbacher Sanofi has done just about everything that a pharma can do to shake things up. Viehbacher has redefined the company's R&D strategy, dropping some diseases and concentrating on others ... Sanofi also spent $500 million for BiPar, which had one of

---

226 Carroll, John (2011) Sanofi chief outlines R&D, biotech investment strategy, *FierceBiotech* 12 April 2011, http://www.fiercebiotech.com/story/sanofi-chief-outlines-rd-biotech-investment-strategy/2011-04-12. In 2010 the headline was Sanofi-Aventis Chops into R&D Budget, Drops Cancer Drug.
227 Carroll, John (2011) Sanofi-Aventis—he world's biggest R&D spenders, *FierceBiotech*, 8 March,2011,http://www.fiercebiotech.com/special-reports/worlds-biggest-rd-spenders/sanofi-aventis-worlds-biggest-rd-spenders. In 2010 the headline was Sanofi-Aventis Chops into R&D Budget, Drops Cancer Drug, http://www.fiercebiotech.com/story/sanofi-aventis-chops-r-d-budget-drops-cancer-drug/2010-02-10.

the most promising mid-stage cancer drugs in the world—until Sanofi investigators tested iniparib in a phase 3 breast cancer study and saw it fall short of its primary endpoints. Viehbacher's outsourced substantial pipeline work to Covance.

The largest pharmaceutical company Pfizer has pursued in the past 2 years, a hybrid of models A and B, by acquiring, for example, Wyeth, Rinat, and CovX to add to a proprietary drug and vaccine portfolio, and also purchasing King Pharmaceuticals, the generic drug manufacturer. Novartis had earlier bought Hexal, at the time the second largest German generic company, which made Novartis with Sandoz, Hexal with Eon Labs the largest generic, surpassing Teva.

To indicate how unsure these strategies might seem to be, shortly after buying King, Pfizer CEO, Ian Read, was reported[228] to consider Pfizer to be a pure R&D-based pharma company, and indeed Pfizer has sold its highly successful veterinary medicines unit to invest more in pharma.

Model As and the hybrids clearly accelerate the trend of divesting or restricting a company's own R&D. In such a prevalent climate of a company that says: "it is better to purchase than to research and develop in our own shop," the best scientists leave the companies before being fired.

However, the pendulum may swing back and in-house research may come into vogue again. Then we will be under the next set of managers armed with a new balance sheet showing the success, or lack of it,[229] of purchases made. While it is a fast process to destroy a top-class R&D facility, it is a slow process to build top R&D capacity back again.[230] The swing may definitely be expected, however.

228 Carroll, John (2011) Will Pfizer divest a big chunk of its operations?, *FierceBiotech*, 14 March, 2011, http://www.fiercebiotech.com/story/will-pfizer-divest-big-chunk-its-oper ations/2011-03-14.
229 As indicated above for iniparib under "Sanofi-Aventis—The world's biggest R&D spenders."
230 If a company decides to revitalize its in-house R&D it may decide to acquire an R&D department via acquisition of a pharma that had not destroyed it. But, if it can afford its acquisition, it is unlikely that the R&D chunk will be big enough.

Purchased projects and companies undergo ongoing, post-acquisition, tricky "due diligence." The results show that the success rate from phase 1 or phase 2 to NDA of purchased biotech projects is significantly lower than the success rate of in-house projects. It is, however, hard to have the managers responsible for these failed purchases of hundreds of millions of dollars, usually from the recently cut R&D budget, to admit these facts. The due diligence would be carried out by the company's own researchers and they might succumb to their fair share of misjudgments and jealousy about the quality of the biotech in-licensing. Sanofi's acquisition of BiPar Sciences, with one PARP inhibitor as its drug candidate, was described by Bloomberg as "looking like a bargain" and hailed as follows:

Sanofi Lands Cancer Drug by Paying $500 Million for 18 People[231]

Viehbacher said the BiPar acquisition came from a new philosophy he's been pushing since he joined Sanofi six months ago.

"The size of teams and the size of their budget [do] not correlate to research and development success," Viehbacher said in an interview at the meeting[232] yesterday. Sanofi is changing the way it conducts research, seeking "true innovation" by shifting more than half of its drug discovery to smaller companies through acquisitions and partnerships, he said.

BiPar's researchers in San Francisco will keep their offices there, and will continue to lead development of the experimental drug, called BSI-201. Viehbacher, who joined the company six months ago, said the new treatment is now one of the drugmaker's most promising drugs.

---

231   Randall, Tom (2009) Sanofi Lands Cancer Drug by Paying $500 Million for 18 People, Bloomberg 1 June 2009, http://www.bloomberg.com/apps/news?pid=newsarchive&sid=aiit 00.KTlIE&refer=us.
232   of the American Society of Clinical Oncology.

Since the original research team continued the development, the failure could not be blamed on a change in R&D; it just shows how hard it is to make successful drugs. Obviously this is not good news for anyone, especially the cancer patients; the first observations had been really encouraging.

These trends point to a stage where three, four, or five research-driven Big Pharma and a number of pharma-OTC commodity giants will dominate in 2025. The biggest problem is that even the companies that follow or profess to follow Model B and rely on their own R&D have stopped working on many indications that society needs because of the development risk, because they want to reduce their risk. This leaves us with a regrettable vacuum of projects aimed at finding drugs to treat stroke, Alzheimer's disease,[233] neuropathic pain, COPD, and schizophrenia as well as finding novel antibiotics, just to mention a few of the most scary omissions or victims of this strategy.

Large biotech

The large biotech companies, which have sales in billions, struggle to make it to the "Big Pharma" class, that is, to have proprietary product line in several disease areas and sales of $20 billion or more per year. It seems hard; Amgen, Biogen-Idec, Celgene, Gilead, and Vertex (see Table 7.2) seem to be stuck in the $3-15 billion sales and two or maximum three disease areas. The progress of biologicals' companies like Amgen and Biogen-Idec into small-molecule drug discovery has been slow and erratic. The much-hyped small molecules such as Biogen-Idec's BG12, a dimethyl fumaric acid—to match Novartis' small molecule oral multiple sclerosis drug Gilenya—are revivals of very old drugs and represent a small increment in genuine novel research, even though they may turn out successful. The majority of small molecule drugs outside of Big Pharma have come from a handful of biotechs such as Vertex, Aurora, and Gilead, which have built a drug discovery machine that is identical in ability, platforms, and chemistry skills to that of Big Pharma, and is even superior in some aspects. If their promising trials lead to NDAs, and these companies continue on this track, they might be

---

233   Notwithstanding the familial Alzheimer trial mentioned in Chapters 00, 05, and 11.

the companies who may fill some of the gaps left by Big Pharma abandoning some important indications. The problem is that these companies already today struggle with financing the phase 3 studies. Nevertheless, it seems that 10-20 publicly traded large biotech companies will survive the patent expiries of beta-interferon, EPO, and so forth, and will remain independent drug developers in the next 10-15 years. If truly profitable, they will inevitably become takeover targets as this year's takeover of Genzyme by Sanofi showed. These takeovers have so far without exception led to cuts of research. While they add to the short-term financial prowess of the Big Pharma, they globally represent a loss of innovation.

Successful large generic and R&D companies like Teva or the large CRO, R&D, and generic company, Dr Reddy, deserve attention as they use the income of the generic arm to enhance their own R&D to create novel medicines. Their skills in medicinal chemistry, process chemistry, and development may serve them well and their stable income basis permits some R&D projects, but their scope is limited and they tread carefully. It is clear that they will continue to present strong competition in the generic arena, but it is not likely that in the next 15 years they become strong, multitherapeutic area R&D-based companies.

Small biotech

These companies are started by academic researchers and serial biotech entrepreneurs with VC funding and/or by angel investors. Serial biotech entrepreneurs carefully canvass any and all university laboratories for new project ideas. New scientific data are the plentiful fuel for starting these companies. Some small-business administration-type governmental grants and some nongovernmental organization (NGO) funding also assist in the first steps.

The two major problems facing formation and progress of these small biotechs, which were the cradle of many of today's medicines, in particular in biologicals, are:

1. severe shortage of VC funding, and
2. lack of exit opportunity.

With the clear abandonment of some disease areas by Big Pharma it is clear that there will be no or very few bidders for drugs in development even if a successful phase 2 is achieved after spending the necessary, but, today, very hard to raise $20–25 million.

Not-for-profit pharma companies

Nonprofit pharma companies have been around for a decade but have not yet become rooted in the pharma landscape. Many are not easily distinguishable for most of us from NGOs also devoted to treatment of tropical diseases and disease associated with poverty.

They often pick up drugs developed by Big Pharma, for example, GSK, Novartis, and so forth. The "for-profits" no longer want to carry out the full trial nor distribute the drugs for the prices that they may be able to charge, nor do they want to accept the potentially large liability.

There are many reasons why nonprofit pharma are not much beloved yet: most importantly because they have not had any big success. In addition, their former pharma executives allegedly continue on high salaries that turn off many potential investors, who would otherwise like to support social entrepreneurs and who might invest in new medicines.

Some known as "public-private partnerships" (PPPs) are working on one or a very small collection of diseases, such as the Global Alliance for TB Drug Development, the International AIDS Vaccine Initiative (IAVI), PATH's Malaria Vaccine Initiative (MVI), and the Medicines for Malaria Venture (MMV).

Nonprofit pharmaceutical companies, such as MannKind and the Institute for OneWorld Health have larger in-house R&D personnel who are planning to take the candidates through to the IND[234] application to the Food and Drug Administration (FDA). They partner, in this case, with universities (UCB) and biotech (Amyris Biotechnologies), and have received funding from an NGO (the Bill and Melinda Gates Foundation).

---

234   Investigational New Drug.

Again some new ventures have a multiple disease focus such as Drugs for Neglected Diseases Initiative (DNDi); others may have a single-disease focus such as the Aereas Global TB Vaccine Foundation.

Even if successful, they will have to partner with pharma for marketing and distribution.[235]

Virtual companies

Many former pharmaceutical and biotech executives, "looking for new opportunities,"[236] are approaching new drug development by looking for the low-hanging fruit in the former employers' garden, and try to out-license and reposition drugs that are known to be safe, but might have failed in the first indication, or where a different formulation may have some medical and/or intellectual property (IP) benefits. The number of these "available" projects is increasing as Big Pharma closes projects, and as biotechs run out of funds. Biotechs with such shortened purse strings fire their research personal to focus on the development of their existing drug candidates with their remaining funds. It is thus not unusual that even some publicly traded biotechs dismiss their entire preclinical research teams, that is, their—and society's—collective longer term future, and invest the remaining funds into clinical trials through a CRO. This is largely in the hope (of investors) that when positive data are produced in a year or several years the biotech will be then acquired. The timing of such a future "acquiescence" would depend upon the stage of the clinical candidate when such a decision drastically to outsource is made.

The CROs will now carry out the actual work instead of it being done by Big Pharma. There are CROs in every area of activity formulation, toxicology, and clinical trials. The outsourcing trend of Big Pharma from 1995 onward has created a CRO industry that is also now found outside Europe and the

---

235 For further reading turn to Hale, VG, Woo, K, and Lipton, HL (2005) Oxymoron no more: the potential of nonprofit drug companies to deliver on the promise of medicines for the developing world, *Health Affairs* July 2005, http://content.healthaffairs.org/content/24/4/1057.full.

236 All firings are described as "[the executive] left to pursue new opportunities, we wish him every success."

United States. Today a substantial portion of CRO activities is carried out in China, India, and, increasingly, Russia. These CROs are an important—although not sufficient—forerunner for a home pharmaceutical industry for these countries. The CROs have so far not shown that they can coalesce into a competitive drug company. Some large clinical CROs now have VC arms that try to steer clinical trial projects their way—but these virtual companies have yet to produce novel drugs in areas of real medical need.

In face of the above trends, which leave us short on developing drugs in some areas where we would need them most, several ideas are being discussed and even actively pursued in the world.

Rescue of phase 2 drugs

The most important item on society's agenda is the rescue of phase 2 drugs in important diseases with a high medical need, and which are being abandoned because of the new therapeutic focus at Big Pharma. This is the most imminent issue and the one with the largest and most immediate possible impact on healthcare.

There are pharma companies and biotech companies that have stopped the development of drugs that have reached a successful phase 2 trial. Thus we have both human safety and some efficacy data regarding these drug candidates. In biotech, these data are the fruits of some $25-50 million spent. But, more importantly, the famous *value inflexion point*[237] so much looked forward to by managers and investors is not materializing because no "white knight" appears with a $300 million or larger funding to put this drug candidate through the phase 3 trials. Similar phase 3 drugs, in Big Pharma, represent even larger investments due to the larger and more extensive phases 1 and 2 these companies conduct as compared to those by biotech companies. "Why should we have six preclinical programs in this indication when we can at best put one through the clinic?" asked the CEO of one of the top four pharmaceutical companies. The philosophically rational answer is: "Because preclinical research is

---

237   or "break-even milestone" in the drug development path at which point the value of the project is (substantially) increased.

cheap, and the attrition rate is high." But while preclinical research is cheap, it is not free. The unfortunate result of such fiscal introspection by fiscal narrators is cutting the preclinical research dramatically in order to save dollars on short-term paper. This is the opposite of biotechs' more fiscally inevitable: "Let's pour all resources into our single program!" For Big Pharma it is a big effort to save and for biotech it is a big effort to survive, albeit with an eye on short- to medium-term fiscal attractiveness to acquisiteurs.

These questions were not formulated before in such a defeatist tone; it just reflects the squeezed atmosphere of Big Pharma board rooms.

The rescue of these assets of biotech and of Big Pharma is of interest to society if the drug candidate is aimed at therapy of a disease where no good drug is yet available. It is not of especial societal interest to rescue a drug when the "novel drug" is not so novel but in reality is a me-too, which might indeed exhibit some real advantages, but does not fill a space of medical need where there are no alternatives available.

The answer to many—not all—problems is more funds: some by deferring tax income, some by spending money now.

Three ideas to revitalize phase 2 to NDA drug development phases in key areas

1. Award orphan drug status to drugs we badly need.
   a. In the short run this costs nothing; it has worked in the past several decades to mobilize private capital and it may also work now.
2. Use the existing governmental clinical-trial machinery to evaluate several of those drug candidates with a successful phase 2 in disease areas of interest that are now being shelved for lack of risk-willing private capital.
3. Create a governmental support.
   a. A public–private partnership in which governments finance or co-finance the development of these drugs through phase 3.
   b. By agreeing in advance to being (one of) the major purchasers of these drugs, and through which government(s) will receive benefits with, for example, better drug prices when successful.

c. Use tax breaks to encourage the development of drugs in the desired areas.

d. Share the financial success of the new drugs with the originators and IP owners.

The resurrection or strengthening of preclinical research to phase 2 stages of drug discovery is being discussed in academia and among VCs. VCs point to the financial crisis of 2008 and the altered tax laws, which make the income of VC partners lower, as the major reasons for the lower VC funding in the United States. The taxation of VCs is a matter of continuous debate and it is safe to say that their situation is like that of bankers, while their usefulness is not disputed, their high remunerations and high-handed treatment of the scientists whose ideas made them rich won them few friends.

The fourth idea for a big incentive: rewrite patent guidelines

The United States is the dominant force when it comes to patent law. In 1984, the Hatch-Waxman Act[238] was enacted to enable the extension of patent life in certain circumstances. It was designed to support the pharmaceutical industry and also generics. The protagonists came from the Senate in Republican form (Orrin Hatch) and the House of Representatives in Democratic form (Henry Waxman). The intentions may be honorable and steadfast, but, of course, and typical for U.S. law, it makes everything so complicated; the result is a mishmash of good intentions, law, science, and regulatory (FDA) authority. The real winners are always the lawyers who carve out yet another patch of turf in the societal garden. Making a change to the "American Way," which supports lawyers above even capitalism, seems to be impossible, but we will suggest it anyway. The patent life of 20 years starts when the putative drug's life begins, quite some time before the phase 3 clinical trials start. A drug's effective patent period during which it has exclusive use in the market is maybe only up to 12 years before the generics arrive. Before this, the competitors will be launching their me-toos with similar—maybe better—efficacy and safety.

---

238   Formally, the Drug Price Competition and Patent Term Restoration Act.

When trials take longer, as they must for preventative medicines of complex diseases—yes, Alzheimer's disease again—the patent life window shortens. A short patent protection period translates as higher initial drug prices and a major, major disincentive to discover new innovative drugs.

This long preamble leads to the radical suggestion that the patent life of the drug candidate starts when the molecule is patented, but is renewed back to 20 years (or some mutually agreeable period) on approval. Think how much lower prices of drugs might be if the exclusive patent time were extended automatically on approval. It would not inhibit competitively priced me-toos, and the effect of delaying generics would be mitigated by competitive pricing during the patent life of the industry's products. There is no need for legislation to favor the generic makers over the innovators. Of course, we cannot be sure that the industry would gravitate toward lower prices, but, if part of the approval process was enveloped in a QALY-like calculation of worth, pricing could be part of the approval process.

Of course, in these few sentences we have upset almost all of our readers who have any fixed idea about how the world should be organized. Radical changes without revolutions are hardly ever successful, especially in countries where the views of the people are truly represented. Multiparty democracies have governments of consensus, which can actually work. The U.S. governmental branches can have differently persuaded administrations, Senates, Houses of Representatives, and a Supreme Court. For example, at the time of writing, we have a Democratic majority in the first two and a Republican majority in the last two. Half of the Congress can change every 2 years, the administration every 4 years (so often effective for only 2 years) with a Supreme Court, which changes less frequently and is not democratically elected, where only one to three votes is unknown before the court case. To objective outsiders it seems that the system is designed to be ineffectual. The so-called Obamacare plan could not go so far as to be an actual equivalent of the cheaper European and Asian national healthcare plans and have individuals protected by being covered by the system, not insurance. In order to pass both the Senate and the House, it had to be "private sector" and so individuals are enforced to buy insurance, rather than extend the perceived reach of Medicare and Medicaid. This meant that its legality could be challenged all the way to the Supreme Court, which, to the surprise of many, declared the compulsory purchase of (affordable) insurance to be a tax, and, therefore, constitutional. Since the internationally recognized first rule of government is to protect the people, it is strange that this applies to defense (and often pre-emptive attack) before healthcare.

Maybe it does not help when, excluding anarchists, all of America's citizens are both republican (there being very few royalists) and democrat (there being very few dictatorial advocates) that the parties are distinguished by these epithets.

We are not revolutionaries and are both European and U.S. citizens. Therefore, we may have an international opinion that is only radical to some and is motivated by a desire to support the needs of society.

We are not being political. Recommending extending patent life and delaying generics makes us, in the U.S. context, Republican. Suggesting government support society and have universal health makes us Democrat. No, we want administration-independent, bipartisan support to facilitate drug discovery in a private enterprise environment. Both U.S. parties support the National Institutes of Health equally well.

So, why not extend patent life to accommodate a change in demands and a moving of the regulatory goalposts?

A "Biotech Projects Stock Market"

The lack of investment capital and not the lack of scientific-clinical ideas nor biotech management is the biggest problem facing biotech companies. There are many people who have successfully started and exited biotech companies in the past 30 years and who would like to do this again. They have in many cases accumulated funds and can be some of the investors. But sourcing the rest of the required funds is harder even if they have the perfect track record; there are few new biotech-focused VC firms with unspent funds. Even the VCs that still could raise a new fund in the difficult post-2008 times have the ability to invest in only 20-30 companies, and they receive for their potential investment consideration several hundred plans a year, with ~20-25% of those being interesting and potentially making a worthwhile investment. Thus there are hundreds of worthwhile ideas and more advanced drug development projects waiting to be tested with appropriate financing.

Governmental small-business grants are assisting biotech companies in Europe and in the United States, and these funds are very important, but very insufficient.

The 2004 tsunami and the 2008 U.S. presidential election have both shown that Internet-based fundraising from small donors can amount to a billion dollars or more. One has therefore started to think of models of biotech stock markets where small investors can become stakeholders and stockholders in projects they believe in at a stage of the project when they deem that their interest and budget is aligned with the offerings.

The idea—advanced by a successful biotech entrepreneur—is that a "Biotech Projects Stock Market" would permit a small investor to invest in a chosen single-drug development project by use of public opinions from an expert panel that describes to investors the medical and financial goals, the risks, and the stage of development for each project. This would present, and advertise, hundreds of projects found worthy by this expert panel of people. The panel should be from a cross section of those with experience in drug development, and should comprise former pharma and biotech employees, VC directors and financiers, and clinicians. Opinion should be objective and the Information should be as current as possible and report on changes in projects' status such as successful toxicology test, successful phase 1, failed phase 1, and so forth. At each point of drug development, information would be available to the stockholders and new stock buyers about how much money is needed to take the drug to the next step toward approval, and how much has been spent so far, what are the possible or probable assumed risks, when the next result is expected, and what might be the assumed value increase if this next step were successful.

This would enable small investors to invest early on a small sum, with a high risk of losing it, or another sum later, when the drug has passed phase 1 or phase 2 and the risk is lower but the unit stock in this drug project is more expensive.

The ability to select to invest in individual projects from a very large number of drug candidates would be interesting to a large number of people as the enormous sums social networking sites can move today, and junk bonds of earlier have shown. The key to the financing of these projects is the credibility and the work of the expert panel as the investors will rely on their knowledge, and opinion, instead of, say, buying stock from BMS, Lilly, or Merck, and so forth, and relying, in a less transparent way, on BMS', Lilly's, or Merck's own management and expert judgment. Behind the closed doors of the industry, decisions regarding projects are determined by a combination of in-house scientific, economical, and clinical expertise added to which are outside experts who consult for these companies, some of whom will now be "public" experts on the Biotech Projects Stock Market.

The liquidity of this market is a question not yet solved; any Biotech Projects Stock Market would have to have liquidity. Can one indeed sell these stocks as they gain in value with increased likelihood of success of the project and, if so, to whom? Who will provide funds if the next step of drug development is not fully funded? If funds were insufficient to take a project forward, would it mean that all that has been invested in this project is lost? If the project as such cannot now be sold to a company, would investment money beyond the last stage be returned? Since we are talking about projects of great importance to society, should governments have the facility to step in?

The small biotech companies, and the larger ones, which may want to finance one or another project in the above manner, face the problem. How will it be guaranteed that monies paid for this particular project are used exclusively, or in an attributable way, to this project, is another question. But no matter how many potential problems we can depict, the idea remains very powerful because it would tap into funds for drug development that society needs and would sell shares in individual projects rather than making the investor trust the whole management philosophy of a large conglomerate. It is also clear that most small investors can never invest in a biotech firm as they simply do not have the funds to become a limited partner in a VC fund. Others are less interested in sustaining the lavish lifestyle of many VC partners and would rather cut them out.

One can imagine that a drug company would want to finance development projects through this mechanism. This would mean that it needs to give updates, project by project, at regular intervals, as any investments by this route would be for the individual projects and not the whole company. Today, these companies give regular updates to stock market analysts and private banks. But these updates concern only the most advanced projects and mostly focus on the successes. However, the spectacular phase 3 failures, because of the large sums, as well as because of the lack of presumed revenue in the near future, cannot be publicly ignored anymore. Thus a company using this financing model would emancipate the small stockholder with the analyst; the small stockholder, using the expert panel, would be privy to the same information and estimates regarding a specific drug development. This is tantamount to a democratization of drug developments, of sorts.

Government sponsored drug development as the way to produce important new drugs is not a desire of anyone who has seen planned economy in the Soviet Union. While it could keep or be ahead in several scientific, technical, and military areas, it failed to provide for many needs, chief among them medical need with novel drugs. But, in this context, government-sponsored basic research already dominates the basis of all drug development projects.

Governments are also acting through the European Medicines Agency (EMA), FDA, and national agencies of other countries as the regulators of drug approval safety and quality control and, besides, governments are indirectly or directly the largest customers of medicine through healthcare plans. If as foreseen herein, they step into the clinical trials and production of strategically important drugs not only of vaccines and antibiotics but also of Alzheimer drugs then it will be the political process that will determine which diseases are representing a strategic threat to society. This is not desirable compared to an expert process such as that of EMA and FDA today, which are kept out from the everyday politics to a surprising extent. However, one can pay this price in the areas of serious medical need that profit driven companies leave.

Safeguarding the future of safe medicines

Neglecting the proverbial writing on the wall, some of it graffiti on Wall Street and Congress, should not be an option. The market alone cannot be relied upon to prevent the looming epidemics of Alzheimer's disease and diabetes, among others. Government and private sector financial backing of scientific endeavor and clinical trials is the way to recover from the impact of the now neglected serious diseases of ever-increasing prevalence. There is still a complex set of scientific, clinical, legal, and financial requirements to safeguard the future of safe medicines.

Index

Note: Page numbers followed by "f" and "t" indicate figures and tables respectively.